Projecting
Britain at War

Projecting Britain at War

*The National Character
in British World War II Films*

Jeremy Havardi

McFarland & Company, Inc., Publishers
Jefferson, North Carolina

LIBRARY OF CONGRESS CATALOGUING-IN-PUBLICATION DATA

Havardi, Jeremy.
　　Projecting Britain at war : the national character in British World War II films / Jeremy Havardi.
　　　　p.　　cm.
　　Includes bibliographical references and index.

　　ISBN 978-0-7864-7483-7 (softcover : acid free paper) ∞
　　ISBN 978-1-4766-0439-8 (ebook)

　　1. War films—Great Britain—History and criticism.
2. National characteristics, British, in motion pictures.
3. Great Britain—In motion pictures.　I. Title.
PN1995.9.W3H38　2014
791.43′658—dc23   2014001597

BRITISH LIBRARY CATALOGUING DATA ARE AVAILABLE

© 2014 Jeremy Havardi. All rights reserved

No part of this book may be reproduced or transmitted in any form or by any means, electronic or mechanical, including photocopying or recording, or by any information storage and retrieval system, without permission in writing from the publisher.

On the cover: *left to right* Donald Sinden and Jack Hawkins in *The Cruel Sea*, 1953 (Ealing Studios/Photofest)

Manufactured in the United States of America

McFarland & Company, Inc., Publishers
　Box 611, Jefferson, North Carolina 28640
　　www.mcfarlandpub.com

To Violette Szabo and the unsung heroes of the SOE, whose courage, resilience and devotion to duty inspired the peoples of Europe to resist Nazism

Table of Contents

Preface — 1
Introduction — 3

1. Our Obsession with 1940 — 11
2. The Development of the English National Character — 23
3. Projecting Britain in the Early Documentaries — 40
4. The Home Front: Muddling Through with a Stiff Upper Lip — 49
5. Service Films: The Triumph of Duty — 67
6. Cloak and Dagger: The Victory of the Amateur — 89
7. Heroic Johnny Foreigner: Resistance and the Triumph of the Underdog — 98
8. History and Heritage as Propaganda — 108
9. The Postwar Interlude: War Films 1945–1950 — 120
10. Obsessive Nostalgia: The British War Films of the 1950s — 128
11. The Critique of Deference in the Aftermath of Suez — 158
12. How We Lost the War: Anti-Heroism and the New Wave — 167
13. The Dominance of Narcissism: British War Films from the 1980s and Beyond — 187

Conclusion — 201
Chronological List of Films Covered — 205
Chapter Notes — 209
Bibliography — 216
Index — 219

Preface

I have been a passionate fan of cinema since the age of twelve, when I became hooked on a diet of Hitchcock thrillers, Ealing comedies, Laurel and Hardy, and film noir. However, this book was originally inspired by an undergraduate course on British cinema and society at the Open University. In my final year I wrote a modest 6,000-word dissertation on British war films of the 1950s which featured an in depth discussion of such classics as *Ice Cold in Alex*, *Reach for the Sky* and *The Cruel Sea*. Subsequently, I assembled a large collection of war movies which I proceeded to watch with increasing interest. I came to believe that these films told us a great deal about national identity, British identity, as well as contemporary historical events, and suddenly the idea for a full-length book emerged. This volume is the fruit of those labors.

Projecting Britain at War surveys how British war films represented, reflected and shaped prevailing ideas about national character. Movies are a rich and often neglected source of historical material for understanding how nations view themselves and how they project a national image to the rest of the world. This is no less true of films about the Second World War, an existential conflict that forced many to re-define their national identity.

Questions about national identity are particularly relevant in twenty-first century Britain. It is undeniable that we now live in a more fragmented community than half a century ago. This has resulted from a number of factors, ranging from changing demographic trends, the influence of consumerist culture, patterns of immigration and the long shadow of the 1960s revolution. There are real fears that devolution may eventually lead to the break-up of Britain, leading many to ask what will remain in terms of the identity of the home countries.

This book discusses almost every major British film made about the Second World War, providing an analysis of underlying ideological themes, as well as the films' plots, actors and cinematography. No attempt is made to compare war films from different countries (the scope is too big for a detailed analysis), though some pictures made in foreign studios that deal with recognizably British themes are mentioned (e.g., *Mrs. Miniver*).

The research material consists largely of the films and documentaries themselves, numbering some 150, together with a multitude of contemporary reviews in newspapers and magazines. Much of my research was carried out at London's British Film Institute. With its wonderful archive of movies, books, articles and ephemera, it is the first port of call for any serious historian of film. North London's Colindale newspaper library was also invaluable for tracking down newspaper articles.

The book is aimed at a variety of audiences. Firstly, there are university students, particularly those in modern history courses that cover film and ideology; next are those with an interest in the British film industry, particularly older readers who are extremely familiar with movies from the '40s and '50s, and who will recognize many of the films and actors mentioned in the book. Also targeted are those with an interest in British identity and how it creates cultural constructs; and finally, anyone with an interest in the Second World War and its cultural representation.

There are a great number of books on the market covering every angle of World War II: different nationally based narratives, biographies of military and political figures, analyzes of specific battles and events and the turning points of the war. There are also some brilliant surveys of the British war film genre, including some fine studies by Jeffrey Richards, Robert Murphy and Anthony Aldgate. A growing volume of books now explore what it means to be English and British too, including the complex question of national character. This book brings together these strands of military history, genre analysis and cultural study in a unique fusion.

Introduction

A familiar joke goes that whereas "they" had Germany, Italy and Japan, "we" had John Mills, Jack Hawkins and Kenneth More. While this may seem an entirely light-hearted cultural observation, it does point to the peculiar British obsession with war films, and with the Second World War more generally. More than seven decades after it started, the war still evokes intense feelings of pride. Dunkirk, the Blitz and the "few" have seared their way into the British imagination, taking on an iconic status that is tantamount to a secular religion. They are symbols of a glorious past when the British nation was united in its defiance of tyranny and remained stoical in the face of adversity. They also represent a period in which the British nation had a surer sense of its collective identity than at any time since. To question British involvement in the conflict is, for many, akin to heresy.

One of the chief ways in which the war has assumed such critical importance is through the confluence of history with popular culture, and by far the most powerful cultural medium has been the cinema. Film has helped shape the public memory of war through its seamless presentation of visual images, sounds and compelling narrative. This is particularly relevant to World War II, which remains, after all, a "cinematic war" par excellence. Photographers accompanied the armed forces of every combatant nation, enabling them to capture powerful contemporary images that could be beamed into their nation's cinemas. It became a war in which governments utilized the resources of the motion picture industry, including the documentary movement, in an effort to mobilize their populations.[1]

The British war genre has certainly spawned a rich and diverse collection of films that feature among the great classics of national cinema, and which provide some of its most enduring images. In perhaps the most famous naval combat film of the war, *In Which We Serve*, the survivors of HMS *Torrin* cling to a life raft while having repeated flashbacks of their lives as civilians. The intercutting between present and past is extraordinarily moving and grips the viewer throughout the film. In *Reach for the Sky*, we see the young RAF pilot Douglas Bader (Kenneth More) hovering between life and death in a hospital after a near fatal air crash. More's stirring performance provides eloquent testimony to the courage of the real-life hero.

The climax of *The Dam Busters* features a dramatic recreation of the moment when Barnes Wallis' bouncing bomb shatters the Ruhr dams in a carefully planned operation. Throughout the film we are reminded of the intense sacrifice of the bomber crews, while Michael Redgrave's subtle and restrained performance lends credibility to the role. Finally, it is hard to forget the thrilling climax to *The Bridge on the River Kwai* when a deluded Alec Guinness collapses onto a detonator, destroying the bridge that he has built so painstakingly for the enemy.

The films are also famous for their leading actors. Jack Hawkins in *The Cruel Sea* is the quintessential British bulldog; with his rasping voice he is indomitable and rugged, a commanding officer who retains the respect of his men. David Niven in *The First of the Few* epitomizes upper-class manners and gentlemanly conduct, while the more dashing and middle-class Kenneth More is equally stirring in *Reach for the Sky*. John Mills, by contrast, is an innocent, salt of the earth cockney in films like *In Which We Serve*. He personifies the understated but visible heroism of the working-class soldier. War films from the 1940s to the 1970s feature a roll call of Britain's finest acting talent, including Laurence Olivier, Michael Redgrave, Dirk Bogarde, Anthony Quayle, Richard Attenborough, Michael Caine, Deborah Kerr and Virginia McKenna.

For those of a certain generation, these actors and their memorable films still summon up visceral emotions. It is as if they are Englishness personified, a microcosm of the national character on celluloid. Jack Hawkins and John Mills seem as familiar as Monty and Slim—the cinematic embodiment of raw English pluck, courage and valor. As Philip Taylor puts it, "Douglas Bader looked like Kenneth More, Rommel looked like James Mason and every RAF pilot should have looked like David Niven."[2] Home grown stars such as Mills, Hawkins and More attracted a patriotic aura as "bearers of British national culture."[3] To merely invoke their names is to evoke a chapter in history, to summon up a plethora of historical associations laden with emotional resonance.

Of course, the power of cinema to move audiences and evoke patriotic feeling has long been recognized. As a mass medium for transmitting national propaganda and history, the cinema has been unequalled in the twentieth century. This is partly because of its mass reach. During the Golden Age of British cinema in the 1940s, 80 percent of the British population went to the movies at least once a year, and 1,640 million tickets were sold.[4] In both 1942 and

1943, more than one billion cinema tickets were sold in Germany, while in America in the 1930s, weekly attendance at cinemas was 80,000,000, representing nearly two-thirds of the U.S. population. But it owes something to the medium itself. With its seamless blend of language, action and music, film has an unrivaled emotional impact on its audiences. It transmits its messages with a unique visual potency, and casts such a glow over its audience that it can cement stereotypes and images in the popular imagination.

The appeal of cinema as a means of disseminating patriotic feeling was not lost on the most famous of all state propagandists, Joseph Goebbels. The Nazi propaganda minister declared that the cinema was "one of the most important and far reaching media that there [was] for influencing the masses."[5] He used his extensive powers to ensure that German films bore the imprint of Nazi ideology, and that they vilified all those (Jews, Slavs, Communists) who were deemed to be enemies of the state. The most famous Nazi productions, such as *Olympia*, *Triumph of the Will*, *Jew Suss* and *Der Ewige Jude* (The Eternal Jew), invoke the familiar themes of Aryan superiority, German greatness and the centrality of Hitlerism to national life. They are a chilling reminder of how a totalitarian state can mold national opinion for its own sinister ends.

As a parliamentary democracy with a free press, Britain has never been in danger of such a stringent level of state control. Nonetheless, propaganda can exist in more subtle forms, and the messages it imparts can be explicit or subtle depending on context. As Alexander Korda once pointed out, "Propaganda can be bitter medicine. It needs a sugar coating."[6]

The key point is that British war films, like those of every genre, have an underlying *ideology*. Ideology can be thought of as a labyrinthine system of social and political beliefs that give meaning to a nation. It can be seen as "a system of ideas that explains, and makes sense of, society."[7] Classic Hollywood films are underpinned by a number of key ideological tenets: the defense of individual rights and citizenship, the championing of heterosexual relations, the preservation of property, the maintenance of law and order, and the sanctity of the family. This philosophical mixture of capitalism, democracy and the rule of law embodies the most cherished values of American society and provides the films with an unmistakable "signature trait." These beliefs represent the status quo and are so fundamental that they call for little reflection.

Durgnat expresses this very point in his now classic *Mirror for England*:

> Even a film which seems uncontroversial to its makers and most of its spectators is loaded with assumption, and so, to someone else it will be a "message" film. Thus we all know that Hollywood exports the American way of life, and similarly British films have often hoped to spread the influence of the British way of life. Merely by being about people, their problems, and how they solve them, they're message films.[8]

British war movies (referring here to those of the Second World War) are no different to Hollywood productions in this sense. They too are permeated by an underlying ideology which reveals much about, and makes sense of, the society from which they emerge. The films are underpinned by varying national identity stereotypes about the English, the most traditional of which are a sense of unflappability, gentlemanly conduct, emotional self-control, cheerful but self-effacing humor, stoicism and devotion to duty. When we watch the myriad of World War II war films made between 1939 and 1960, this depiction of the national character is unmistakable. Yet, crucially, our ideas of national identity are not fixed or immutable but remain "modifiable."[9] They vary with changing historical events, so that when circumstances change, so too do perceptions of national character, altering films in the process. That will be a key contention of this book.

Films with ideologies revolving around national identity are worth studying from a historian's viewpoint. They reflect the society and culture in which they are created, and they are also informed by a set of literary and historical influences which make up a nation's story. This means that they become powerful historical sources capable of revealing much about how a nation sees itself, how it portrays itself to others and how it shapes subsequent social perceptions. And because such a large percentage of the public watches movies, it is likely that their perceptions of historical events, characters and eras will be influenced by what they have seen. For good reason the cinema has been termed the most successful historian of the twentieth century. Thus, as one historian puts it, the study of film will reward historians because "however flawed the results in terms of accuracy and nuance, to those not reading into the subject it is the dominant means of communicating what happened in the past."[10]

Like literature, film is therefore a valuable historical source because of what it reveals about the society that produces it. It is a representation of an underlying social reality and helps to socialize us in ways that we can find hard to discern. It can reveal the ways we relate to each other, and the state of our laws, customs and mores. It is also a barometer of the prevailing social values in any generation. The narratives of film, the choice of characters and the manner in which characters are portrayed all help to reflect existing values and reinforce them through the powerful visual medium of cinema. Jeffrey Richards rightly points out that the "study of a nation's self image" is "a crucial element in understanding its actions."[11]

In Chapter 1, I examine the peculiar British obsession with the war, or rather a part of the war. I explain that certain events of the war, primarily but not exclusively "The Finest Hour," are ones that are remembered with the greatest fondness in Britain. Indeed, what is remembered is a consensus myth, created at the time and embellished ever since, which elevates a selection of events because they fit a predetermined national narrative.

War films had the feel of the familiar and the domestic: the behavior of the British war film hero typified certain recognizable traits associated with the national character. In Chapter 2 I examine four of these major traits: stoicism/personal restraint, understated humor, improvisation and the underdog mentality, showing these to be central to the common conception of the English. These traits developed over a number of centuries in national culture and mythology.

In the next six chapters I show how these traits imbued Britain's wartime war films with a distinctly national ethos and gave them a recognizable "signature trait." It was the understated tone of the films, their characters' bullishness in adversity, their willingness to improvise against the enemy and an underlying good humor which made them quintessentially English (and British) productions.

After a brief survey of the immediate postwar period, the 1950s war film is given thorough treatment. In this period, some of the most familiar classics of war cinema were produced, including *The Cruel Sea*, *Reach for the Sky*, *The Dam Busters*, *The Colditz Story*, *Carve Her Name with Pride*, and *The Malta Story*. They unapologetically celebrated not just a national victory but the self-sacrifice, heroic courage and sense of duty that made it necessary. But Chapter 11 shows how national self-perceptions began to change shortly after the Suez crisis. If glory had been achieved, then it had come at a price which some were ready to question.

These films are analyzed in the context of declining British power in the world and a growing mood of international uncertainty. In the simplest sense, war films reminded their audiences of a previous epoch of unparalleled greatness and moral certainty. With the 1960s revolution fast approaching, they also harkened back to a time when English manners, mores and values were taken for granted. An analysis of films made from the '60s until the present follows in the remaining chapters.

Many books have been written about the British war film genre, many others on representations of English identity, and literally thousands on the experience of World War II. This volume brings the three together for the first time.

What Do We Mean by a British War Film?

This apparently straightforward question is, in fact, incredibly difficult to answer. Must a British film include a British star or stars, or just a predominantly British cast? Must it have a British director? Must the financing be British and not involve outside money? Must it be set in Britain or feature quintessentially British landmarks? Must it be based on a British theme, novel or story? Or should it include all or most of these? The U.K. Film Council (now defunct) rated films by certain criteria in order to determine whether they could qualify as British. Films could be awarded cultural test points depending on their content, cultural contribution and practitioners; and if they scored 16 out of 31 points by these criteria, they could apply for U.K. Film Council funding and tax relief. Some of these criteria made more sense than others, such as whether the film was based on original British subject matter or whether its lead characters were British citizens. Ultimately, there is no sound, objective answer to the question "What makes a film British?"

One might think that the starting point is the control of production—which studio controlled the film, an American or British one? There are, however, a number of wartime films which are set in Britain, feature a British actor or director, and revolve around an aspect of the British wartime experience, but which are still controlled and produced by Hollywood. Classic examples include William Wyler's Oscar-winning *Mrs. Miniver* (1942) and Alexander Korda's *Lady Hamilton* (1941). In addition, foreign actors have frequently performed iconic representations of English identity, as much as English stars have embraced roles as foreigners. To add to the complications, English is, of course, a global rather than a distinctively national language.

The vast majority of the films I have included possess a combination of the factors listed by the U.K. Film Council. They mostly feature British directors and actors; they are frequently set in Britain; they are made by British studios; and are usually based on British literary works or a historical narrative. In particular, they revolve around the British wartime experience, whether on the home front or on the front line. But most importantly, there is a unifying ideology centered on stereotypes of English national identity, which gives the films a cultural "signature trait." It is the combination of all (or most of) these features that define a film as British. Where appropriate, I have made references to a number of pictures that were made in Hollywood but which have an unmistakable British theme. I have also cross-referenced all films with Denis Gifford's admirable reference work *The British Film Catalogue 1895–1985*, which includes every British movie since 1927 registered with the Board of Trade.

One final point needs to be made. The national character that this book refers to was essentially an English one, dating back centuries before the union that joined Scotland, Wales and England. However, the words Englishness and Britishness became synonymous during the time that England emerged as the dominant component of the British "political" nation. Englishness came to define British character; it was the essence of Britishness. Naturally, any talk of a unified British identity is automatically contested and invites recrimination from non–English Britons who cling proudly to their own rich cultural heritage. But the fact that English traits were projected onto the wider British nation makes the confluence of these terms inevitable.

Chapter 1

Our Obsession with 1940

The front page of *The Sun* on October 30, 2007, screamed national treason. Gordon Brown had just signed the Lisbon Treaty which was, as Valery Giscard d'Estang admitted, the proposed European constitution in all but name. The Prime Minister had just "stitched up British voters over the new Brussels power grab," and in an attempt to summon up the paper's deep distaste for this political chicanery, the editor had borrowed the iconic language of the Churchill years. Gordon Brown was pictured doing a V sign while the headline stated, "Never have so few decided so much for so many."[1] Casting itself in the role of national savior, the paper invoked images from the past to rally the faithful against perceived Continental despotism.

A few years earlier *The Sun* invoked memories of the Second World War in an entirely different context. On the eve of England's semi-final clash with Germany in Euro '96, its headline screamed "LET'S BLITZ FRITZ" with barely disguised echoes of the British experience of 1940. *The Sun* was certainly not the only tabloid paper with a touch of racy jingoism. *The Star* led with an amusing front page headline, "MEIN GOTT: BRING ON THE KRAUTS." *The Mirror*, meanwhile, carried pictures of two of England's leading players wearing tin helmets and bearing the headline "ACHTUNG, SURRENDER."[2]

At the game itself, England supporters whistled the theme tune from *The Dambusters*, much to the bemusement of the visiting German fans. On the eve of England's World Cup game with Algeria in the 2010 World Cup, the spirited references to World War II continued. The England team was urged to give the nation "their finest hour (and a half)," while after a disappointing 0–0 result, the paper followed up with: "Never in the field of World Cup conflict has so little been offered by so few to so many."[3]

More than 65 years after it ended, the war continues to exercise a powerful hold over the British imagination. Nobody knows this better than the unfortunate foreigners at whom British bile is frequently directed. According to the

German foreign minister Michael Naumann, "England is obsessed with the war. It is the only nation in the world that has decided to make the Second World War a sort of spiritual core of its national self, understanding and pride."[4] His objection is typical of those who think that "war mania" has produced an insular nation of little Englanders.

If popular culture is anything to go by, this mania is unlikely to abate very soon. Every year a proliferation of books, museums, television programs, biographies and newspaper stories testify to a deep level of popular fascination with the war years. In 2002, Churchill was named the Greatest Briton, with the primary emphasis falling on his role as prime minister. In his series on the *Secrets of Leadership*, Andrew Roberts discussed Churchill's wartime leadership skills in one of four illuminating programs. Television series were made on the Battle of the Atlantic and on the relationship between Churchill and his generals.

A plethora of books have appeared in recent years on a variety of British wartime stories. Among the topics covered are the exploits of the Dambusters, the escape from Colditz, the evacuation of Dunkirk, the heroics of Douglas Bader, Walter Shellenburg's document for the Nazi invasion of Britain, a revisionist view of the Battle of Britain, and numerous biographies of the major political players in Britain at the time.

Nowhere do we see more British passion raised than when the integrity of our war heroes is questioned. On May Day 2000 a protestor defaced the statue of Churchill in Westminster. A piece of green turf was placed on the statue's head and red paint daubed on the mouth. The political outcry came very quickly. No less than the prime minister declared that "the people responsible for the damage are an absolute disgrace. Their actions have got nothing to do with convictions or beliefs and everything to do with mindless thuggery. To deface [the Cenotaph and] the statue of Winston Churchill is simply beneath contempt."

A recent BBC2 Dunkirk TV series sparked controversy when it was claimed that the program was trying to debunk myths. Jane Root, the Controller of BBC Two, decided to release a public statement denying that the documentary had set out to question "the heroism and sacrifices of those involved in the evacuation." Instead, the documentary was "a testament to the bravery and sacrifice made by those involved in the evacuation."

There was a similar furor when one of Germany's most controversial historians, Jörg Friedrich, published a photo book called *Brandstätten* (Fire Sites). The volume contained images of the mutilated bodies of women and children who died in the RAF bombing campaign. Friedrich argued that the RAF's relentless campaign against Germany during the final months of the war served no military purpose, and he denounced Churchill as a war criminal. Winston Churchill's grandson was led to reply that we should not forget which country had "started" the war.

But in a more lighthearted vein, the Second World War has also guaranteed a joyful poke at the enemy. Hilarious stereotypes of the Germans as robotic and humorless appeared in one of the most popular of British sitcoms, *Fawlty Towers*. In a famous episode, "The Germans," we see hotel proprietor Basil Fawlty doing the goose step and impersonating a Nazi officer, much to the chagrin of his German guests.

There may have been predictable outrage when Naumann made his complaint, but in one sense it missed the point. The war, for many, is truly the "spiritual core of our national self, understanding and pride."

It is not hard to see why. The British have memorialized World War II as a period of undeniable achievement and unambiguous moral purpose. Britain, unlike her allies, fought against Nazi Germany from the first few days of the conflict and survived to inflict defeat on a barbarous regime. Hitler was a uniquely evil foe whose political ambitions threatened the very fabric of Western civilization. Left unchecked, his Nazi empire would have engulfed the whole of Europe and Russia, leading to decades of slavery, massacre and plunder. That Churchill's government stood up to Nazism when pragmatism might have counseled an isolationist policy is much to its credit. The war years were also a period when the country was relatively united, despite the enormous prewar disparities of wealth, class and education. While the degree of social solidarity can be exaggerated, it is clear that the prewar hierarchies came under tremendous strain between 1939 and 1945, paving the way for the rise of a postwar meritocracy.

Yet not every aspect of our war evokes equal pride among modern Britons. The deliberate and indiscriminate bombing of German cities, the policy known as area bombing, was responsible for nearly ten times as many civilian deaths as those caused during the Blitz. Major German cities, such as Hamburg and Dresden, were crushed beneath the weight of Allied bombs. For many, this appears to be a war crime comparable to the worst excesses of the totalitarian powers. Bomber Harris' behavior is most often regarded as unsporting, uncivilized and distinctly un–British.

Other episodes appear so embarrassing that they have been airbrushed altogether from popular memory. One is the decision of the British government in July 1940 to attack the French fleet at Mers-el-Kébir in North Africa. This attack on a former ally left 1,297 French sailors dead and stained Anglo-French relations for years to come. While many celebrate military victory in the Egyptian desert in 1942, it is often forgotten that this was preceded by numerous humiliating setbacks. The worst was the surrender of Singapore in February 1942, a setback that Churchill would later describe as "the worst disaster and largest capitulation in British history."[5]

Then there are the uncomfortable episodes from the home front, chief among them the decision to intern "enemy aliens," many of them refugees from

Nazi Germany, in 1940. Such a suspension of habeas corpus sits uneasily with the British self-image of a free people struggling against Continental tyranny. Clearly only selective aspects of Britain's overall war experience summon up a sense of national pride.

The period of World War II that is most fondly remembered, the period that matters most in British memory, is the Finest Hour of 1940. Our Finest Hour, as coined by Churchill in one of his revered speeches, refers specifically to the period when Britain (and her Empire) stood alone against the might of the Nazi empire. It was the year of Dunkirk, the Battle of Britain and the Blitz; the year of the Spitfire and Hurricane; the year of pugnacious Churchillian rhetoric and of a beleaguered population coming together despite the barriers of class and creed. A powerful *consensus myth*, reinforced through various elements of popular culture, was constructed around these events at the time and now forms a popular memory of the war years. One might even call it a hallowed "national memory."

The word "myth" needs to be used with care here. To describe a popular or official reading of the war as mythical is not to imply that it is false. On the contrary, there will be much within the myth that relies on established facts and very real events, personalities and narratives. In this sense, myth and reality do not belong to mutually exclusive categories. Of course, there are wartime "myths" which are simply false, such as the notion that an actor read Churchill's speeches in 1940 to the British public.

When history becomes myth, it is usually because some of the facts have been elevated and heightened in importance, raised to a level where they become the essence of, rather than a part of, the historical narrative. This is because they represent some deep truth about a nation, its most cherished values or its underlying "character."

As such, myths possess an extraordinary power to simplify historical explanation because they reflect widely held assumptions about a nation. They can become "central to the common sense of the period in which they hold sway."[6] If all this seems abstract, it will become clearer after identifying the basic elements of the Finest Hour "myth."

The Myth of the Finest Hour

The period from May 1940 until the end of the year revolves around three separate but interrelated events: the Dunkirk evacuation, the Battle of Britain and the Blitz. A simplified account would run along the following lines.

Following Chamberlain's disastrously complacent leadership of Britain in the "phoney war," Winston Churchill became prime minister by popular acclaim in May 1940. He reached No. 10 just as German forces were invading Western Europe, with their Blitzkrieg operations quickly overrunning parts of France, Belgium, Holland and Luxembourg. British troops had been sent to France to help defend against this possibility, but, owing to poor French morale and strategic incompetence, it became obvious that they would have to be withdrawn.

A carefully coordinated plan was conceived for evacuation in line with the strategic plans of Britain's allies. The "miracle" of Dunkirk then occurred, as most of the BEF were escorted from Dunkirk and surrounding beaches, with a great deal of help from small boats manned by volunteer civilians. While it was initially feared that only 40,000 men would be withdrawn, the final tally was 338,000, including more than 100,000 French soldiers. The "little ships at Dunkirk" were a symbol both of plucky British resistance and also the huge civilian contribution to the war effort. In Churchill's words, Dunkirk was "a miracle of deliverance."

When France fell in June 1940, Britain stood alone against Nazi tyranny. Churchill rejected a compromise peace with Germany and promised to defend the island "whatever the cost may be" and never to surrender. His speeches in the summer of 1940 inspired the British people and summoned up a spirit of unyielding defiance in the face of Nazi tyranny. He formed the Local Defense Volunteers, the Home Guard, who were tasked with offering resistance in the event of a German invasion. But the air force was now called upon to save the nation in its greatest ever trial.

This was epitomized in the heroic struggle between the pilots of the RAF and the Luftwaffe, known to us as the Battle of Britain. Churchill eulogized the efforts of RAF pilots, "the few," in their daredevil exploits with the enemy. It was he who coined the phrase "the Battle of Britain." Every day, thousands could look up at the summer skies and see great aerial duels being fought between the two opposing air forces, while the results of these battles were displayed as if they were cricket scores. Despite being outnumbered by superior German technology, the Dunkirk spirit prevailed, and by September 15 the RAF had inflicted grave losses on the Luftwaffe. The aerial "few" had outfought the many.

A week before "Battle of Britain day," the Germans launched a raid on the heart of London's East End, marking the start of the Blitz. Over 400 civilians were killed and thousands more made homeless. Thus began the nightly bombing of London and other British cities by the German air force, causing over 60,000 deaths by the middle of 1941.

Many shops and businesses refused to close, despite suffering massive bomb damage. Many people began to gather in communal areas, such as underground stations and underground shelters, in order to avoid the devastation of the German bombing onslaught. Neighbors took in homeless people, and fire-fighters and volunteers scrambled amid bomb ruins to find survivors of an air raid. This highlighted the camaraderie and sense of shared purpose animating the people of the big cities.

Government policy also became crucial in generating social leveling. Millions of people were affected on a day to day basis by conscription, food rationing and food controls, the death of loved ones and friends, the destruction of property and the omnipresence of war propaganda throughout the media. But by May 1941, Britain had survived the German Blitz, and its people remained unbowed. The nation would fight on until victory was assured.

This is a simplified, basic account of the myth of the Finest Hour, which has been written about on many previous occasions. There are plenty of revisionist texts which explain the limitations of this account, such as Clive Ponting's *1940: Myth and Reality* and Angus Calder's *The Myth of the Blitz*.

They reveal how Britain was far from a united nation in 1940; how the Blitz was characterized as much by looting, strikes and a black market as it was by genuine social solidarity; how the RAF enjoyed certain strategic advantages over the Luftwaffe in the Battle of Britain, and how much victory was owed to German miscalculation; how morale sank among the British forces at Dunkirk, and how it was the Royal Navy, rather than the little ships, that carried away most of the BEF; how people affected by the Blitz displayed panic and terror instead of the fabled stoicism and sang-froid.

But none of these revelations are enough to shatter the fundamental consensus myth of 1940. This is partly because the two are not mutually exclusive. It is perfectly possible for "popular history" to accommodate instances of dishonorable behavior, particularly from marginalized sections of the community. Such stubborn facts exist at the periphery of the main narrative. As long as they do not alter the "big picture," then the myth remains intact.

When it comes to 1940, the central narrative centers on "Dunkirk," the "Blitz," "the few" and "Winston," words which are, as Malcolm Smith put it, "totemic." These form a potent narrative which has become deeply etched in the popular memory, reinforced by powerful visual images from contemporary and modern representations of war. No revelations about misconduct from British soldiers, selfishness during the Blitz, or political machinations can alter this narrative. As Smith says, "The exposure of counter factual details misses the point that the meta-narrative surrounding Britain's rebirth in 1940 explains such exposures as simply details, explicable and redeemable given the larger, more positive story."[7]

The 1940 myth can be supplemented by other episodes from the war, which, though not part of the big myth, are nonetheless significant. The Battle of the Atlantic refers to the period from 1939 to 1945 when the Royal and merchant navy fought a constant battle to protect the Atlantic from the lethal threat of German U-boats. This was essential, not only to ensure the constant supply of food and raw materials that would guarantee British survival, but to enable the build-up of American forces and tanks for the D-Day landings. Over 30,000 British sailors lost their lives in these years. Many of those who lived through these U-boat attacks have left us with inspiring tales of survival against the odds. Their stories of weeks spent in lifeboats stranded in the Atlantic appeal to our sense of the underdog, and of men facing the prospect of imminent death with stoicism and dignity.

Similarly inspiring are the many tales of heroic prisoner escapes from POW camps in occupied Europe. More than 100,000 Britons found themselves prisoners of war in Germany, Austria and Poland between 1939 and 1945. Many made determined efforts to escape their captors, some defying the enemy on multiple occasions. The most famous escapes were from the supposedly impregnable Stalag Luft III in Germany, which were later immortalized in *The Great Escape*. These episodes also appeal to something in the national psyche—a story of plucky prisoners surmounting incredible odds to escape captivity, and of men using guile and improvisation to evade a technologically superior enemy. Successful prisoner escapes are the ultimate triumph of the underdog. Though not based on actual events, the numerous fictional accounts of English spies outwitting the Nazi regime are part of much the same genre.

Outside of 1940 there were, of course, numerous battlegrounds in which British forces were involved. These ranged from the war in the North African desert to the Normandy landings, from the operations in Italy and Sicily to the war in the Far East. Those episodes likely to be memorialized are not the great successes against weaker enemy forces, or, for that matter, the surrender of Hong Kong and Singapore. They are more likely to be the many stories of courage, pluck and survival against the odds.

Why do these particular episodes remain so totemic today, and why do they inform the popular national memory of the war? Here we need to remind ourselves about the function of historical myths, which is to simplify historical explanation and make episodes meaningful in terms of some deeper, underlying factors. It turns out that Dunkirk, the Battle of Britain, and the Blitz (together with stories of POW escapes and survival in the Atlantic) are special because they reflect deeply ingrained elements of Britain's self-image and national identity.

Dunkirk

The Dunkirk evacuation was totemic on many levels. It appeared to follow a long-established convention about how the British army fought in war:

she started off badly, only to eventually emerge triumphant at a later date. In one sense, Dunkirk exemplified just such a bad start. Despite spending nine months defending France, the British Expeditionary Force was forced to evacuate her ally after failing to stop a heavy German advance into Western Europe. The soldiers also lost their heavy weapons in the process.

But the bad start, as Connelly has pointed out, preceded even Dunkirk. Indeed, one can date it to September 3, 1939, the day Britain declared war on Germany. It marked the start of the phoney war, the period of national complacency when Britons on the Home Front tried to laugh off the German threat and carry on with life as normal. It was a period overseen by the arch appeaser, Neville Chamberlain, the man who famously declared in April 1940 that "Hitler had missed the bus."

That Chamberlain was indelibly associated with the Munich agreement made it easy to deride him as an ineffective, even spineless war leader who was not up to the job. He was the "warm up for the main act"—namely, Winston Churchill.[8]

Churchill was Britain's "man for the hour" who emerged to save his nation from imminent and certain catastrophe. Like a phoenix from the ashes, he provided the inspiring leadership and oratory to galvanize the nation in its darkest hour.

Dunkirk also reinforced the notion of the plucky Englishman outwitting the technically superior German foe. While the BEF could not outmuscle the Wehrmacht, while they were no match militarily, their guile and initiative prevented certain defeat. After all, such a formidable undertaking as a mass evacuation required boldness of thought as well as the ability to improvise.

That improvisation was provided by the armada of small vessels (barges, steam boats, fishing boats) which were provided by civilians and used to ferry men to the bigger Royal Navy vessels. In popular memory, the lives of the BEF were owed as much to the daring of the volunteers manning civilian vessels as to the professionalism of the Royal Navy. The small boats have become totemic in themselves, a powerful reminder that the "island race" had a love of the sea in their blood. These brave civilians were thus worthy heirs to the gallant tradition of Drake and Frobisher. They were also a powerful sign of the newfound unity between civilians and the military, and of how Britons were pulling together for the heroic struggle ahead. The "ordinary people" rallied to the news of evacuation by becoming part of the rescue effort; war was too important to be left to the Navy. Thus the famous description in the 1940 polemic *Guilty Men* of "heroes in jerseys and sweaters and old rubber boots."[9]

It certainly appeared miraculous that so many Allied troops could be withdrawn in a short time while the Luftwaffe was mercilessly pounding the

French beaches. After all, even Churchill assumed that only 50,000 men could be rescued. Thus when 338,000 men were plucked from French beaches in the face of terrible attacks from the Luftwaffe, it seemed that disaster had been staved off in the face of truly overwhelming odds. The BEF had been cast in the role of underdog—but survived. Thus was born the legend of the Dunkirk spirit, a celebration of a particularly English "backs against the wall" mentality. One could read a Christian narrative into the events at Dunkirk: a people seemingly doomed to destruction were rescued at the last minute, allowing for the possibility of national redemption and rebirth.

This underdog heroism was spectacularly reinforced after the fall of France in June 1940. While the collapse of France led to French recriminations of "perfidious Albion," for the British it was a sign that she would have to continue the struggle without allies. As Churchill put it at the end of the Dunkirk speech, Britain would carry on "if necessary for years, if necessary alone." In one famous cartoon by David Low, a soldier stands on top of the cliffs of Dover shaking his fist in defiance at the Continent. The caption aptly summarizes his feelings: "Very well, alone." It was Britain against the might of Continental tyranny, but the bulldog would prevail. George VI declared, "Personally I feel happier now that we have no allies to be polite to and pamper."[10] Then there was the *Express* editorial which made much the same point: "All right. We can take it. Now we are on our own."[11]

Dunkirk also reinforced a long held and somewhat xenophobic belief, fostered by centuries of warfare with Catholic nations, that Britain was separate from and superior to Continental powers. If these foreigners were suspect, then Britain was better off without them. Therefore the Dunkirk myth spoke volumes for the national self-perception of insularity, apartness and self-reliance. As Jeremy Paxman said of Dunkirk, "It demonstrates to the English what they have known for centuries, that the European Continent is a place of nothing but trouble and that their greatest security is behind the thousands of miles of irregular coastline around their island home."[12]

The Battle of Britain

Dunkirk can be seen as the prelude to the epic aerial battle fought over English skies in the summer of 1940. The Battle of Britain, named by Churchill before it had even begun, had all the hallmarks of a glorious campaign. The heroes were the young pilots of the RAF, immortalized by Churchill as "the few" who would come to the rescue of the many.

In popular memory, a few thousand dashing young pilots, seemingly unfazed by the daunting task ahead, were all that stood in the way of a German invasion. These were the romantic knights of war whose individual heroism and technical prowess was to stir the imagination of an avid population. Conceptualizing the Battle of Britain as an exercise in chivalry was important, for it created a contrast between healthy Anglo-Saxon individualism and the excesses of Teutonic efficiency. On the one hand, the British pilots controlled machines of immense sophistication which could launch grievous blows against the massed ranks of the enemy. On the other, the pilots were plucky, skilful and ingenious, with their aerial exploits likened to a sporting contest.

After one raid, a newspaper vendor wrote, "Biggest raid ever—Score 78 to 26—England still batting." To liken war to cricket served a number of purposes. For one thing it was typically English in its eccentricity and understatement. What could be more lighthearted than a form of jousting in the sky between two aerial knights? Sport was also about teamwork, self-discipline and self-sacrifice, and to depict the few as part of a team only reinforced these very English virtues. Finally, the sporting metaphor worked because it showed that the pilots were prepared to play by the rules—unlike their Prussian counterparts. Cricket was, after all, the quintessential embodiment of English fair play.

But the Battle of Britain myth also reflected something more fundamental: the victory of the Dunkirk spirit. Central to the myth is the notion that the beleaguered "few" of the RAF were outnumbered by superior German firepower. Years of capital spending on "guns, not butter" had created a colossal German air force, which was believed to be more powerful than its British counterpart. Yet despite the perceived odds against a British victory, the RAF prevailed, armed as they were with a "backs to the wall" mentality.

The Blitz

While the Battle of Britain has been mythologized as the victory of the few and a paean to masculine heroism, the Blitz was the victory of the many. It was "the people's war" lived on the "Home Front." The defining myth of the Blitz was that the British people came through the ordeal of mass bombing with their dignity intact and remained "the sole nation in arms against the Nazi Empire."[13]

During the Blitz the reality of war was brought home to the people of Britain in a manner never seen before. While German raids in World War I had caused a small number of civilian casualties, the Zeppellins represented only a tiny fraction of the threat posed by the Luftwaffe. The Blitz was lived collectively; potentially everybody within Britain's large cities was vulnerable to an air raid. The raids were indiscriminate in nature, causing death and destruction to members of the middle and working classes, the rich and poor alike. If you were not personally affected, it was highly likely that you knew someone who was.

This brings us to the central, almost defining myth of the Blitz: that it helped engender a unique sense of social solidarity among the population. It is widely believed that the Blitz marked the start of the great social leveling which would eventually lead to a sustained postwar emphasis on social reconstruction and welfarism. It is not hard to see why. Images of people sheltering collectively in underground stations, and the perception of a common threat, were bound to iron out some of the prewar class and social distinctions in Britain. Not only did Britons endure the horrors of bombing, they re-discovered themselves as a socially united nation. According to the myth, the Blitz created a newly "democratized" people.

According to the popular accounts of the Blitz, the population under fire behaved with impeccable English spirit: they were calm, stoical, resilient, phlegmatic, good humored and tight-lipped throughout their ordeal. To use the well known phrase, they simply "muddled through."

Of course there is evidence of a breakdown of morale in some quarters, of hysteria and terror among sections of the beleaguered population, of the looting of bombed houses, and of resentment towards the government, even Churchill. This much is clear from the reports of Mass-Observation which collected evidence from Blitzed cities in 1940. But it is also undeniable that the myth stems from a core of truth—that people did display stoicism, good humor and high morale, precisely because this is how they thought they were expected to behave under duress.

Thus numerous reports from Mass-Observation note the general cheerfulness, humor and defiance of London's population despite the bombing raids. Other reports note the same characteristics among the inhabitants of provincial cities.[14]

These glorious episodes have become mythologized to the extent that they provide a simple overarching narrative which is readily understood without further embellishment. The mythical narrative simplifies events because it provides a story of the country in miniature; it is a microcosm of something we "know" about the English: they are underdogs opposing tyranny ("backs-to-the-wall mentality"), they are phlegmatic and emotionally tight lipped in adversity ("stoicism"); they prefer eccentricity, improvisation, guile and ingenuity to mechanized efficiency and planning ("English amateurishness"), which is why they often start wars so badly; their humor is modest, ironic and often self-effacing ("ironic humour"). Thus we have a "core truth" about the events of 1940 which buttresses a core truth about the nation. In Connelly's words, "1940 was the remake of the national epic."[15] And all the other episodes from the war in which these characteristics were displayed (such as the POW escapes) tap into the wider myth of 1940.

But just where did these national traits—of indomitability in adversity, stoicism, amateurishness and understated humor—actually come from? Who invented this "grammar" of Englishness? It is to this subject that we turn in the next chapter.

Chapter 2

The Development of the English National Character

Nations are rather curious entities. They are an abstraction, a somewhat amorphous collective entity, yet we like to invest them with a persona, a character, a soul—in short, with "cultural DNA." In everyday life we make stereotyped observations about entire populations on the basis of their perceived behavior, attitudes and values. Thus the French are often derided for their arrogance and extramarital affairs, the Germans for their coldness and lack of humor, the Italians for their "warm-blooded" passions, the Spanish for their indolence, and Americans for their bravado and tactlessness. For their part, the English are most often seen as cold, private, insular and obsessively polite. Every national community appears to have characteristics that set it apart from the rest, as if it had embedded within it some unique behavioral DNA. National character just seems to be one of those ideas we take for granted in common discourse.

Yet for all that, some critics believe that there is no such thing as "national character." In his book *The Illusion of National Character*, Hamilton Fyfe derides the idea as "among the popular errors and superstitions that have confused and injured mankind," and which has caused "immeasurable suffering and ruin." Character, he points out, "implies fixed traits" and "a uniform behavior." But these traits and behaviors are affected by influences, and as "there are many different influences," there are too "many different characters." He goes on:

> There are no qualities which can be said to distinguish a group, such as a club or profession, much less a nation. No one would say "Doctors are rash or cautious," "Bricklayers are polite or boorish," "Members of the Carlton Club are generous or stingy." Yet, while recognizing that a small group cannot be generalized, almost everybody has until recently taken it for granted that the characteristics of a very large group can be accurately ascertained and set down."[1]

Fyfe goes on to dissect contemporary views about various nations, showing how opinions about those nations have been in flux with every major historical convulsion and political change. Thus in 1890

> the national character of the Germans was generally supposed to be intelligent, kindly, peaceable, gently patriotic, home-loving, music-loving, studious, agreeable. From 1914 to 1919, your life was not safe in Britain, France, or the United States if you did not call them bloodthirsty savages, cruel, aggressive, unfit to be in Europe. From 1933 to 1939 they were poor fish, trembling at the nod of pinchbeck despots, enthused by flatulent oratory, forced to shout in obedient unison their approval of whatever their tyrants might do. Then they became devils again.[2]

Now Fyfe, writing at a time when extreme nationalism had already led to two global wars, makes a number of nifty observations. If "national character" is taken to indicate invariable patterns of behavior applying to every member of a national group in perpetuity, it is indeed illusory for the reasons he cites. National identity, as Andrew Higson points out, is not "a fixed phenomenon, but constantly shifting, constantly in the process of becoming."[3]

Surveying impressionistic accounts of the English over several centuries, one finds that opinions about them have been many and various, often contradictory, and that is without taking into account important local and regional variations. The English are not an undifferentiated biological unit which has a separate DNA from other nations. There is no English gene which propels us to act according to a pre-set design and which is at odds with the predetermined behavior of other national groups.

But there are observable patterns of behavior within any national group that do stand out and which reflect a specific and unique set of cultural influences. These may be myths insofar as they are not attributable to a "cultural DNA" and insofar as they have shifted over time. But, as George Orwell pointed out, these myths generally *become* true because "they set up a type or persona which the average person will do his best to resemble…. Traditionally the Englishman is phlegmatic, unimaginative, not easily rattled, and since that is what he thinks he ought to be, that is what he tends to become."[4]

Skepticism about national identity mirrors, in part, a much deeper skepticism about the nation state. Left-leaning intellectuals remind us all that we live in a "global village" where political boundaries between peoples have become artificial. We live in an age of increasingly powerful multi-national corporations which are creating, so it is alleged, a rather homogenized, culture-free McWorld. Instead of the old traditional loyalties, the world is awash with a new allegiance to consumer brands that know no country or heritage. Indeed, their very lack of historical context is the stamp of modernity. The internet has come to transcend national boundaries, giving us a sense of proximity to people who are otherwise physically distant.

So too the global marketplace has expanded. Vast financial transactions are made every day on the stock markets, further eroding the ability of nation states to manage their own economic affairs. To make matters even more complicated, there are numerous multilateral agencies that compete with nations in the sphere of politics, such as the EU, the World Bank, the IMF, the UN and the WTO. These supra-national entities are often seen as the embodiment of political virtue precisely because their focus is on the global, not the local. Nations, according to the chattering classes, are as redundant as the horse and cart—or so we are led to believe.

In fact, the nation state remains the most powerful political unit of modern times. Modern nations harness enormous economic and political power, and create a vibrant focus for communal allegiance. They produce "mass" societies which, imbued with patriotic sentiment, have been willing to sacrifice themselves for a national cause. This sense of allegiance and communal togetherness is the most potent aspect of the national idea. For it is often unforced, arising from the human desire for communal bonds among perceptibly similar beings. Among the myriad of social identities today, there is no doubt that "national" identity has an intoxicating power.

Across the world, the effects of nationalism are hard to miss. In recent years, ethnic rivalry has torn apart the former Yugoslavia, while the break up of the old Soviet Union has released the pent-up separatist feelings of various nationalities. In Britain, devolution has created new political representation for the Scots and Welsh, and led to repeated calls for full national independence. Not a day goes by without hearing of Kurdish, Chechen or Basque problems, all of which testify to the many flashpoints in world politics where national feeling plays a decisive role.

It would surely be pointless to ignore the consequences of globalization in the twenty-first century. Even in the most traditional societies one does not have to look very far to find satellite phones, CNN reporters, Nike footwear or chain restaurants, such as McDonald's. But, ironically, globalization may actually have strengthened national forces in some cases. There are certainly more nations in the world today than ever before—the number of sovereign states is currently around 200, depending upon the measurement criteria one employs—and the drive for separatism and independence seems insatiable.

Tradition, custom and ritual, while not unchanging, prove highly resistant to modernity. As Claire Fox observes, "Just because people everywhere want to wear Nike trainers and drink Coke does not necessarily mean that they are any less fiercely concerned about their cultural identity."[5] Quite simply, the increasing proliferation of global forces has failed to dampen the attachment to tradition, nation and heritage.

What Is a Nation?

A nation is not the same thing as a country. A country is a self-governing political entity occupying a given space and possessing internationally recognized boundaries. This gives its rulers a sense of externally recognized sovereignty in that no other state can legitimately exercise power over that country's territory, resources or population in the absence of a sanctioned war. A country or state has a body or population who live and work there on a permanent or semi-permanent basis, and whose activity generates economic growth.

A nation is not just a body of people in a given territory but a culturally homogenous community whose bonds are strong enough to imply a form of comradeship, regardless of the social, class and religious differences in that society. The community is bonded by its connection with a clearly defined territory, though this is far from coincidental. The territory clearly possesses a profound significance for the nation. It is imbued with a variety of historical associations, and provides a set of psychological and cultural contours for the community.[6]

With the civic conception of nationalism there is an additional element of legal equality. All members of a nation will be equal before the law and have a set of rights that flow from a political constitution. But they will also have corresponding political obligations and duties, with the state emphasizing the need for citizenship and social solidarity, particularly in times of emergency. Ethnic theories of nationalism, by contrast, emphasize the organic nature of the community and stress the binding ties of common descent and racial kinship.

But while a nation is a definable, culturally homogenous community, it is also, in the words of Benedict Anderson, an "imagined community." This is because "the members of even the smallest nation will never know most of their fellow members, meet them or even hear of them." Nevertheless, in the mind of each person "lies the image of their communion." So I may never know more than a tiny fraction of my fellow Englishmen, but I am capable of imagining their simultaneous activity and how, together, they form a collective of which I am a member.

An imagined community is always aware of both its past and future. Nations are communities formed by a matrix of cultural, historical and literary forces. These forces are the cumulative product of previous generations which "demand" to be passed on to future generations. It is impossible to understand the national idea without sensing the importance of this link between past, present and future. The current generation is seen as the inheritor of ideals and values which are themselves the product of centuries of custom, tradition and law.

These national values are often underpinned by a rich repository of mythology, symbols, traditions and folklore. Most nations will possess one or more "founding myths," which are events or episodes of great symbolic significance and which come to be seen as a source of national pride. Often they revolve around one individual who is regarded as the embodiment of a nation's genius and character. By their nature, founding myths involve exaggeration, distortion, selective focus and plain untruths, yet they fulfill their function. The historical accuracy of the legends matters less than the value derived from them and the sense of identity that they impart.

Christopher Columbus is lauded as a discoverer of the land now occupied by the United States. His voyages are the stuff of popular legend, and he is frequently depicted in the nation's stamps. In fact, Columbus never set foot on what is today U.S. soil, visiting instead the lands of Central and South America on his four voyages. He was on a voyage to find a shorter route to the Orient, meaning that his discovery of the Americas was far from intentional. He always claimed that the areas he had discovered were Asian, which explains why he named the Native Americans (the indigenous population) "Indians." In any case, the notion that Columbus was a "father" of the United States belies the fact that he lived centuries before the creation of the country's constitution and first government.

England too has a rich and varied mythology which continues to inform the national psyche. One of the most popular English myths concerns the exploits of King Alfred, the first proper English king. He is credited with many achievements, from improving the navy and founding Oxford University to establishing schools and creating fortified towns. The most enduring story told about him, however, is almost certainly apocryphal.

Alfred was at a low ebb in his fight with the Danes, a group of invaders who had overrun numerous areas of England in the 9th century. In 877 he was pushed back to Athelney in Somerset, and Anglo-Saxon resistance was minimal. According to legend, Alfred was so low in his fortunes that he was forced to travel anonymously and seek lodging in the hut of an old swineherd. After being told to mind the griddle cakes cooking on the fire, Alfred started reflecting on his many troubles. The cakes burned, and the peasant woman gave her King a good scolding for his carelessness.

The tale illustrates the depth to which the young Alfred had sunk in his battle with the Danish invaders. Indeed, at one point he was forced to hide in Somerset's tidal marshes with his bodyguards and small army of Thegns. Thereafter, Alfred had victories against the Danes before eventually forcing the surrender of Gunthum. The ruler of Wessex had prevented England from becoming another outpost of the Viking Empire.

It matters little that some of these tales are embedded in myth. What ultimately matters is the psychic affinity between past and present, the extent to which Alfred's deeds, values and character resonate with later generations. Alfred's behavior makes sense to us because the idea of being resolute in war and not admitting defeat, of improvising in emergencies, and of emerging triumphant despite starting badly, seems very English.

As Maureen Duffy writes:

> Alfred has that ability to hold on, not admitting defeat, until he can make a spectacular comeback, which informs both our myth and our modern national epic ... there is something unheroic, rather Dad's Army, about Alfred with his piles, being ticked off by the swineherd's wife, or strumming through the enemy camp, and this is part of the English tradition of irony, eccentricity and muddling through.[7]

When we talk about the "embedding of myth in national memory" it is precisely these tales that are important. Underlying them are the deepest ideas that any community can possess about its identity, its values and its "character."

But English national character was not created in the 9th century, remaining unchanged until 1940. Over a number of centuries the development of England (later Britain) as an isolated, Protestant nation added new layers of depth and meaning to the original myth of Alfred the Great, the quintessential Englishman. It helped to foster a lasting myth of English national character and a specific set of character attributes that remain familiar today.

Indomitable Underdogs

For centuries the English have pictured themselves as a persecuted people, nobly embattled against various forms of Continental tyranny. Whether their enemies were the French, the Spanish or the Papacy, the English were always the chosen "few" who would stand up for what was just and true.

St. George was therefore a highly appropriate patron saint. According to Catholic tradition, he became a martyr when he protested the murder of fellow Christians by the emperor Diocletian. In England he was popularized after the Crusades when the George and the Dragon myth became the defining monument to his courage and perseverance. The slaying of the dragon symbolized a fight against the odds, a David-versus-Goliath struggle in which the weaker side would emerge triumphant. In short, St. George was the ultimate symbol of an underdog people.

Allied to the underdog mentality was a sense of England as a nation apart, and the English as an isolated, self-contained people. This unfortunately bred a noticeable distrust of foreigners, a characteristic noted by observers down the centuries. The English, said one Venetian ambassador, "think that there are no other men than themselves," and the best compliment that could be paid to a foreigner is that he "looked like an Englishman."[8] For Pepys, the Englishman possessed an absurd nature in that he could not "forbear laughing and jeering at everything that looks strange." For Sorbiere, the English were "united amongst themselves against strangers."[9]

Such xenophobia stemmed, at least in part, from their status as an island people. For one thing, this bred a mental insularity and sense of self-assurance, particularly where foreign powers were concerned. For centuries the English must have breathed a sigh of relief that their country was not joined to the European landmass, or subject to its territorial and political convulsions. The boundaries of the "sceptred isle" seemed immutable to most Englishmen, something that must have bred a settled and self-confident disposition.

Shakespeare, the greatest English propagandist that has ever lived, summed up the sense of separateness in *Richard II* when he described England as a "fortress built by nature" which protects it "against infection and the hand of war." The "precious stone set in a silver sea" was clearly protected from the evils emanating from the Continent, and its isolation was a blessing and a privilege. More to the point, all Englishmen knew that foreigners had been unable, despite many attempts, to invade and defeat England since 1066. That the mighty European Goliath had been unable to subdue the English David was clear testament to the courage and fighting spirit of the English.

Shakespeare used this David-versus-Goliath imagery powerfully in *Henry V*. It is September 1415, and Henry listens to his troops on the eve of the Battle of Agincourt. The English realize that they are hugely outnumbered by about seven to one, and Westmoreland cries out for more reinforcements. But Henry prefers things as they are, sensing that his band of underdogs will acquire a heroic status if they succeed against mightier forces. As he tells Westmoreland, "If we are mark'd to die, we are enow to do our country loss; and if to live, the fewer men, the greater share of honour" [*Henry V*, Scene 3]. Henry's band of crossbowmen was the medieval equivalent of Churchill's few.

In the following centuries the Reformation transformed England into a Protestant nation at loggerheads with the Papacy. Protestants pictured themselves as persecuted martyrs who were forced to suffer horribly for their beliefs. They even had their own Bible of suffering, namely Foxe's *Book of Martyrs*, which offered a detailed and gruesome account of Protestant oppression at the hands of the Catholic Church. The martyrs in chief were Archbishops Latimer and Ridley, who were burnt at the stake by Mary I for their faith. As Owen Chadwick put it, the "steadfastness of the victims ... baptized the English Reformation in blood and drove into English minds the fatal association of ecclesiastical tyranny with the See of Rome."[10] If Catholicism was indelibly associated with despotism and corruption, then the Protestant Church was its moral counterpart: the embodiment of virtue, freedom and compassion.

But this new Protestant England was also a chosen nation, a "new Israel" whose civilizing mission was to confront the Catholic dragon in its many guises. Catholic plots were duly defeated in the reigns of Elizabeth I, while James VI/I crushed Catholic subversion in the Gunpowder Plot. Ireland too was subdued, particularly during the rule of Oliver Cromwell.

In 1588 England fought off the challenge of the Spanish Armada, crushed homegrown tyranny in the Glorious Revolution of 1688, and defeated the French in Canada during the Seven Years War. These great victories reinforced the sense of difference between, on the one hand, a freedom-loving, tolerant and civilized people and the "other," defined as an oppressive, absolutist Catholic tyranny. And there was no doubt whose side God was on.

In the nineteenth century a series of events powerfully reinforced the British sense of being a righteous underdog nation. The Battle of Trafalgar destroyed any chance of a French invasion and laid the foundation for a century of unchallenged naval supremacy. Yet Nelson, Britain's greatest combat hero, is chiefly remembered for his death at the hands of a French sharpshooter, as well as his unfailing sense of duty. It was his gallantry, more than his victories, that turned him into an enduring icon for the British people.

The siege of Lucknow during the 1857–8 Indian Mutiny stands out as one of the most significant episodes in the history of the Raj. In the British garrison at Lucknow, some 1,700 people, among them 1,000 Europeans, were besieged by more than 30,000 Indians from June until the middle of November. The defenders faced a barrage of artillery and musket fire, and various attempts by sepoys outside to tunnel their way into the compound. During this period the defenders had to look after hundreds of sick and injured women and children, with dwindling supplies of food and medicine. Despite the early loss of their commander, Henry Lawrence, the garrison fought off determined attempts by Indian sepoys to storm the Residency until, at last, they were rescued. Lucknow was a classic case of a beleaguered British force surviving against the odds.

The Zulu war of 1879, a notable success for the British military, is little remembered today apart from one incident, the Battle of Rorke's Drift. On January 22, 1879, 139 British soldiers, who had been left to guard a garrison near a ford known as Rorke's Drift near the Buffalo River, were attacked by up to 4,000 Zulu warriors. Despite being badly outnumbered, the soldiers managed to survive the Zulu onslaught and defend the garrison. In the process, 11 men were awarded a Victoria Cross, the highest ever number for one regiment in a single action. The story of a plucky British "David" outwitting an imperial "Goliath" quickly became the stuff of legend, which was just as well,

2. The Development of the English National Character

considering that Rorke's Drift occurred shortly after a disastrous British defeat at Isandhlwana.

Imperial self-sacrifice, so crucial to the Victorian self-image, was powerfully embodied by the fate of General Gordon. Gordon had been governor-general of Sudan, an Egyptian possession, until 1880. In 1881 the self-proclaimed Mahdi led an uprising against Anglo-Egyptian rule and destroyed a British-led Egyptian force in the country. Gladstone sent Gordon to Sudan with orders to evacuate British and Egyptian nationals. However, Gordon was reluctant to withdraw in the face of this revolt and disobeyed his orders, installing himself instead in the Sudanese capital. He intended to await relief and re-establish control of the Sudan.

Gladstone delayed making a final decision about relieving Gordon for ten months, and the General was killed two days before a relief mission arrived. Gladstone was pilloried in the press as "the murderer of Gordon," while Gordon himself became an overnight legend. In boy's magazines and newspapers, Gordon's disobedience was airbrushed from the record. According to the popular record, a brave Christian had taken a lone stand against tribal savages and died a martyr's death. As Paxman has so astutely observed, "Those military events which have the greatest imaginative resonance in the English mind are not necessarily triumphs at all."[11]

Muddling Through, Improvisation and Amateurism

For Englishmen of an older generation, the words "muddling through" seemed an apt summation of the English national character. They denoted that ability to resolve problems not through superior organization or professional efficiency, but rather improvisation and amateur flair. There was a peculiar English tendency to achieve the right results without a masterplan, and often after a string of embarrassing setbacks.

In part, this is what one would expect of an underdog nation beset by technically superior adversaries. But it also reflected a "down to earth," common-sense approach to resolving everyday problems. For observers down the centuries, among the defining features of English national identity were earthiness, practicability and common sense.

Goethe believed that practicality was the "main secret of their [the English's] ascendancy among the various races of the earth." For Van Gentz, England was nothing more than a "theatre of practical wisdom."[12] Dickens himself wrote of his countrymen in 1850 that they were "a steady and matter of fact sort of people," while for George Meredith the English people wished "to be thought practical."[13] At least from the eighteenth century onwards, the

English were thought of as being endowed with the spirit of empiricism and of being "doers" rather than thinkers.

Practicability and an empirical outlook could certainly be found in all forms of culture and thought. They formed a huge part of the English philosophic tradition, while a rejection of *a priori* deduction and abstract speculation had long underpinned the English legal tradition.

The English philosophic tradition is saturated with what can only be described as an "empirical outlook." For Roger Bacon the deductive methods of scholastic reasoning could not provide true knowledge. Convincing conclusions about what we could know had to submit to the test of experiment. At the same time, Duns Scotus took a swipe at intellectual approaches to theology, while William of Ockham was of the view that ultimately all knowledge was derived from experience. There was a medieval preference for fact over abstraction, and this was to continue into the Elizabethan era.

Francis Bacon sought a transformation of our understanding of nature by the rigorous use of the empirical method and a belief in experimentation. For this he required an inductive method that would start not from abstract principles but the investigation of particulars. Axioms had to be tested by experience and by practical experiment, and the subsequent truth value of a theory depended on its degree of success. Bacon's method could be regarded as the intellectual foundation of experimental science.

There is definite empirical earthiness in what he writes. The same can be said of John Locke, the greatest of the English empiricists. He offers us a comprehensive account of how knowledge is to be gained by experience alone. Our minds at birth are tabula rasa (blank slates), and all subsequent ideas come from experience, either from sensory perception or a reflection on the mind's workings.

Thomas Hobbes also disdains philosophical systems based on pure abstraction and seeks a system of socio-political philosophy which is worldly and earthbound. His political project, *Leviathan*, is concerned with the cut and thrust of political life and the nature of man. His brutal assessment and his grim reading of how people would live without proper governance reflects a definite pragmatist outlook. *Leviathan*, which argues for a strong, centralized authority in order to contain man's baser instincts, is very much a work of practical philosophy, offering a realistic solution to conditions in the real world.

Both of the nineteenth century's greatest British philosophers, Mill and Bentham, shared the empirical cast of mind. Bentham was interested in social and civic reform. His utilitarian maxim was that "it is the greatest happiness of the greatest number that is the measure of right and wrong." As a result, he produced an empirical ethics which derided *a priori* speculation about natural rights. Mill's empirical outlook was naturalistic, holding that humans were part of the natural order of things, and that, as minds were also natural, we could not possess *a priori* knowledge of the world. Like Bentham, Mill was concerned with concrete political change. Thus he became an MP and sought to bring about universal suffrage and the enfranchisement of women. Earthiness, empiricism, pragmatism, practicability and worldliness are qualities deeply rooted in the English philosophical tradition.

Some of these characteristics can also be found in the legal system. There is a relation between the English Common Law and the down-to-earth character of the English. For unlike other legal systems, common law is not based on a top-down model of abstract reasoning in which first principles are expounded and then applied to individual cases. Instead, it rests on precedent, custom and tradition. Roman Law worked deductively from first principles which could then work down to the individual case. Common law is empirical, seeing justice instantiated in the individual case, whereas untried and merely abstract principles lack authority.

Common law is a process of discovery, a discovery of the law of the land. As Scruton puts it, this willingness to work from particular cases, not theoretical principles, ensured that legal thinking was "concrete, close to human life" and connected to "the realities of human conflict."[14]

Where might the disdain for abstract principles, clever sophistry and intellectual theorizing have come from? In one of the many engrossing passages of *The English*, Jeremy Paxman suggests that a stable political system was at its heart. Being island dwellers meant possessing a degree of insulation from the theoretical tides that swept the rest of Europe. While other countries on the Continent were being ravaged by religious wars, revolutions and political re-inventions, England's institutions "changed gently, incrementally and often at the last minute." Sedimentary and unchanging political structures are not, he argues, the ideal breeding ground for intellectuals who prefer "a more changeable world where anything seems possible."[15]

If a people reject deliberate intellectual calculation from first principles, they will respond to problems based on tried and tested solutions. Custom and experience are better guides to policy than abstract speculation. If new situations arise, they will improvise novel solutions, whether this applies to law, war or business. But the "cult of the amateur" is also tied up with notions of gentlemanly conduct and stoicism, which are dealt with later.

Ironic Humor

The English have long placed a value on having a sense of humor and using it in the most adverse circumstances. Of course, they are hardly alone in this respect. Wit is clearly a universal quality that manifests itself in the narratives and customs of all nations. It is a matter of interest, though, that the English pride themselves on the fact that their humor is rarely appreciated by other nations. In popular culture it is often regarded as a secret weapon to be used on unsuspecting foreigners. If foreigners describe the English as lacking in humor, so much the better, for it merely proves that this superior wit is inaccessible to them.

Historically, the English sense of humor has had a self-effacing quality, which is often lost on those used to literalism. Irony, as Kate Fox indicates, is "the dominant ingredient in English humour" and consists of two central ingredients—understatement and self-deprecation.[16]

One might almost say that understatement has been a dominant theme in all English discourse. It is that ability to substitute simple, modest, unassuming language for that which is pompous, earnest and exaggerated. It is the tendency to feign indifference to hide emotion. It is the ability to modestly underplay one's own achievements or downplay the importance of a situation, particularly one of great danger. Self-deprecation is a species of ironic wit which involves "saying the opposite of what you mean" in order to convey to others the appearance of modesty. Both irony and self-deprecation are based on restrained, self-mocking humor, for they involve a subtle poke at our national obsession with appearing modest.

They are strongly connected to other features of the national character, in particular earthiness and anti-intellectualism. In the previous section we noted the historic English aversion to pomposity and earnestness, and the consequent love of practicality and common sense. Those who were "too clever by half," who were intoxicated by their own sense of self-importance, were not behaving according to the unspoken rules of English behavior. As Priestley once pointed out, this bluff "matter of fact-ness" gave the English the ability to expose "fanatical claims to certainty" that were "monstrously out of proportion, and so [were] ridiculous."[17]

Understated humor is also connected to stoicism and emotional restraint, which both discourage exaggerated displays of emotion and encourage individual privacy. The English brand of humor finally reflects a quality the English love to see in themselves: that they possess both individuality and (by implication) liberty.

Tales of English eccentricity abound in the stories of foreign visitors to English shores. The term came into vogue in the eighteenth century and came to imply a sense of caprice, whim and folly. Numerous plays, novels and caricatures of the time testify to this eccentric character, and this was "permanently to affect the language and imagery of Englishness."[18] According to Steele, originality or eccentricity was also intrinsically connected to the "legal and political rights which Englishmen enjoyed." The lack of political interference was cited as the means by which the eccentric Englishman could go about his business unmolested. It was seen as a positive and uniquely amusing maladaption to the life and the world in general.

Stoicism and Duty

If one quality has come to typify the Englishman more than any other, it is stoicism or emotional restraint. True English gentlemen were stereotypically composed and impassive, rarely given to overt displays of emotion. Instead, they relied on their famed stiff upper lip to ensure self-control in a crisis.

According to Princess Lieven, England was "not the country of emotions," while Karamzin noted that "to live here for the enjoyment of social life would be like seeking flowers in a sandy desert."[19] The English were long noted for their taciturnity compared to their European counterparts. Many foreigners, unable to understand this aspect of Englishness, took it for xenophobic incivility or bad manners. Others, such as Elizabeth Grenville, said it was a form of social awkwardness or "unease when confronted with strangers."

But this picture of emotional continence and personal restraint only came to be seen as the *embodiment* of national character during the nineteenth century. Perkin writes that "between 1780 and 1850 the English ceased to be one of the most aggressive, brutal, rowdy, outspoken, riotous, cruel and bloodthirsty nations in the world and became one of the most inhibited, polite, orderly, tender minded, prudish and hypocritical."[20] Undoubtedly the context for this radical alteration in behavior was the series of social, economic and religious upheavals resulting from the industrial revolution.

The age of industrialization brought with it both physical and social transformation, and the latter greatly concerned the minds of nineteenth-century moralists. The rapid urbanization of the nineteenth century, the growth of the factory system and the disintegration of traditional rural communities led to the creation of a newly industrialized working class. This new mass of people in the heart of Britain's cities would need moral fiber and self-control to ensure that they did not upset the social order; various movements would provide this.

One central religious influence was Methodism, which preached the goals of respectability and hard work, and ultimately reinforced the puritan values of the middle class. Another spur came from the evangelical movement. With a burning sense of missionary zeal, the evangelicals preached the virtues of a Spartan lifestyle that eschewed all forms of worldly pleasure. Instead they promoted the values of respectability, education, duty and hard work.[21]

The moral revolution, to which Evangelicalism made a major contribution, was not solely the prerogative of religious reformers. The utilitarian creed of Bentham and Mill emphasized the benefits of education, intellectual endeavor and non-hedonistic "experiments in living." Bentham and Mill, with their denunciation of indolence and waste, and their emphasis on education, intellectual endeavor and service, appealed to those of a puritanical mindset.

Into this mix came the mutual improvement societies, led by their Victorian spokesman, Samuel Smiles. Smiles believed that some vital ingredients were necessary for success, among which were punctuality, early rising, orderliness, thrift, piety and the avoidance of bad temper. Above all, he emphasized the critical importance of application and industry, which would ensure the individual's independence in life. This was a puritan social morality directed to the middle and respectable working classes. His book *Self Help*, which preached the virtue of self-reliance, became a Victorian bestseller. Out of these nineteenth-century creeds there began to emerge a definable portrait of the English: they were orderly, decent, honest and dutiful people who showed concern for others and exercised personal restraint.

The notions of stoicism, personal restraint and responsibility are also embedded in the English obsession with gentlemanly conduct and chivalry. Though the idea of a gentleman had been around since the time of Chaucer, it was not until the eighteenth century that a gentlemanly "code" of behavior was developed in the aftermath of the French Revolution. The revolutionary currents from overseas and the increasing demand for democratization at home struck a degree of fear into the governing classes. Ever aware of the subtleties of class and of the threat to the social order from the lower orders, there was an increasing emphasis on "minor aspects of social behaviour" that would help separate the classes.

Gentlemen knew what their code had to be. They had to be "brave, show no sign of panic or cowardice, be courteous and protective to women and children, be loyal to their comrades and meet death without flinching."[22] One code that was increasingly stressed was solidity and stoicism. "It was important not only to bear physical pain without squealing but also to repress all signs of emotion." It could be picked up, at times unconsciously, in a number of important ways—"through advice, through example, through what they had been taught at school or by their parents, and through endless stories of chivalry, daring, knights, gentlemen and gallantry which they had been read or been told by way of history books, ballads, poems, plays, pictures and novels."

Moreover, as the nineteenth century wore on, the demand grew for an "imperial class of officers who must appear impassive, god like impartial in the eyes of the chattering natives." The stiff upper lip was part of the mask of stoicism designed to avoid unwanted displays of emotion. As Mason observes, the nineteenth century cult of the gentleman "provided the English with a second religion" and one "less demanding" than Christianity.[23] One could certainly subscribe to it if one did not subscribe to Christian dogma, a position many Victorians found themselves in.

Combined with this came the revival of the (related) cult of chivalry, another ideology that provided a moral underpinning for the English notions of duty, restraint and self-sacrifice. Chivalry had been deeply ingrained in most forms of English culture. The patron saint of England, St. George, appears as a knight in armor destroying dragons and rescuing people in distress. This image perfectly symbolizes a nation which is divinely chosen to spread God's word by courageous and unselfish actions.

Throughout the Middle Ages and into the Elizabethan era, the chivalric ideal was kept alive by a spirited retelling of great epic stories. Thus characters like Parsifal, Tristan, Gawain and King Arthur continually crop up in medieval literature. While the medieval and Elizabethan periods saw a flourishing of literature in which the romance of chivalry was celebrated, it was not until the early nineteenth century that there was a general revival of interest.

Sir Walter Scott's novels are an instinctively romantic celebration of the chivalric ideal, with references to Arthurian legend. His great characters show bravery, loyalty and hospitality, treat women decently, and show a magnanimous attitude towards enemies. His novels take a medieval code and reinvent it for modernity, suggesting a set of "desirable standards, not just for young gentlemen but for gentlemen of all ages." Kingsley's *Westward Ho*, Arnold's *Tristan and Iseult* and Tennyson's *Idylls of the King* were the most notable among a host of literary projects that dealt with Arthurian legend. By the mid–nineteenth century images of chivalry had become absorbed into the pattern of everyday life through their infiltration of Victorian art, architecture and literature. Within 50 years, chivalric ideals had seeped into mass culture and were readily understood by gentlemen of all classes.

The religion of chivalry and gentlemanly conduct was aided by the growing influence of the public schools. They transmitted an ethos which promoted character formation and moral outlook, rather than the pursuit of academic excellence, as their key aim. For Thomas Arnold, headmaster of Rugby School for 14 years, the most important role of the public school was to instill religious and moral principles, then gentlemanly conduct, and finally the intellectual elements of scholarship. In *Tom Brown's Schooldays*, a novel about life at Rugby written by one of its former pupils, Tom's father muses on his reasons for sending his son to the school: "I don't care a straw for Greek particles or the diagamma.... If he'll only turn out a brave, helpful, truth-telling Englishman and a gentleman and a Christian, that's all I want." Nothing better epitomizes the spirit of the great English public schools in the eighteenth and nineteenth centuries.

One way that schools transformed student "character" was by toughening up those in their care. Cold baths and dormitories, a meager supply of food (one proper meal a day) and runs in the rain were designed to harden the new future elite. Another was school sport and games. According to the Royal Commission on the Public Schools, cricket and football fields were "not merely places of exercise and amusement. They help to form some of the most valuable social qualities and manly virtues."[24]

Through playing these games, it was believed that a certain toughness of character would emerge. "Hardiness, self composure, coolness in the face of pain and danger, confidence in one's own decisions." According to Punch, a true sportsman is not merely steely and tough, but one who can "control his anger," "be considerate to his fellow man," "take no mean advantage" and "never know himself defeated until the last breath is out of his body."[25]

Games encouraged not just self-discipline, self-control and physical steel, but also an adherence to the team ethic, to following rules and to playing fair. The alternative, of course, was just "not cricket." The chivalric code in football and cricket implied a sense of honor and sportsmanship—in short, a gentlemanly code of conduct. From this notion of "playing the game" one derives the cult of the amateur, and the idea that fairness in sport is intricately connected with being an untrained and non-professional player.

Self-restraint naturally had to be extended to sexuality, that vice against which Victorian schoolmasters were constantly battling. The pleasures of the body had to be suppressed, with physical exercise sublimating young boys' sexual energies into more acceptable channels. Here one finds perhaps the ultimate rationale for the ritual of the cold dip. As far as sex was concerned, the Victorians believed in purity, an ideal which dictated that the male lover remain pure until marriage and then faithful after it.

This English stress on stoicism, self-control and self-sacrifice provided a justification for imperial activity. The public schools needed to produce an elite of future imperial leaders, but this would be an elite defined by manners and character, not brains. Britons were empire builders, and, guided by a visionary zeal and a belief in their status as a chosen nation, they would go on to conquer the world and pretend it was for the benefit of the natives. If a foreign colony was incorporated into the British Empire, so much the better for the "unenlightened" heathen. They would soon be reaping the rewards of Christianity, commerce and civilization.

In this way, Evangelicalism provided a fertile base for the secular nationalistic zeal of the late nineteenth century. The zeal continued into the twentieth century, except that the ideology was increasingly targeted at the middle classes and not just elite sections of society. Boys magazines were no longer dominated by a cavalcade of stoical aristocrats but instead by middle-class protagonists, "ordinary boys learning to fit into a society over which they had little control."[26]

In all these ways, a distinct narrative about English identity and behavior, built around an underdog status, ironic humor, the cult of the amateur, stoicism and duty, had been implanted in the nation's imagination by the time war broke out in 1939. Over time, what was an originally English identity came to be seen as a British one, as if the traits of one nation had somehow been projected onto the regions. It remains to be seen how war films incorporated national character stereotypes within the specific context of the Second World War.

Chapter 3

Projecting Britain in the Early Documentaries

The Second World War is often regarded as the golden age of British cinema. During the war years, a homegrown cinema with a truly national flavor emerged that was to give an overarching purpose and thematic unity to its productions. It became, as Robert Murphy noted, "an essential part of wartime culture."[1] Instead of trying to replicate Hollywood productions, as was the case throughout the 1930s, British cinema would come to focus on problems unique to the Home Front, while creating a lasting visual monument to the stereotypical national character. The notion of the People's War, in which stoic heroism, humor and "muddling through" were seen as indomitable values, became a central ideological component of many wartime productions.

The golden age was centrally about an increase in film quality. A number of highly talented writers and editors became well established, with the list of names forming a formidable roll call of creative talent: David Lean, Carol Reed, the Boulting Brothers, Cavalcanti, Anthony Asquith, and Powell and Pressburger. This certainly raised high quality patriotic productions to greater prominence, with the films themselves receiving a deeper level of critical scrutiny. Paradoxically, while quality was improving, the quantity of films produced was decreasing. Between 1933 and 1937 an average of 150 British films were made per year, with this number decreasing to as low as 46 in 1942. This reflected a number of factors: the requisitioning of studio space, the call up of actors and technicians, the scarcity of film stock and the increase in taxes affecting the film industry.

But whether or not we accept that there was a golden age between 1939 and 1945, cinema was certainly an incredibly important element of wartime British culture. People generally desired escapism in the form of light entertainment, especially comedies, with such films offering a temporary respite from the grim reality of the Blitz. The reduced number of consumer goods on the domestic market enabled people to use spare money on alternative forms of entertainment. Thus weekly film audiences increased from 19 million in 1939 to 30 million in 1945.[2] Box office receipts trebled in that period, though the cinemas did not reap the full financial benefit, partly due to significant rises in entertainment tax.

Second World War British cinema was characterized by the pervasive role of official wartime censorship and propaganda. As it turns out, this was not wholly unexpected or even repugnant to filmmakers who had long been used to a system of political censorship. It had been run by the British Board of Film Censors (BBFC), a body financed by the film trade and whose certificates of approval were essential if movies were to be shown to the public. Its primary concern was to preserve middle-class standards of behavior and a sense of decorum, and, in political terms, to exclude any discussion of controversial topics, such as fascism or industrial unrest.

Propaganda had also been used as early as the First World War. In 1918 the Ministry of Information had been established under the watchful eye of Lord Beaverbrook and in conjunction with Lord Northcliffe's Department of Enemy Propaganda at Crewe House. Many later believed that the department had significantly aided the war effort, among them Adolf Hitler, who thought that Lord Northliffe's work was a significant part of the British war machine.

Many interwar British politicians would have agreed with Professor Leonard Doob, who wrote of the "bad odour" attached to the word "propaganda."[3] Sam Hoare found himself "unable to show propaganda by this country" and believed it could not be a substitute "for calmly getting on with the business of government."[4] For Christopher Addison, "This kind of thing is repugnant to the British spirit," with propaganda seen as the prerogative of the undemocratic and totalitarian regimes like Stalinist Russia and Nazi Germany.[5]

Nevertheless, the potential usefulness of promoting British policy at a time of increasing international crises was accepted by Anthony Eden in 1937. He wrote that propaganda involved the task of "interpretation and persuasion," and that the country would suffer "if we leave the field of foreign public opinion to our antagonists." What was required was "equally energetic actions on our part on behalf of the truth."[6] Eden was aware of the almost Herculean efforts being made by the totalitarian states' propaganda machines. In particular, in 1933 Goebbels had created the Ministry of Popular Enlightenment and Propaganda. The concern that the public face of Britain, its institutions and its international role would be left to the machinations of a foreign demagogue was not one that a responsible government could ignore. The energetic actions that he had mentioned were being put in place shortly before he wrote these words.

In 1934 the British Council was created to respond to the rise of totalitarianism in Europe. With British interests under threat from foreign propaganda, the Council projected a more favorable image of a democratic and fair Britain. A year later a powerful CID subcommittee was formed to prepare plans for the establishment of a Ministry of Information (MOI) in time of war. The function of the new MOI was to "present the national case to the public at home and abroad in time of war."[7]

The Publicity Department, one of the five main divisions of the Ministry, was charged with ensuring that "the national cause is properly presented to the public." In order to achieve this, it was vital to "disseminate the national point of view in a guise which will be attractive and through channels which will ensure that it reaches persons who are likely to be influenced by it."[8]

Sir Stephen Tallents, a high-ranking civil servant who had gained considerable experience in publicity work with the GPO and the BBC, was named as Director General Designate of the Ministry. The Ministry was held responsible for the transmission of all official information and propaganda, and the release of news, media censorship, radio and films, and other official publicity campaigns, both at home and to foreign countries. He would later declare that cinema was "the greatest agent of international communication," and it was thus the ideal instrument by which to project the national self-image to the outside world. His view was echoed by the authors of a 1936 report from the Board of Trade committee which stated that film was "undoubtedly a most important factor in the education of all classes of the community, in the spread of national culture and in presenting national ideas and customs to the world." The report concluded that "the propaganda value of the film cannot be overemphasized."[9]

The notion that film could transmit a powerful national self-image to the rest of the world, that it had a patriotic, educative and even civilizing purpose, was shared by a number of key figures in the British cinema industry of the 1930s. John Grierson, the founder of Britain's documentary movement, conceived of film as a tool to educate and enlighten the masses rather than a means of providing cheap entertainment. The son of a headmaster, Grierson believed in the profound importance of education in order to advance the individual and society, and saw in cinema the means by which to provide knowledge and enlightenment for the masses. Perhaps this is why he once described film as "the only democratic institution that has ever appeared on a world wide scale."[10]

Other than Grierson, the two most influential figures in British cinema at this time were Alexander Korda and Michael Balcon. As with so many of the children of immigrants, both Korda and Balcon were intensely patriotic and desired to promote favorable images of Britishness abroad. During the

1930s both men produced a series of films extolling the British Empire, including *Sanders of the River*, *The Four Feathers* and *Rhodes of Africa*. These pictures champion the exercise of British imperial rule, justifying it on the basis of the perceived superiority of national character and conduct rather than any economic argument. They projected the image of a benelovent Empire that was dependent upon the loyal service and selfless duty of those sent to govern it.[11] They would have shared Kipling's view that Empire was less a bounty and more a "White Man's Burden." Korda also enjoyed close links with two unrepentant imperialists in the 1930s—Winston Churchill and Sir Robert Vansittart—the latter of whom was employed to write scripts for pro-imperialist films.

In 1938, Balcon, now chief of Ealing Studios, sent a memorandum to the government stating his belief that "films could serve to fight against fascism both in this country and elsewhere, and to project the democratic idea for which all right minded people, as well as the left minded people, are fighting today."[12] Instead of concentrating on making films for the American market, the usual commercial imperative for British filmmakers, he campaigned for movies that reflected British values. Michael Powell, one half of the incredibly important Powell/Pressburger partnership, was much like Balcon in his contempt for cheap escapism and lowbrow entertainment. At an early stage of the war he made it clear that he and his colleagues would not work on "tuppeny-halfpenny subjects about blondes and jazz and what happened down Argentine way."[13] What he wanted was serious subject matter at a time of dire national emergency. From this it is easy to discern that there was a commonality of concern to project Britain, its character and its values to the world, with cinema now an indispensable medium for propaganda.

Given this readiness to use films as a vehicle for patriotism—from civil servants and filmmakers alike—it must have come as a shock when, on September 3, 1939, a decision was taken to close all public places of entertainment. This owed much to a long held fear that enemy aerial bombardment would kill vast numbers of civilians and induce unprecedented panic and trauma across the population. Governments throughout the 1930s were animated by the belief that the "bomber will always get through," helping to shape the appeasement policy at the time. Cinemas were thus considered to be potential death traps. After several days in which the Luftwaffe's raids failed to materialize, and under understandable pressure from the commercial exhibitors, the cinemas re-opened. It would, however, be some two months before all cinemas were permitted to remain open until 11 p.m.

The Ministry of Information was not slow to grasp how cinema could be mobilized for the war effort. The MOI's task was now to "present the national case to the public at home and abroad," which put it in charge of issuing news, preparing national propaganda and controlling information in the interests of security. The early PR disasters of this ministry (dubbed the "Ministry of Disinformation" by its detractors) have been well enough documented over the years and there is little need to dwell on them here.

In 1940 Sir Kenneth Clark, the newly appointed head of the MOI's films division, produced a "Programme for Film Propaganda." The program envisaged the use of feature films, newsreels and documentaries as propaganda in terms of three themes: "What Britain is fighting for," "How Britain fights," and "The need for sacrifice if the fight is to be won." Clark was naturally aware that Britain had a rich documentary tradition which, in the 1930s, had provided a gritty and realistic depiction of working-class life in Britain. The documentarists stressed the serious, educative function of cinema and deprecated the notion that cinema should merely be a tool for Hollywood-style escapism. Thus he specifically called for documentaries about the ongoing war effort, films that celebrated British ideals and traditions, and pictures that dealt with British life and character.[14] What follows is the briefest survey of some of the more famous wartime documentaries made in the first two years of the war.

Before the war started the GPO produced *If War Should Come* (re-named *Do It Now* when the war started). Shown to audiences across the U.K., this was an instructional documentary that told people how to respond in the event of a wartime emergency. With Elgar's "First Pomp and Circumstance" march playing in the background, the film opened with stirring messages about how democracy would triumph if war came to Britain. People were then offered a series of simple messages: they must not pay attention to rumors, they must construct air raid shelters, they must avoid the panic of buying and hoarding, they have to listen to important messages on the radio, and they must carry around gas masks and ID. This was a didactic short designed to raise morale and provide some reassurance that if the worst happened, Britain would be prepared.

The documentary *The First Days*, made shortly after the outbreak of war in 1939, was designed to boost morale by reminding people of their endurance under fire, their stoicism and their sense of humor. The England depicted here is a quiet, peaceful and introspective place. The camera pans across England on the Sunday that war is declared, showing ordinary folk walking to church and a vicar preparing for the morning service. The gentlefolk seem undisturbed by Nazi tyranny and will need to be roused from their bucolic idyll to fight evil.

Yet roused they are as soon as war is declared. We see people filling sandbags and digging trenches in a heartening display of social solidarity. Filling sandbags is described as everybody's business, and class distinctions, which would have been insurmountable barriers in peacetime, now scarcely matter.

"The thousand classes of London, some from their damp basements, some from their luxury flats came to work for the public good." This may be the earliest depiction of the People's War in British film.

One message that this documentary strongly conveys is that Londoners' lives will not be fundamentally altered by the Nazi menace. People will continue to go to work and aid the war effort. They will continue to keep their shops open and put up barricades, in some cases with paper and glue. The British are resilient and muddle through. Their defiance is symbolized by a heap of sandbags piled on top of a tank with a flag on top saying "Let em all come." For in London there is "adaptability and enterprise," and "the plodding round of labor in dangerous places." The Blitz "myth" merely built on these pre-existing ideas of English muddling through. In a curious echo of the later documentary *London Can Take It*, the voiceover at the end pays tribute to the London front, "the front of the anonymous millions, a civilian people whose name has gone spinning across the world."

The Humphrey Jennings and Harry Watt short *London Can Take It* (later called *Britain Can Take It*), captures this Blitz spirit nicely. In the film, the American correspondent Quentin Reynolds reports back home after witnessing a typical day in the life of London's citizens. He pays fulsome tribute to the "greatest civilian army ever to be assembled," while images depict ordinary people adapting to life during the Blitz. It is the sheer incongruity between the terror of the Blitz and the normality of behavior that Reynolds seeks to explore. After a lethal raid, Londoners go to work through the rubble-filled streets; shops open as usual, with some, as he wittily puts it, "more open than others"; people move about without fuss or demur. At night, people sleep in an underground shelter, leading Reynolds to ask: "Do you see any signs of fear on these faces?" Londoners are depicted as a model of stoicism and perseverance. Reynolds concludes: "I can assure you that there is no panic, no fear, no despair in London town; there is nothing but determination, confidence and high courage among the people of Churchill's island." In essence, London could "take it."

The Front Line (1940) does for Dover what *London Can Take It* does for the capital. In this short documentary, directed by Harry Watt, we meet a number of Dover's ordinary inhabitants who speak directly to the camera about their wartime experiences. One housewife says she has no intention of leaving the town for "that rat Hitler" and will have to be thrown out before consenting to depart. Another man quietly tends his gardens despite his house suffering recent bomb damage. The town's fishermen carry on their daily business, though they admit that they are getting "proper fed up at fishing Jerries out of the sea." The picture is of an unruffled, phlegmatic and peaceful people whose spirits remain high despite living only 20 miles from German-occupied Europe. Of course there is more than a small element of caricature here but the overall message is unmistakable: "The key of Britain is strong because its people are strong."

A short film that also attempts to identify the character of the British is *Island People*, a documentary from 1940. In 10 minutes we encounter a cross section of British people from all walks of life: dairy farmers in villages and market towns, coal miners in Northumberland, shipbuilders in Liverpool, international traders in London, a naval captain, and many others. The workers are all masters of their trades and play an essential role in the functioning of the economy. But the film also shows how British people crave time for leisure, whether it is taken up in spectator sports, gardening, hunting or family entertainment. This is an island whose abiding characteristics are a love of liberty and tolerance, where individuals freely associate without the clammy hand of an interfering state. The war is not even mentioned here, but the essential message of the unity of the British people, despite their individuality, is clear enough.

Christmas Under Fire (1941) celebrates the fact that despite the horrors of the Blitz, which by then had seen the destruction of regional cities like Coventry, the British people still celebrated their religious traditions. Again featuring narration by Quentin Reynolds, this is another patriotic tribute to British resilience, but it also shows another side of national character: adaptability. Families are forced to modify their celebrations because of wartime restrictions. The Christmas trees this year are shorter so that they can fit into air raid shelters; the church bells are silent so as not to generate fear of an invasion; and model RAF planes are now much favored presents. Nonetheless, the most enduring image is of young carol singers in King's College, Cambridge, keeping the Christmas flame alive. Reynolds tells his American audiences not to feel sorry for the British because "England does not feel sorry for herself." It is just the sort of spirited message that the MOI wished to convey to those across the Atlantic.

While many of these shorts are set in urban centers, Humphrey Jennings' *Spring Offensive* (1940) brings to life the quaint ways of rural communities. It deals with another aspect of the home front—the production of food during wartime. As a result of attacks on British shipping and reductions in imported food, it was essential to ensure that farmers increased output wherever possible. The film looks at the War Agricultural Executive, a body which was tasked with offering farmers incentives to plough derelict land and boost food supply. We see farmers respond to the call, using a variety of technological tools to transform the countryside. They do a job "as vital to national defence as that of the armed forces" and perform heroic feats in three months that would have taken three years to perform before the last war. What is implicit throughout is a sense of community purpose: men, women and children working with nature and driven by a patriotic instinct to work for the national interest. The documentary ends with a stirring call to nurture the land not just in war but also in peace.

The image of a quiet, cooperative and deferential populace animates *War and Order* (1940), a short film that acknowledges the vital importance of police work within the wartime community. The documentary highlights the multifaceted role that the police are now playing and celebrates the community cohesion that has resulted. Like the armed forces, the police are ever alert to enemy action, and during one raid they rapidly spring into action to save civilian lives. They enjoy genial relations with the local community who follow police instructions to the letter. Law enforcement is pictured as a calm and orderly business in which the police show steadiness against the backdrop of the Blitz. Naturally in a propaganda piece like this, no mention could be made of the real crime waves of the Blitz that included looting, hoarding and a variety of darker crimes.

Two short films concentrated on Britain's defenses in 1939 and 1940. *Squadron 992* (1940) looks at the work of the balloon squadrons and shows how necessary they were in countering the threat of dive bombers. The documentary, which is introduced by Air Vice Marshal Boyd, features a re-creation of a raid on the Forth Bridge with some visually impressive sequences of this important event from 1939. By contrast, *The Story of an Air Communiqué* focuses on the events of September 15, 1940, a pivotal day in the Battle of Britain when, according to official reports, 185 enemy planes were downed by the RAF. The documentary is at pains to show the accuracy of these figures by tracing the process of investigation at every stage, from the pilot's initial testimony to the Air Ministry which collated the figures. The most recent evidence suggests that the figures were inaccurate and exaggerated, though we can understand why the MOI wanted the public to think otherwise. The film's pilots fit the class stereotype, with their Home Counties accents and clipped delivery setting the standard for later films in the air war subgenre.

Leslie Howard had played a vital role in producing Allied propaganda, including starring roles in films like *Pimpernel Smith* and *The First of the Few*. *From the Four Corners* (1941) features an encounter between Howard and three soldiers from Canada, Australia and New Zealand. Over a pint at a local pub, he asks them why they chose to enlist and then, dissatisfied with their answers, gives them a history lesson from the top of St. Paul's Cathedral. From this position he points out various landmarks of historic significance, such as Runnymede, Tilbury Docks and the Houses of Parliament, in order to draw out the message that this is a war to establish the universal rights of liberty and tolerance, not to gain territory or simply fight for the "motherland." His language is stirring and eloquent, even if his moralizing approach may have alienated contemporary audiences.

Some of these documentaries were crude and didactic in approach, offering clear moral messages about the country's social cohesion and united purpose. But in all of these documentaries a familiar picture of the English emerges. It is of a quiet, stoical, determined, patriotic community that regards the Nazi menace as an inconvenience that needs to be defeated. The populace under fire revels in the immortal spirit of the underdog. Despite the terror of war, people find within themselves a stoical courage and resilience. They do not show fear or hysteria; they are phlegmatic but determined, cheerful and prepared. Above all, they are imbued with a simple patriotism and an abiding love of liberty. Despite the perception of themselves as underdogs, they will muddle through with all their usual inventiveness and amateurishness. Above all, they work together as a team. The military, police and civilians operate as one seamless unit even if the ideology of the classless People's war has yet to fully take root. These and other themes came to manifest themselves in the many feature films made during the war. But this was only the case because the English sense of national identity, which had long enthused many an English novel and poem in the preceding centuries, was now more sharply in focus than ever before due to the emergency conditions of the war.

Chapter 4

The Home Front: Muddling Through with a Stiff Upper Lip

The war years saw a sharp divide in terms of how British films represented the nation. Early service productions like *The Lion Has Wings*, *Convoy* and *Ships with Wings* harked back to the social divide of the 1930s. In these films leadership was provided by upper-class officers whose authority for conducting the conflict was rarely questioned by the respectfully deferential lower orders. But films about the home front started to adopt a model of social democracy from almost the start of the conflict. They focused on the "People's War," the central notion of which was that ordinary citizens were "doing their bit" regardless of their class or social background. In these films the ordinary citizen aided the war effort and worked for a common purpose, despite the terrors of enemy bombardment. Civilians on the home front were shown making an essential contribution to the war effort. Naturally the extent of social leveling has been disputed by historians, but it did have some grounding in reality. In this war, unlike any other, there was a deeper level of participation from all social classes.

The move towards a cinematic representation of the People's War is usually associated with Ealing Studios. Ealing will forever be linked with Michael Balcon, one of the most influential figures in the history of British cinema and a man who strove to create a truly national cinema. Balcon was a self-confessed admirer of the documentary movement, which he regarded as the "single greatest influence on British film production."

He particularly admired the documentaries of Robert Flaherty, with their emphasis on ordinary people in adversity, and was determined that the "documentary approach" was one that his own work should take.[1] The marriage of documentary realism and Hollywood-style narrative film was made possible at Ealing by Balcon's recruitment of some key figures: Alberto Cavalcanti, a

Brazilian filmmaker who had worked at GPO and the Crown Film Units; Harry Watt, who directed several famous documentaries in the 1930s; Thorold Dickinson, who had experience making documentaries during the Spanish Civil War; and Robert Hamer, who worked under Cavalcanti at GPO. They were to work on a number of important feature films which dealt with problems of the home front. These pictures would see the emergence of greater realism, defined as the insertion of "narrative-documentary techniques into commercial feature film production." No longer would there be class stereotypes but a focus on "groups of people in authentic situations."[2]

Ealing's sense of social conscience could be found in one of the earliest wartime productions, *The Proud Valley* (1940). The film was directed by Pen Tennyson, great-grandson of the Poet Laureate, whose interest in social issues was discernible in his first movie, *There Ain't No Justice*. Paul Robeson played David Goliath, a black American merchant seaman who leaves the Navy and goes looking for a job in a small, close knit mining community. Goliath has a great singing voice, and in one memorable scene has a solo role in a rehearsal of *Elijah*. He ingratiates himself with the miner-choirmaster, who offers him some employment.

Not surprisingly, he encounters some hostility from other miners, both as an outsider and as a black man. In the latter case, the hostility is defused when the men are reminded that they are all black while they are down in the pits. Tragedy strikes when an explosion kills the choirmaster and forces the pit closure. In the original prewar version of the film, Michael Balcon had wanted a small number of unemployed miners to defy their masters by opening up the pits. But Balcon thought this was "neither tactful nor helpful propaganda when the country was at war," and he changed the emphasis.[3]

The miners decide to pay a surprise visit to London to persuade the owners to re-open the pits. The miners' dedication is not matched by the mine owners, who provide only bureaucratic objections and red tape when hearing of the scheme. Yet the case for opening the mines is powerfully spelt out and forms the central propaganda element of the film: "Coal in wartime is as much a part of national defence as guns or anything else." With some reluctance the pits are re-opened, which both alleviates the miners' distress and serves a vital national interest.

The last half hour of the film brings the ideas of solidarity, community and courageous self-sacrifice to the fore. Paul Robeson, the outsider who becomes a part of the small community, now sacrifices himself to keep the community alive. After four of the men (including Robeson) are trapped down the mine, an escape is only possible if they blast their way out, though it will mean certain death for one person. The men draw lots but Robeson ends up being the sacrificial lamb, allowing the men and the coal to come to the surface.

When the coal emerges, it is draped in the Union Flag in a display of patriotic symbolism. Coal is a national possession as much as a reward for the people of the village. Wartime camaraderie has healed old wounds and divisions, while the stereotypical notions of English selfless devotion, duty and chivalry are of paramount importance.

The transition from self-interest to national interest is not immediate, however. When the miners first hear about Hitler's demands for Danzig and the Polish corridor, one of the men asks what this has to do with them. The march to London is more about relieving their immediate dire circumstances than meeting the threat from Nazism. Slowly it dawns on them that the two might be linked.

Unfortunately, the film became mired in controversy after Robeson made critical comments in America about the "imperialistic ambitions of the Allies."[4] The actor's pro–Soviet sympathies angered Lord Beaverbrook, who decided not to mention the film in three of his newspapers, ensuring that it did not receive the critical publicity it deserved. *The New Statesman* was fairly uncompromising in its critique: "The dialogue is both flat and false ... and the direction and photography uninspired."[5]

Welsh miners also featured in Humphrey Jennings' drama-documentary *The Silent Village* (1943). The film is set in the Welsh village of Cwmgiedd but modeled on the Czech village of Lidice, which was destroyed by the Nazis in 1942 as retaliation for the assassination of Reinhard Heydrich. The Welsh villagers, like their Czech counterparts, find their village coming under foreign occupation. The sound of marching, gunshots and amplified orders conveys the brutality of the repression, but ordinary people choose to resist their oppressors. Modeling their day-to-day activities on the Czech underground, they publish a Welsh language paper and listen defiantly to their radios, despite fear of reprisals. When Welsh locals are forced to register at the village hall, they choose to reveal their actual names. At the end, the men are lined up against a wall and shot, though Jennings chooses not to show this act of murderous violence. The film suggests the universality of patriotism and unwavering courage in the face of tyranny.

Old Bill and Son, directed by Ian Dalrymple in 1940, is a light-hearted production which has much in common with the early war comedies. But it is also infused with a gentle patriotic sentiment and sends out a clear message about the democratizing nature of the People's War.

Morland Graham stars as Old Bill, the loveable Blimpish figure created by Bruce Bairnsfather during World War I. When war breaks out, Old Bill goes to the recruiting office to be signed up but is disappointed when he is rejected for his age. Nonetheless, he gets sent to France where he meets up with his son (John Mills) and adopted daughter. After a series of comic escapades, Mills and his pals take part in a daring raid on German lines. When Mills fails to return, his father sets out for him and discovers a group of stranded German soldiers that his son has just captured.

Old Bill is certainly a Blimpish figure who initially finds it hard to adjust to the contingencies of modern warfare. He understands little of air raid shelters and the black out, and ridicules his son when he is told about the mechanization of modern warfare. While in France he causes mayhem by crashing a tank into the wall of a bar owned by an old French friend of his. He is very much an "old school" figure who understands the value of tradition. He tells his friends and fellow WWI veterans: "War is just like boxing. You can let a stronger fellow punch you all round the ring for nine rounds and then flatten him in the tenth." He believes this pretty much sums up Britain's historic status as a heroic embattled underdog. As he says, "Fighting is all they [the Germans] think about. It's just a sideline with us."

The notion that this is a People's War, which may rapidly accelerate social leveling and the shattering of class barriers, is evident from the start. Mills is hard pressed to accept women entering the war effort and takes the line that "girls should be girls." Mills' mother laments her personal sacrifice in seeing both husband and son go off to war, screaming to Old Bill that she will never do anything as undignified as war work.

Later on we see her dressed up in uniform at an army camp, marching about and directing others in authoritative fashion. Mills himself is eager for social advancement. He has none of the other soldiers' dignified deference for higher orders and tells Ray, "You don't have to be a toff to be an officer nowadays." Yet in *some* respects this is a socially conservative production. As with other films of the period, upper class accents predominate among those in charge, typified by the self-assured and tight-lipped Ronald Culver.

Salute John Citizen (1942) chronicles the life of an ordinary suburban family headed by the "everyman" Mr. Bunting. He is a simple and unpretentious man, rarely given to emotional extremes, and animated by a quiet but unshakable patriotism. Just before war breaks out he is sacked from his work after nearly 50 years service and replaced by a younger man. Together with his children, one of whom, Ernest (Jimmy Hanley), is a pacifist, he experiences the Blitz first hand and hides in an Anderson shelter in the back garden. Mr. Bunting is later reinstated and becomes a fire warden, helping to tackle incendiary bombs. He helps lead his family through the war in a calm and dignified manner, showing that he is, in the words of the opening narrative, "the backbone of the nation."

He and his wife are stoical throughout, for, as she tells him, "I suppose that's the one good thing most of us ordinary people are good at—sticking it out." Given that this is 1942, the English everyman is depicted as a salt of the earth, lower-middle-class gentleman without any trace of a Home Counties accent. The film harks back to the early stages of the war with contrived speeches from the younger generation about fighting to build a better world. This surely reflected the "democratic realism" induced by the Beveridge Report, with its promises about creating a universal welfare state and eradicating the evils of want and squalor. Indeed, this had been the radical message of J.B. Priestley in his broadcasts of 1940, but they had proved too controversial and he was taken off the air.

In some respects, *Salute John Citizen* could be seen as a family drama, an appealing attempt to chart the life of a typical suburban lower-middle-class family that had come to personify the English nation. *This Happy Breed* (1944), directed by David Lean and based on the Noël Coward play, explores much the same theme. The film follows the Gibbonses of 17 Sycamore Road, Clapham, and provides a fascinating chronicle of the inter-war years. The everyday concerns of the family's central characters—Frank and Ethel Gibbons (Robert Newton and Celia Johnson), and their children (Reg, Queenie and Vi)—are shown against the backdrop of key events: the Wembley Exhibition of 1924, the General Strike of 1926, the emergence of Hitler's dictatorship and the rise of fascism, both in the East End and abroad. Like Mr. Bunting, Frank remains a staunch patriot and rejects political extremism, symbolizing the English love of moderation and common sense. But he is sufficiently political to distance himself from the policy of appeasement in the 1930s. The film would prove popular at the box office and was seen as a valuable attempt to depict the lives of ordinary people in England.

Another film that celebrates the stoicism, humor and decency of the British, as well as the emerging Anglo-Soviet alliance, is *The Demi Paradise* (1943), directed by Anthony Asquith. Laurence Olivier is convincing in the lead role of Ivan Kouznetsoff, an engineer who creates a revolutionary design for a propeller to be used on ice breakers.

A quote at the beginning serves as the motto for the entire film: "Joking decides great things stronger and better oft than earnest can." The quirky English sense of humor, that ability to laugh in the face of adversity and "make do" in times of trouble, will enable the country to survive the rigors of war. Kouznetsoff comes to see humor as the essence of English tolerance and sense of fair play, but not before he has overcome a deep skepticism about polite society.

On his first visit to England, Kouznetsoff finds reason to dislike English life, and is, by turns, puzzled, dismissive and contemptuous of what he sees. His arrival is marred by the grim English weather, while he finds English people to be cold, brusque and impolite. His landlady treats him with suspicion, warning him that he has entered a respectable establishment and therefore expects no trouble. He is befriended by Ann Tisdall (Penelope Ward), the granddaughter of the manager of the shipbuilding firm that he has come to see. But when he visits her house, misunderstandings abound. There are fears that Kouznetsoff is a revolutionary terrorist, while the Russian, steeped in Communist tradition, cannot understand why Tisdall's father has not joined a trade union.

Kouznetsoff's encounters with polite society leave him somewhat baffled. He is bewildered by the English propensity for eccentricity: their love of cricket, train timetables and endless cups of tea. He lectures his English hosts on the evils of capitalism, believing that all employers are exploitative and obsessed with profit. He is promptly contradicted by the shipyard manager, who tells him that the company's motto "Duty and service" could be a Communist slogan.

He is taken to a theater, which he considers outrageously expensive, and fails to find its star turn, Leslie Henson, particularly amusing. Once again the English sense of humor is paraded as England's secret weapon, inaccessible to "closed-minded" foreigners. He fails to see any point in the town's annual pageant, with its re-enactment of scenes from British history. "You are hidebound, convention filled," he tells his English hosts.

Kouznetsoff's disillusionment with England is sealed when Tisdall, the object of his affections, rather impolitely rebuffs his request for marriage. Kouznetsoff believes she is heartless, a perfect reflection of her moribund and unfeeling people.

When Kouznetsoff returns to England later in the war, his perception of the country is gradually transformed. Despite being at war, there are few signs of panic. English stoicism and calm during an air raid both surprises and impresses him. When Germany invades his homeland, he is welcomed as an ally, with promises of support for Russia's military needs.

The pageant now has an international flavor, featuring some of Britain's wartime allies, while proceeds are donated to Kouznetsoff's home town. The shipyard manager promises him that shipping contracts will be completed, no matter what obstacles stand in the way. And at the end, when a new propeller has to be fitted in record time, the shipyard workers perform Herculean labors to complete the task. Even Kouznetsoff senses that "the English never know when they are beaten."

The film is an elaboration of the English character—the ability to muddle through, stoicism in adversity and unfailing humor—for foreign ears. While finding English reserve puzzling, idiosyncratic and unfriendly, the Russian hero comes to appreciate its warmer side. At the end his rousing peroration celebrates the English sense of humor:

> If you can laugh at life and at yourselves, you can be tolerant. If you can laugh, you must hate persecution. You must love decency; above all, you must love freedom. For there is no laughter where there is no freedom.

However, this is England seen through the eyes of the upper middle class, with little deference to the People's War.[6]

An interesting MGM take on the English class system is provided by *Mrs. Miniver* (1942), a classic MGM production directed by William Wyler that received six Academy Awards, including Best Film. The film deals with the lives of a suburban middle-class family in Kent and how they adapt to the demands of total war. Though affluent, they lack the pretensions or haughty manners with which the aristocracy were associated in American eyes. The Minivers behave with stoic fortitude and come to accept the privations that war brings. During one air raid they content themselves with reading *Alice in Wonderland* as menacing German bombers fly overhead.

They are set against the film's upper-class figure, Lady Beldon, a woman who is always inclined to view her social inferiors with disdain. She regards the war as one big intrusion by the working class and regrets having to follow the instructions of an air raid warden during a raid. At one point she says, "The worst thing about this war is the chance it gives to little people to make themselves important." However, her haughtiness and sense of superiority eventually give way to a feeling of social solidarity. She invites the villagers to take shelter in the cellar of Beldon Hall, and at the end of the film, having lost a daughter in an enemy raid, sings with the other villagers in the local church. The parish priest calls this "a war of the people," and in the closing shot we peer through a gaping hole in the church roof as RAF bombers head towards Germany.

Mrs. Miniver is at once a depiction of a typical middle-class family who show resilience in adversity and also a representation of social leveling. A former class antagonist of the aristocracy, Mrs. Beldon comes to condone the egalitarian ethos of the People's War and the classless assumptions that underlie it.

It is a series of Ealing productions, including *The Bells Go Down*, *The Foreman Went to France*, *Nine Men*, and *San Demetrio, London*, which truly glorify the "democratic spirit" of wartime Britain. All feature ordinary citizens turned heroes, and focus on a small, tight-knit group of individuals from differing backgrounds who are bound together by a common duty.

The Bells Go Down (1943), like Humphrey Jennings' classic *Fires Were Started*, celebrates the work of the Auxiliary Fire Service. The AFS had been created in 1938 as a back-up service and was designed to help out in emergencies, such as the bombing that was expected in a prolonged war. The film tells the story of a group of recruits to the AFS who are trained in fire-fighting before being put to the test during the Blitz. The men come from a variety of backgrounds: Sam (Meryvn Johns) was a petty thief, Brooks (William Hartnell) was a veteran of the International Brigade, and Tommy Turk (Tommy Trinder) was a gambler.

The film shows the camaraderie between the men and emphasizes the importance of teamwork and duty. There is no stuffy, upper-class type in charge, and no-one receives promotion through hereditary entitlement. The cooperation of these characters, despite their very different backgrounds, symbolizes the merging of all classes in the war effort—the real spirit of the People's War.

One fireman describes his experiences of fighting in Madrid during the Spanish Civil War. His paean to the work of the fire-fighters could have been a motto for the People's War: "...they never gave in, they died for each other or went on living for each other..."

The scenes of firemen tackling blazes are a mix of dramatic studio-based reconstruction and documentary footage from the Blitz. The Blitz images have an iconic status all their own—of cheerful, humorous, working-class people defying the bomb damage to open up their businesses, the anti–Nazi slogans on shop windows, the brave death-defying firefighters tackling blazes amid carnage and destruction. For those watching this film in 1942, such images were still fresh in the mind and evoked powerful memories.

Throughout the film, Trinder provides his trademark Cockney cheerfulness and optimism, a humorous relief from the bombing. Yet his death at the end, when a wall collapses on him, seems strangely inappropriate, and is, in the words of James Chapman, "a shocking and unexpected reversal of the audience's expectations."[7]

The film is more than the story of brave fire-fighters. Throughout, the unit's activities are seen against the background of their local community. The film opens with a simple paean to the inhabitants of an ordinary village in the East End. We see images of people going about their daily business, shopping at the local market and mingling with each other. A voiceover tells us that "London isn't a town, but a group of villages ... a community bounded by a few streets, with its own market place, its shops, its church, its police station and its fire brigade." We follow the community as its church is bombed, the local pub takes a hit, and the hospital is blitzed. Yet the stoical cheerfulness of the community remains unaffected.

The Bells Go Down suffered from the fact that it was released so soon after Jennings' acclaimed masterpiece *Fires Were Started*. According to *The Sunday Times*, the feature seemed "gimcrack after the magnificent *Fires Were Started*" and lacked the documentary's "astonishing spontaneity and truth."[8]

A shift towards greater realism and more credible storylines was provided by *The Foreman Went to France* (also known as *Somewhere in France*), a 1942 film based on a story by J.B. Priestley. Alberto Cavalcanti joined the Ealing team, determined to use his background in documentaries to lend his films authenticity, while Charles Frend directed.

Essentially, the film is a tale of how determined foreman Fred Carrick (Clifford Evans) volunteers to rescue machinery in France which is vital to the war effort. Along the way, he and some companions encounter a variety of obstacles, whether bureaucrats in his firm, fifth columnists, Nazi dive bombers or fleeing refugees. Managing to outwit the enemy, the foreman and his colleagues get the machinery to the French coast where it is transported to Britain. It is a tale of courage and plucky resistance suffused with the democratic flavor of the People's War. The characters are human and believable, with the film eschewing stock characterizations and caricatures.

Carrick's mission is undertaken "against the odds," and his pluck and resourcefulness must win the day against a technically superior adversary. In his path lie Blimpish managers and bureaucrats in his firm who, thanks to a mixture of complacency and adherence to official procedure, threaten to delay the mission before it has started. The civil servants he encounters are more interested in form filling than winning the war. With good reason Charles Barr comments that the threat comes "as much from English complacency and amateurism ... as from enemy operations."[9]

When he arrives in France, he encounters fifth columnists and Nazi sympathizers who also try to hinder his progress. Indeed, the plot is dominated by the corrosive effect of wartime collaboration. Nonetheless, he reaches the factory and sees the machines that need to be transported out of the country. But he has no perambulator, no cycle and little idea of how to accomplish his goals. His chief weapon is a never say die attitude and an amateur's ability to improvise. When he teams up with an American secretary, she points out that his half-baked plans are "what the English call muddling through."

Later Carrick teams up with two soldiers, Tommy (Tommy Trinder) and Jock (Gordon Jackson), as well as an American nurse Anne Stafford (Constance Cummings), who all promise to help bring the machine back to England. In doing so, the film emphasizes the unity of civilians and the military, even if at times this means working against strict military rules. Evans is told that to load a military lorry with a machine in this way would be contrary to King's regulations, with Evans merely pointing out that there is nothing in King's regulations that rules out using common sense.

Neither Trinder nor Gordon Jackson can be described as Blimpish types. Trinder, who featured in a number of Ealing productions, was the archetypal cocky Cockney whose songs and one-liners had brought him fame among British audiences throughout the war. This film is full of his youthful exuberance and native wit.

The only British officer we encounter is aiding the enemy, giving the film a different emphasis to that of *Ships with Wings* and *Convoy*. The characters have a practical, gritty patriotism which is about getting the job done efficiently. If their mission had been entrusted to men of higher rank, one wonders if it would have ever got off the ground. At one point Carrick declares that "the people at the top think they're fighting the last war all over again," echoing the kind of radical sentiments that so upset Churchill.

Balcon was quite clear about the film's central message: "It showed how the civilian population, particularly those engaged in the manufacture of essentials for wartime purposes, were just as much in the front line as the troops."[10]

But the film also celebrates the spirit of wartime cooperation from different national groups. Carrick and Jock work together, showing how the Scots and English had put aside their historic rivalries, while Stafford's cooperation reminded audiences of the newfound Anglo-American alliance. At the end, the small group reaches a French fishing port where they must rely on local goodwill to transport the machine back to England.

With German forces closing in on the town, the townsfolk are about to board with all their possessions, but the machine can only be transported if the possessions are left behind. In a poignant final scene, the trawler sails with the machine on board after the villagers decide to leave their worldly goods behind. The skipper's final remarks are testament to the belief in Anglo-French solidarity: "We shall owe everything to your country when France lives again—one day."

One theme in *The Foreman Went to France* was the insidious threat from collaborators. Many believed that Germany's success in overrunning Western Europe in 1940 was partly due to homegrown enemies within each of the defeated countries. They were said to form a lethal "fifth column" which spread despondency and passed on information vital to the enemy. The rapid collapse of Belgium, Holland and France persuaded many that this threat was real and that the same forces in Britain could cause a national capitulation in the event of invasion.

In the middle of 1940, thousands of suspected German and Italian collaborators (many were actually anti-fascist refugees) were rounded up and shipped to the Isle of Man, following Churchill's order to "collar the lot." At the same time, poster campaigns were warning people about the dangers of careless talk, with such titles as "Keep Mum, she's not so dumb" and "Keep it under your hat." Exaggerated concerns about the presence of German agents and sympathizers persuaded many that unguarded conversations and gossip could inadvertently aid the enemy, endangering lives in the process. It would not be long before a feature film would deal with these connected concerns.

Michael Balcon was approached by General Hawkesworth, the director of military training, about making a film dealing with army security. He was told that the War Office would provide financial support (£20,000), while serving men would be released for the duration of the film. The resulting production, *Next of Kin* (1942), was an important success for Ealing, though it nearly fell foul of Churchill. When the Prime Minister saw the film prior to its release, he expressed the view that "it would cause unnecessary alarm and sorrow to a great number of people"[11] and wanted its release delayed. Fortunately for Balcon, the Prime Minister's views did not prevail.

In the film we are told that this is a "story of how you unwittingly worked for the enemy—you—without knowing gave him the facts—you—in all innocence—helped to write these tragic words." The tragic words in question are "the next of kin of casualties have been informed," which became a standard BBC announcement.

At the start, a commando raid is carried out on a German submarine base in Brittany. It is successful, but this is tempered by the fact that the Allies suffer heavy casualties. We discover that the Germans had been given advance warning of the attack through the unwitting help of well-intentioned individuals. The rest of the film elaborates on how the Germans received, and then acted on, this vital intelligence.

Throughout the film we are shown alarming examples of complacency at every level. Senior officers are given helpful directions to a military installation with no questions asked, prompting one man to comment on how easy it would be for a German spy in England. A private reveals to his Dutch girlfriend where his military training is taking place, little realizing that her employer will then blackmail the information out of her. A wing commander, meeting his date at a restaurant, leaves sensitive aerial photographs in a briefcase, only for Nazi agents to switch briefcases and pass copies of the photographs on to Berlin. As Barr points out, the film highlights the "underside of those British qualities of insouciance and understatement: amateurism and complacency."[12]

The film works by humanizing the spies and suggesting how easily they can masquerade as upright members of the community. Barratt (Stephen Murray) is a respectable bookseller who blackmails his employee Beppie (Nova Pilbeam) by threatening to kill her Dutch family. Davis (Mervyn Johns), a seemingly harmless Welsh evacuee, is actually a murderous Nazi agent, while a theatrical dresser, is another dangerous blackmailer. Fifth columnists are presented as a pervasive threat that lurks "in any walk of life, grocers, pubkeepers, barbers, politicians … [or] people the enemy has bribed or blackmailed."

The film ends by showing the consequences of all this indiscretion. During the British raid on Norville, countless soldiers are shot, bayoneted and hacked to death by German troops. The scene is filmed in harrowing fashion, with snatches of documentary footage showing dive bombers in action. Together they form a visually compelling reminder of the price paid for careless talk.

In general the film was well received by the critics. Dilys Powell of *The Sunday Times* described it as "a tale told with authority and conviction," while C.A. Lejeune said it was "meticulously done in every department of writing, direction and acting."[13] For General Alexander, the picture's value was far greater. He told Dickinson, "This film was worth a division of troops to the British army."[14] However, not all reacted to the movie's realism in such a positive fashion. Writing of the film's preview at London's Curzon cinema, director Thorold Dickinson commented, "The first version of *The Next of Kin* was so explicit that it sobered the troops who saw it and sickened many of the civilians, some of whom were carried out in a dead faint."[15]

Another film that tackles the threat of the fifth column is *Unpublished Story*, made in 1942 by Two Cities. It focuses on Britain's annus mirabilis of 1940 when the country saw off the threat of invasion and put up solid resistance to Nazi tyranny.

But this is far from an unvarnished panegyric to 1940, for no attempt is made to glorify the retreat from Dunkirk. We see a trainload of soldiers returning from France, bewildered by the events they have witnessed. Far from returning in a blaze of glory, they appear disillusioned, weak and washed out. The men are accompanied by sports reporter Bob Randall (Richard Greene), who has witnessed first hand the tumultuous events of the previous month. He tells his bosses that the British army had been fighting not just an enemy army but "panic and confusion behind their lines, fifth columnists giving false orders ... traitors within the gates."

Warning of similar dangers in Britain, the reporter sets out to expose the leaders of a British organization, "People for Peace," which he suspects may be a dangerous collaborationist front for Nazi Germany. However, his stern account of one of their meetings falls foul of the Home Security censors, and a more restrained piece from a rival reporter is published. Greene later finds the censor cavorting with the leaders of "People for Peace"; but far from being a traitor, the censor is actually an MI5 agent tracking the group's activities. The agent's suspicions are well founded, for the group is indeed being used by Nazi agents posing as English businessmen.

This production, like *Next of Kin*, intersperses the narrative with an impressive array of wartime footage, this time centered on the wreckage of the Blitz. We see buildings crumble from the vast firestorm created by bombing raids, with the iconic image of St. Paul's Cathedral standing tall amid the debris. But the focus here is very much on the enduring stoicism of the British people as they cope with adversity.

After one raid a pub owner finds his premises "more open than usual" but insists on business as usual, even ejecting a defeatist peace agitator. His cheerful demeanor is in striking contrast to the physical destruction inflicted by the Luftwaffe. During another East End raid, journalist Carole Bennett (Valerie Hobson) visits an underground station where people have settled down for the night. People walk along in a calm, ordered manner while others engage in an impromptu sing-along. Together they exemplify the calm and cheerful exterior so characteristic of popular mythology.

When the newspaper offices are devastated by a bombing raid, the editor (Brefni O'Rorke) is informed that the paper will still go to press, using lamp-light if necessary. He is warmed by this resilience and exhorts his fellow workers to greater efforts with this fine peroration: "Bombs will never break us, panic will never stampede us, Britain will stick it out." Nothing better sums up the spirit of resistance of the People's War. Randall shows stealth and resolution in unmasking the German agents. But the film also serves as a warning to avoid complacency at home and to unmask the dangerous foes of the war effort, whatever their disguises may be.

Fifth columnists would have posed the greatest security risk in the event of an enemy invasion. Given the proximity of the German army to mainland Britain, the threat of a cross–Channel landing seemed very real during the summer months of 1940, though fears of an imminent attack receded once the Battle of Britain had ended. However, in February 1942 there were renewed concerns over an enemy assault, brought about by the fact that three German warships were able to sail through the English Channel with impunity. Amid growing public anxiety, Ealing started work on an adaptation of a Graham Greene short story from 1940 ("The Lieutenant Died Last") called *Went the Day Well?* (1942). The film was designed to give people a sense of what an enemy invasion might be like, and how a fictional community under occupation would react.

The community in question lives in Bramley End, a tranquil and quite idyllic village in the English countryside. Indeed, the very tranquility of the setting suggests a cozy complacency in which thoughts of invasion are far from people's minds. The village squire laughs at the idea that the village has been put in a state of general defense. We are cheerfully told that the fifth column is "one thing we haven't got to worry about."

But there is a fifth column, and leading it is the respectable leader of the community, Oliver Wilsford, played by Leslie Banks. Secretly he has arranged to help a group of Nazi parachutists, disguised as Royal Engineers, to settle in Bramley End, where they will be billeted. The enemy troops duly arrive and are welcomed into the village before being billeted in various homes. The task of this gang is to install some piece of apparatus which will disrupt the radar system and thus make an imminent German invasion much easier.

Though no match for the Germans in physical strength, the villagers "do their bit" by the simple use of intelligence and quick wits. The Germans give away small clues to their identity: one soldier chastises a child for touching some sensitive equipment, another draws some unusual figures on a telegram, and Nora Ashton, the vicar's daughter (Valerie Taylor) comes across a bar of Viennese chocolate in a soldier's kitbag.

Wilsford is told of the deception and immediately informs the German captain. In turn, German Kommandant Orlter (Basil Sydney) decides to occupy the village and chooses the community's church to announce his intentions. The church, as in so many other films, is at the heart of the community and expresses its Protestant English identity.

As if to demonstrate the enemy's fundamental indecency, Orlter storms into the church while the community is at prayer. The camera cleverly moves from a shot of the villagers, in pious submission, to that of Orlter, whose menacing figure fills the frame. His barking and aggressive tones are in stark contrast to his solemn surroundings.

But this film has a darker edge too. For, under pressure, the contented villagers are capable of matching their captors for sheer ruthless violence. The postmistress, Mrs. Collins (Muriel George) hacks a German soldier to death with an axe before she is herself bayoneted. The men, after breaking out of the church, spare no time in killing as many Germans as possible. Their desensitivity to killing is symbolized by the intentional inclusion of women in the firing line at the end. For most of the film, women have played largely nurturing roles, either tending to the injured or looking after children. By the end, when the villagers are barricaded in a house, two female characters are involved in the shootout. The vicar's daughter is not exempt from this violence. She comes across Wilsford trying to dismantle defenses in the manor house and, realizing that he is a pro–Nazi traitor, shoots him dead.

The film has been taken as another attack on the upper classes, with the treacherous Wilsford and the deceitful Orlter contrasting with the ordinary heroes of Bramley End. In this sense, the picture appears superficially similar to *Foreman Went to France*. But the extent to which the film offers a radical critique of the class system is questionable. Certainly the upper-class Wilsford is the real villain of the piece, a pro–German agent who betrays the trust put in him by the villagers of Bramley End. And there is no doubt that the movie highlights the vital role played by working-class heroes in saving Bramley End from destruction. The working-class George Truscott helps unmask the "British" soldiers as Nazis in disguise. The poacher, Bill Purvis, sacrifices himself after raising the alarm, while ordinary members of the community, such as the postmistress, take the fight to the Nazi occupiers.

But Nora is of the same class as the treacherous Wilsford, and she does not hesitate to kill him at the end after she learns about his pro–Nazi leanings. The vicar, another representative of Britain's leadership class, sacrifices himself

Went the Day Well? (1942) depicts the aftermath of a Nazi invasion of England. Here two villagers of Bramley End (Elizabeth Allan, left, and Thora Hird) take up arms against the brutal intruders (Anchor Bay Entertainment, Photofest).

heroically after his futile attempt to raise the alarm by ringing the church bells. This act of conspicuous valor scarcely goes unnoticed by the rest of the villagers. Thus, what the film really suggests is not that there is something rotten about Britain's class structure per se, but that leadership at a time of crisis must come from all sections of society. Heroes can be molded as much from a working-class as an upper-class background, a quintessential element of the People's War. The central message is that the village community, like the nation, must guard against complacency and rally together in the event of an enemy invasion.

Some reviewers took the film as a serious indicator of what might happen in the event of a real attempted occupation. "If England is ever invaded," wrote Dilys Powell in the *Sunday Times*, "this is what the inhabitants of countless Bramleys up and down the land may expect to happen." She added that it was refreshing to see the English people "shown as capable of individual and concerted resourcefulness in a fight and not merely steady in disaster."[16]

Nonetheless, the relish for violence shown in the film, particularly juxtaposed against the imagery of rural beauty and churches, gives the movie an unsettling quality. As one reviewer wrote, "Even people like the fair minded, quiet living people of Bramley End could turn very nasty indeed if pushed."[17]

For the most part the war genre is a gritty exploration of masculine virtues, with the majority of heroes (Jack Hawkins, John Mills, Kenneth More) demonstrating solid, unflappable and very masculine qualities. As Frank Jackson noted, in British films women are generally "pushed into the background." He wrote:

> They are wives, waiting anxiously at home for their tired heroes to return. They are sweethearts trying, but in vain of course, to water down our fighting spirit. They are nurses, tending our wounds, smiling bravely, giving us badly needed injections of courage ... and then fading decently out of the picture.[18]

Gainsborough's *Two Thousand Woman* (1944), written and directed by Frank Launder, breaks the mold by having exclusively female stars. Among them are Patricia Roc, Phyllis Calvert and Flora Robson. It is also unusual for being set in an internment camp and featuring the escape of Allied servicemen. Such films were rare during the war, and ones featuring daring escapes were rarer still. As Robert Murphy points out, "Jack Beddington of the MOI had requested producers not to deal with escapes in case this goaded the Germans into making conditions in the camps harsher."[19]

A group of British women arrive at a chateau used to guard people who have been interned. Later a group of Allied airmen, whose plane has crashed, seek sanctuary there, and the women have to use their guile to keep the men hidden from the Nazis. Here we see soldiers dependent for their survival on women, a direct challenge to the convention that heroism is exclusively male.

Miss Manningford (Flora Robson) epitomizes the women's resilience and unswerving sense of duty. When initially brought before the German whose task it is to apportion rooms, Manningford insists on being given a room with her elderly friend. She fearlessly threatens to report him to the commandant if he refuses, leading the indignant officer to grant her request. Later she defies the blackout in order to help an Allied air crew bomb their target and then land safely. She and her companion, Miss Meredith (Muriel Aked), admit to their "crime" without demur and accept their subsequent punishment with equanimity. As they are led away, their companions sing "For they are jolly good fellows." Later the women put on a cabaret performance, and while the guards are being entertained, the airmen flee, disguised as Nazis.

Manningford and Meredith's robust defiance of authority mirrors that of the group as a whole. They are forced to use their collective guile and ingenuity to protect the Allied airmen, outwitting German officers and a Nazi member within their own group.

These female heroes demonstrate much of the ethos of "the People's War," even though their war is in French territory. They display an abundance of pluck, stoicism and, above all, unending good humor. But the setting is too unreal and far too cozy to shed any real light on the horrors of the POW experience.

Just as revolutionary for its assertion of a feminist viewpoint is *The Gentle Sex* (1943). The film, directed by Leslie Howard, traces the lives of seven women who enroll in the Auxiliary Territorial Service (ATS). The ATS was set up in 1938 as the women's branch of the British army. At first women signed up on a voluntary basis, but from 1941, conscription meant that they had to join one of the auxiliary services. Contrary to the popular image promoted, the ATS did not offer women glamorous jobs, though the range of roles (drivers, cooks, radar operators) was diverse.

In the opening voiceover we are told that these women are "flippant, vain, inconstant, childish, proud and full of flavor." Their early exposure to military training seems to bear this out, as the new recruits, from different class backgrounds, struggle to work together as a cohesive unit. Slowly they begin to shrug off their "gentle nature" by performing a vital war duty with diligence and efficiency.

They are asked to transport a large quantity of vital war material for use in an imminent military operation. The women have to battle a variety of dangers, including tiredness, low visibility, poor weather and defective tires. In a quasi-military operation the women perform as well as any male unit, acting as an ideal complement to those in the fighting field. As one soldier comments, "This is a women's war."

The Gentle Sex thus belongs in the subgenre of "the People's War" and reminds us of the sacrifices made by those on the Home Front. The narrator tells us that whereas before the Battle of Waterloo women organized a ball for the officers, now the war could not be fought without their contribution. But it is also forward looking and radical in its implicit call for female equality.

While *The Gentle Sex* celebrates the contribution of women to army life, *Millions Like Us* (1943), directed by Sidney Gilliat and Frank Launder, looks at their role on the home front, specifically within an aircraft factory. It does this by focusing on a typical factory worker, Celia (Phyllis Roc), and using her to represent a vast number of other women engaged in similar work. But it does not attempt to present factory life as inherently glamorous or romantic. Instead it is simply presented as a vital component in keeping the armed forces supplied and winning the war.

At the outset Celia virtually begs not to work in industry and harbors dreams of joining the ATS. But she is rebuffed at the recruiting office and told that "Mr. Bevin needs another million women, and I don't think we should disappoint him at a time like this.... You can help your country just as much in an overall as you can in uniform these days." Despite her initial reluctance, she soon takes to factory life with aplomb and wins the approval of the foreman, Charlie Forbes (Eric Portman). She also falls in love with and then marries an air gunner (Gordon Jackson), but their romance is short lived when he is killed flying over Germany.

The film demonstrates that while women may regard such work as mundane and monotonous, it is nevertheless fundamental, and their role should not be overlooked. But whereas *The Gentle Sex* asserts a feminist viewpoint by making an implicit call for equality, *Millions Like Us* takes a more skeptical view of the postwar world. This is reflected in the film's other romance, that between Forbes and the upper-middle-class and somewhat snooty Jennifer Knowles (Anne Crawford). Forbes tells her that he cannot commit to marriage until he is certain that the wartime consensus is maintained after the war. As he puts it, "The world's roughly made up of two kinds of people—you're one sort and I'm the other. Oh, we're together now there's a war on, we need to be. But what's going to happen when it's all over?" The wartime consensus was something that Gilliat and Launder were not prepared to take for granted.

Chapter 5

Service Films: The Triumph of Duty

At various times before the Second World War, British motion pictures had dealt with life in each of the three armed services. Perhaps the earliest recruitment film for the services was *Army Life: How Soldiers Are Made* (1900), which featured footage of cavalry, artillery and infantry. The film was made during the second Boer War and at a time when recruitment to the army was being considerably affected by the inadequate fitness of male volunteers. The War Office, aware of the need to raise the public profile of the armed forces, commissioned a series on both the British army and the British navy.

But it was not until the First World War that full-length films projected the power and influence of the navy and army. *Britain Prepared* went into release in February 1916 and showed audiences scenes of submarines and battleships, together with footage of HMS *Queen Elizabeth*. *The Battle of the Somme* was a lengthy documentary that dealt with the great British offensive of 1916. Though it could hardly reveal the scale of the carnage on the first day of battle, when nearly 20,000 British soldiers perished, it did show audiences shots of artillery and an exploding mine, as well as soldiers going "over the top." The film was a huge popular success, aided by the fact that cinema attendance had reached a weekly total of 20,000,000 by 1917.

By the 1930s each branch of the armed forces was aware of the huge potential offered by the cinema. They were also dismayed by the pacifist mood that prevailed in popular culture and the low esteem in which the armed forces were held. The Admiralty cooperated in the production of a number of naval films, including *Our Fighting Navy* and *Sons of the Sea*. The War Office, too, cooperated fully with three army films in the 1930s, one of which, *OHMS*, featured a youthful John Mills, later a key fixture in British war films.

The air force, the newest of the three branches of the armed forces, was also quick to exploit the popular medium of commercial film. The RAF lent men and aircraft for a number of productions, including the Formby comedy *It's in the Air* and the espionage thriller *Spies of the Air*. Thus, before the outbreak of war, all three services had lent their support to the commercial film industry.

If there is one overriding theme in the service films, it is the paramount value of duty. In a war, one's primary loyalty was to the nation, symbolically represented by a military, naval or air force unit. No war film ever questioned that this was the ultimate source of allegiance for anyone in the services. Selfish individualism was eschewed and seen as a reckless assault on the values of the wider group. However, individual self-sacrifice had a redemptive quality, and, indeed, the war could be seen to depend on it. This core value naturally built on earlier ideas of chivalry and gentlemanly conduct, personal concern for others and the importance of emotional (personal) restraint. Discussions of these wartime films will be divided into three sections, each one corresponding to the three units of the armed forces. By and large, service film documentaries are not discussed.

The Royal Navy

During the "Phoney War," the only branch of the armed services that saw action was the Royal Navy. Its first major success came in December 1939 when three British cruisers engaged the German pocket battleship *Graf Spee* in the South Atlantic, forcing the damaged ship to seek refuge in Montevideo harbor. Four days later the German captain scuttled the ship.

The first film to feature these events was Gainsborough's *For Freedom* (1940), starring the Scottish comedian Will Fyffe. Much of it is concerned with pointing out the evils of Nazism—its censorship of opponents, persecution of minorities, assassination of rivals and aggressive foreign policy—and also, by implication, the bitter futility of appeasement. It takes a particular dig at those who used the Munich agreement to advance their own anti-militarist agenda.

In the film, Fyffe's pacifist son, Stephen, buoyed by Chamberlain's "peace" agreement and his own internationalist outlook, persuades his father to make a film that shows how the scientific and artistic achievements of Western nations can build a better world. This, he argues, will contribute more to peace than a documentary designed to stir opposition to fascism. Accordingly, we see footage of great sporting, scientific and technological triumphs which are the product of every race and nation.

But Hitler's invasion of Czechoslovakia, in defiance of the Munich agreement, shatters any further pacifist illusions. We now follow newsreel footage of events until the invasion of Poland, with Fyffe determined that Germany will be defeated by the forces of civilization.

Fyffe's son, disenchanted with utopian internationalism, redeems himself by returning footage from Montevideo of the sinking of the *Graf Spee*. The Admiralty cooperated with this part of the film, allowing officers and men from the British cruisers *Ajax* and *Exeter* to reconstruct their actions during the battle of the River Plate. The audience was treated to an interesting mixture of reconstruction, narrative (from a retired Vice-Admiral) and a series of newsreel clips. At the end we hear a segment of Churchill's speech at the Guildhall where he pays fulsome tribute to the naval crews. The film is imbued with an infectious patriotism and is enlivened throughout by Fyffe's zestful contempt for Nazism. Fyffe would go on to star in the little known *Neutral Port* (1940), where he played a bad tempered captain of a merchant ship whose vessel is sunk by a U-boat.

The next big naval hit was the Ealing production *Convoy* (1940), the third and final film of talented director Penrose (Pen) Tennyson. The movie is made in semi-documentary fashion, and this owed much to a demand for realism and authenticity. Balcon writes, "Before completing the script, Pen, still a civilian, went off on HMS *Valorous* with a convoy down the east coast from Scotland ... to pick up wonderful actual background material."[1]

The film tells the story of how a cruiser, *Apollo*, tackles a German ship, *The Deutschland*, in order to relieve a convoy which is under threat. While at sea, the cruiser receives an SOS from a ship, the *Seaflower*, that has detached itself from the convoy. It has actually been bombed by the Germans, who are sending out false distress signals. Captain Armitage (Clive Brook) refuses to provide assistance, but Lieutenant Cranford (who earlier ran off with Brook's wife) uses his own judgment. Disobeying orders, he sends a destroyer and a plane to rescue the *Seaflower*, a ship that his ex-wife happens to be traveling on. The plane is shot down, but the U-boat is sunk. Cranford is arrested for disobedience but is later redeemed when he sacrifices himself for the convoy.

Unlike Tennyson's previous film, *The Proud Valley*, *Convoy* concentrates on the actions of the officer class, represented by the tight-lipped Clive Brook and John Clements. Working-class characters, by contrast, are presented in somewhat stereotypical fashion. They are salt of the earth, plucky types who engage regularly in jovial anti–Nazi banter. For this reason William Whitebait wrote in *New Statesman* that "the lower deck of *Convoy* swarms with caricatures which might have come out of Punch."[2]

If the film does not feature social leveling, it does at least promote notions of duty before individual pleasure, and self-sacrificial duty. When the *Seaflower* sends out its fake distress calls, Armitage is guided by duty to the convoy rather than personal feeling. Indeed, duty to maritime life has cost him his marriage for, as his ex-wife reveals, the ships are his "whole existence." The Lieutenant derides him for his lack of common humanity and, in detaching a destroyer, prioritizes his personal selfish feelings. For this act of disobedience he must pay the ultimate price to redeem himself.

In *Convoy*, Germans are depicted in the sterotypical manner of *The Lion Has Wings*. The captain of the German ship is willing to torpedo the *Seaflower* despite the heavy presence of women and children refugees on board. The pleas to the German captain to desist fall on deaf ears. The captain responds robotically and unthinkingly by quoting the Fuhrer's approval of blood-letting in defense of the Reich. Lucy Armitage responds by quoting Nelson's prayer on the eve of Trafalgar. It is a choice between simple piety and humanity or blood and iron politics that disregards common humanity; a stark choice that the audiences of 1940 were all too aware of.

As with so many war films, *Convoy* ends with a religious service. Brook offers up a prayer for the safe return of his ship and crew. Despite the outstanding courage of the men, it is the Protestant religion that symbolizes the unity of England at war.

Ealing's next naval venture was "dedicated to the Fleet Air Arm" and, in particular, the *Ark Royal*. Sergei Nolbandov's *Ships with Wings*, made in 1941, has a strong documentary feel to it, owing much to the footage captured by cameraman Roy Kellino on board HMS *Ark Royal*. Models of ships and aircraft, as well as of an island, had to be constructed, and, in hindsight, the attempt was embarrassingly poor.

In a sense, the film is a continuation of *Convoy* in its representation of class. While the movie is dedicated "to the officers and men of the fleet air arm," it is the officers who receive the central roles. John Clements, Leslie Banks and Basil Sydney all fit into the upper-class mold with consummate ease.

In *Convoy* the overriding theme was the destructive power of individualism, of disregarding the group to follow individual desires. *Ships with Wings* similarly eschews selfish individualism, and when a guilty party violates this code, he must atone for his misdemeanor by sacrificing himself.

Lieutenant Stacey (John Clements) is one of a trio of air arm pilots, the other two being Lieutenant Maxwell (Michael Rennie) and Lieutenant Grant (Michael Wilding). Stacey has asked Celia Wetherby (Jane Baxter) for her hand in marriage and, partly to impress her, takes off in a plane for a display of aeronautic skill. The plane, though, is not up to this grueling display, and Stacey bails out, leaving the plane to crash. Unknown to him, Wetherby's brother is in the plane and is killed. For this reckless display, Stacey is court-martialed and dismissed.

During his court-martial, Stacey learns that the real damage he has inflicted is more than the death of one individual. Captain Fairfax tells him, "What matters to me is the harm you have done to our branch of the service, to this ship."

Now the film switches to wartime and the Greek island of Pamos. Stacey has a job flying for a local airline run by a lazy and incompetent Greek, played by Edward Chapman. His fellow pilot, a German called Wagner (Hugh Williams), is in league with a Nazi agent on Pamos who poses as a Yorkshire businessman. The SS soon take over the island, but the Greek refuses to submit to their barbarity. He rouses himself to deliver a speech that celebrates Greek ideals of freedom and democracy before he is beaten to death. The fact that the Greek government in 1941, being a fascist dictatorship, was far from freedom-loving or democratic was deemed inconsequential.

Stacey escapes the island and flies back to the aircraft carrier, but not before he has spotted the Italians laying some mines in the path of the *Ark Royal*. The attack now switches to the island of Panteria where the Allies aim to destroy a huge dam.

Stacey seeks to make up for his earlier misdemeanors by taking off in a plane to engage the enemy. This time he does so with official sanction. In the air he encounters Wagner, who is on a mission of his own to destroy the carrier. Approaching Wagner's plane from behind, Stacey locks his plane onto Wagner's fuselage and, in an improbable climax, crashes both planes into the dam, breaching it in the process. His final suicidal act grants him the redemption he craves and reasserts the core values of the film.

While documentary footage lends the film an air of authenticity, it is anything but realistic. The island, with its remnants of a Greek temple, looks like a cardboard cut-out. The models of ships and aircraft had to be hastily constructed and look shabby. Another weakness of the film is its lack of realism and fondness for stereotype. Germans behave with unmitigated savagery, fanaticism and lack of humor, Greeks are lazy and incompetent, and Italians are weak and cowardly.

Interestingly, the movie might never have got to the screen if the Prime Minister had had his way, for Churchill believed that the film could cause alarm and despondency. Fortunately for the producers, the decision on whether to approve the picture was handed to Admiral Sir Dudley Pound, the First Sea Lord, who gave it his seal of approval. The film proved tremendously popular with the public and received, according to Tom Harrison of *Mass Observation*, an approval rating of 80 percent, increasing to 96 percent in naval areas.[3]

By 1943, with the Battle of the Atlantic at full height, there were concerns raised about Britain's survival prospects. As Balcon put it, "There was an alarming amount of news at the time about our losses at sea, and consequently about the general petrol shortage. There was much talk, too, of the misuse of petrol by the general public."[4]

Having produced *Convoy*, with its emphasis on individual officers, it was now time for Ealing to produce a service film imbued with the spirit of the People's War. The theme of ordinary men fighting in adversity against tremendous odds was taken up in *San Demetrio, London* (1943).

As with so many of their productions, Ealing based the film on real-life events. *San Demetrio* was "an oil tanker which was practically cut in half in Mid Atlantic and heroically brought home by its stricken crew." For Balcon, *San Demetrio, London* fulfilled a number of different purposes. It would help to highlight the essential work of the merchant navy and make the public realize the human sacrifices that were neccessary to ensure the flow of oil to Britain.[5]

Like *Convoy* and *Ships with Wings*, much of the shooting was studio based and required the construction of elaborate sets. This time the officer class was largely absent, with the heroes comprising a group of working-class seamen.

The tanker *San Demetrio* is carrying 12,000 tons of much needed petrol from the U.S. to the Clyde in autumn 1940. While less than 1,000 miles from home, the convoy she is sailing with is caught by the German cruiser *Admiral Scheer*. The tanker catches fire, and the crew is forced to abandon ship and escape in lifeboats. Two lifeboats are picked up, but the third drifts on until they see a ship on the horizon. It happens to be the *San Demetrio*, still burning and utterly abandoned. Taking a chance, they re-board the ship, put out the fires and sail her back to England in triumph.

The film comes closest to celebrating the true populist spirit of the People's War. It was one thing to show civilians cheerfully doing their bit on the Home Front, and quite another to see this happen on a ship when military hierarchy would normally dictate an inegalitarian division of labor. Yet the men, from diverse backgrounds, are molded into an effective unit, working together against daunting odds.

Every task they carry out is the result of team effort and collective decision making. While stranded in the lifeboat, the captain admits that he can "take orders as well as give them." The decisions to re-board the ship and sail it to England are not decided by anyone of senior rank—they are effectively put to the vote of all crew members. "The crew is democracy in action," as Barr observes.[6] This radical ideological component has little danger of being subversive, however. The idea that a crew could take joint responsibility is subsumed in the ethos of the People's War. The paramountcy of the group and the submerging of individual and national interests for the good of the ship are dominant themes.

Ealing's social democratic ethos displayed on board the stricken tanker *San Demetrio* (*San Demetrio London*, 1943). Here men disregard rank and work collaboratively to extinguish the fire (Twentieth Century–Fox, Photofest).

The spirit of self sacrificial concern for the ship is symbolized by the spirit of duty shown by greaser John Boyle (Mervyn Johns). Even as he lies dying from exposure, his only thoughts are for the repercussions that his death will have on the deck below. The captain says he "never knew a little scrap of a man like that could have so many guts." War has raised a scrawny man to heroic status, but the heroism is typically understated and matter of fact, as if boarding a burning vessel was an everyday occurrence.

In many films the spirit of communal duty is threatened by a potentially subversive outsider who does not share the interests of the group. The American visitor Yank Preston (Robert Beatty) is at first dismissive of rules and regulations, and shows minimal concern for the ship. He disregards the warning from the ship bo'sun that he would be prohibited from entering the tanker if he were drunk. When told that bo'suns enforce such regulations, his brash reply is "I eat em raw." His reckless streak of subversive individualism causes him to be shunned and treated as an outsider. But by the end of the film he has abandoned his thoughtless disregard for rules and even arranges a funeral service for the dead Boyle.

The journey back on the stricken tanker seems improbable, and the odds against the crew are multiplied by the fact that they have "no bridge, no charts, no wireless, no signal flags, no compass and … no steering gear." They have to steer "by guess and by God." In no other film perhaps (save *The Foreman Went to France*) is the English spirit of muddling through and indomitability so apparent.

Balcon described the movie as "a wonderful epic story of human endeavour" which "brought home to the public that thousands of lives were at stake in keeping the pipelines flowing."[7] Yet it was less commercially successful than earlier productions, indicating that the tastes of the British public had started to move on.

In Which We Serve (1942), written and produced by Noël Coward, and co-directed by David Lean, remains the definitive tribute to Britain's fighting services, specifically the Royal Navy. It was based around events in the life of Coward's friend, Lord Mountbatten, whose ship *Kashmir* was sunk during the Battle of Crete in May 1941.

The film revolves around three central characters, each representing a different strand of English society: Captain Kinross (Noël Coward), Chief Petty Officer Walter Hardy (Bernard Miles) and Ordinary seaman Shorty Blake (John Mills). While Kinross is charming and unflappable, the epitome of upper-class manners and reserve, Hardy hails from a respectable middle-class background, and Mills is an authentic, salt of the earth cockney.

The three are bound together by HMS *Torrin*, an incomparable symbol of Britain's naval might. During operations in the Battle of Crete on May 23, 1941, the ship comes under attack by German dive bombers and sinks. The crew swim to safety where they cling onto a life raft, and the rest of the film consists of flashbacks in which they reflect on their civilian experiences as well as their earlier wartime experiences on the ship. From this moment onwards the men suffer equal hardship as they struggle to survive the onslaught of German bombers. In this sense the picture contains a powerful message about social leveling. Class differences, which created barriers during peacetime, are now irrelevant because the men have to pull together in a situation of unprecedented adversity.

HMS *Torrin* is a powerful symbol of the nation at war. She unites men from disparate backgrounds and becomes the focal point of their wartime loyalties. Even the families of the servicemen acknowledge that their husbands' (and their own) overriding duty is to *Torrin*, not their family. At a prewar Christmas party, Kinross' wife, played by Celia Johnson, declares, "The wife of a sailor is most profoundly to be pitied.... Wherever she goes, there is always in her life a permanent and undefeated rival, her husband's ship.... It holds first place in his heart. It comes before wife, home, children, everything." Yet while bemoaning her lot, she finds it extraordinary that she remains "so fond and so proud of her most implacable enemy."

With good reason the *Observer*'s C.A. Lejeune remarked how the film showed "the way timber and steel can become a person and dominate the lives of everyone connected with her."[8]

Like in other war films, death is handled with typical English restraint. In a moving sequence, Shorty Blake learns that Hardy's wife, Kath, was killed in a German raid during the Blitz. Hardy, who is in the middle of writing a letter to his wife, responds dispassionately, acknowledging the news before going up on deck and discarding his letter. The absence of histrionics lends subtlety and power to his performance. Not surprisingly, Kinross is the master of emotional understatement. When he is reunited with other survivors of the *Torrin*, he merely tells them there is "Nothing like a good swim before breakfast."

Noël Coward, the epitome of upper class manners, reserve and tight-lipped professionalism, starring in the 1942 naval classic *In Which We Serve* (United Artists, Photofest).

Though Coward was never a class warrior, he sought to "highlight the strengths of each individual class and to show how by pulling together they could win through." The film remains a powerful tribute to the emotional fiber of the British people and the qualities of "endurance, self sacrifice, stoical humour and team spirit."[9] Yet the movie offers a different perspective to its Ealing counterparts like *San Demetrio, London* and *The Foreman Went to France*. Here the men are never equals, despite their heroic effort at survival. Kinross's sympathy and benevolence is paternalistic in nature, and he never allows the men to forget that he is ultimately in control.

The semi-documentary style of *For Those in Peril* (1944), a lesser known Ealing production, looks fondly at the work of the Air Sea Rescue Service. This service regularly patrolled the Channel and the North Sea in an attempt to save airmen who had been shot down by enemy aircraft. The film centers on a new recruit, Private Rawlings (Ralph Michael), whose perceptions of the service are gradually transformed. Rawlings is a reluctant recruit, having previously served as a pilot. The first time he goes out to sea, little happens and he makes no attempt to hide his boredom. He is promptly upbraided by his mentor, Flight Lieutenant Murray (David Farrar), who reminds him that in war, "95 percent is boredom."

Rawlings becomes so disillusioned that he asks Murray if he can apply for leave after only two weeks. The tension here is between the desire for excitement (heroic individualism) and the more mundane requirements of war (selfless duty). The turning point comes during a mission in which Rawlings and Murray run into a minefield while coming under sustained air assault by enemy planes. Rawlings is asked to go out on deck to steer the ship past the mines, a task he completes adeptly and without demur.

Later he helps rescue sailors from a burning ship, a genuine baptism of fire for the young recruit. When Murray dies in the ensuing gunfight, Rawlings takes control and helps bring the ship back home. Murray lives long enough to congratulate his once doubting colleague, and with characteristic understatement, tells Rawlings that he has had "a tricky first show." But he then adds, "You'll do." Like other service films, *For Those in Peril* celebrates the virtues of understated heroism, pluck, coolness in adversity and a sense of unfailing duty.

The Citizen Army

Three films took a forward looking view of the British army and suggested that it had to adapt to the democratic spirit of the People's War. The most controversial of these three (perhaps the most controversial of the entire war) was another Powell/Pressburger collaboration, *The Life and Death of Colonel Blimp* (1943).

This was the famous film which ran up against the stern opposition of the War Office and then Churchill himself. He derided it as a "foolish production" which would be "detrimental to the morale of the Army" and wanted it stopped. Indeed, he was even prepared to give "special authority" to the MOI to ensure that this happened, though in the end, War Office representatives saw the film and raised no objection to its release. Nonetheless, such was Churchill's displeasure that he sent a memo to Brendan Bracken, his Minister of Information, asking him to stop the production.

Blimp was the creation of the famous cartoonist and critic of appeasement, David Low. For Low, Blimp typified everything that was wrong with the British establishment. He was reactionary, pompous, class obsessed and thoroughly complacent. In short, he typified outdated attitudes, values and ideas. Thus the film, which satirizes these outdated attitudes, is essentially forward looking insofar as it argues that a full-throttled and uninhibited assault on the enemy will alone bring victory. But it also attempts to downplay some of Blimp's negative qualities. The audience comes to appreciate, even empathize with, a noble, chivalric figure whose code of honor has been trumped by the demands of total warfare. Blimp becomes a "dear old bumbler" instead of a figure fit for derision.[10]

The film chronicles the military career of a Blimpish figure, Major-General Clive Wynne-Candy (Roger Livesey), from the Second Boer War in 1900 until the Second World War. At the start we see a military exercise in which the Home Guard are required to defend London against the regular army. Second Lieutenant "Spud" Wilson (James McKechnie) decides to begin the attack at 6 p.m., six hours earlier than scheduled. With the help of his girlfriend, Angela "Johnny" Cannon (Deborah Kerr), Wilson discovers that the head of the Home Guard (Candy) is at a Turkish bath and promptly goes there to arrest him. Candy is put out by the surprise, declaring that "war starts at midnight." A confrontation develops, and both men fall into the bath, leading to a lengthy flashback of Candy's military life.

Over four decades we see Candy transformed from a young, hot-headed soldier into an old-fashioned defender of traditional values. His experiences during the First World War reinforce his belief in a code of chivalry, decency and honor, and he is proud that British soldiers still adhere to "clean fighting" and "honest soldiering." He also befriends a German prisoner of war that he first encountered in South Africa, Theo Kretschmar-Schuldorff (Anton Walbrook), symbolizing his belief in fair play and magnanimity. Theo is resentful of Germany's defeated status and rails against those who seek a punitive peace. This is bound to reflect, in no small measure, the postwar cynicism in high British circles about the harshness of the Versailles Treaty.

But it is Theo who warns Candy that Nazi Germany cannot be defeated without "dirty methods." Learning that the BBC have banned a proposed talk by Candy, in which he says he would rather be defeated than win by German methods, Theo speaks to him with the voice of experience: "If you let yourself be defeated by them just because you are too fair to hit back the same way they hit at you, there won't be any methods but Nazi methods.... This is not a gentleman's war." He adds that if Blimp loses this war, "there won't be a return match next year or perhaps for a hundred years." Candy is persuaded to join the Home Guard, bringing us back full circle. Some were unhappy with the portrayal of a "good German," but this more balanced portrayal was typical of the Powell/Pressburger productions.

Churchill's belief that the film portrayed the British army in a bad light was shared by some critics. *The Daily Mail* wrote, "To depict British officers as stupid, complacent, self-satisfied and ridiculous may be legitimate comedy, but it is disastrously bad propaganda in times of war."[11] But Candy is hardly ridiculed in the film, nor is he made to look stupid. He is a genuinely likeable character who is given a warmer edge by the gentle performance of Walbrook. True, his Blimpish code of chivalry is an unhelpful relic from a bygone age, but that scarcely makes him a figure of fun.

It might be better to describe him as a tragic hero whose sense of honor, so laudable in itself, is simply ill-adjusted to total war. Dilys Powell, in *The Sunday Times*, got it right when she described him as "a soldier holding in the midst of a totalitarian war to the rules of a game which to his romantic, if imperceptible, mind was never deplorable."[12]

World War II films have often been thought of as the British equivalent of the "Western." This no doubt has less to do with plot or location and more to do with the gritty exploration of heroic masculinity. However, *Nine Men* (1943) is a war film that has the genuine feel of a Western. It is set in the Libyan Desert though it was actually shot in the Margam Sands in North Wales. It was Harry Watt's first film for Ealing and, in its dogged realism, austerity and stark approach to war, directly reflected his background in documentaries.

Jack Lambert, playing the tough Sergeant Watson, tells the men under his command about the need for "that little bit extra" (un petit peu) in wartime. He recalls a time earlier in the war when a patrol, of which he was commander, was attacked in a German air raid. With their lorry destroyed, Watson and his men run into a sandstorm in the desert while trying to get to their lines. They stumble across an ancient tomb which they use for temporary shelter and soon find themselves besieged by Italian troops and heavily outnumbered.

Despite repeated attacks by the enemy, the men are able to hold out and successfully launch a counterattack against superior numbers. Eventually they face the enemy in hand to hand combat, and just when it appears that all is lost, the men are relieved by a British command unit. The film is gritty and tense, with some superb cinematography and effective performances.

Nine Men stands alongside *The Bells Go Down* for its superb evocation of the common spirit of ordinary people under fire. Jack Lambert, the robust and no-nonsense sergeant, is a world away from the tight-lipped professionalism of John Clements. The recruits also come from a variety of very ordinary backgrounds: a bookie, a policeman, a cabbie, a miner and a coffee store owner are among some of the characters assembled here. Their dialogue, as one critic noted, was that of "citizens in uniform."[13] However, unlike *In Which We Serve*, it does not dwell on the men's backgrounds or home life. It is designed to be a taut and gritty piece of realism which focuses on how men under fire cope with the strains of war.

The paramountcy of the group is the film's dominant theme. Spurred on by the determined Lambert, the men form an effective and cohesive fighting unit who work for each other and show enormous discipline. And in its depic-

5. *Service Films* 79

Jack Lambert exhorting his soldiers to give *un petit peu* in *Nine Men* (1943). This film has the genuine feel of a British Western (United Artists, Photofest).

tion of the gallant few against the many, the film celebrates the stereotypical English love of the underdog. The odds facing his patrol are daunting, as Lambert points out: "60 against 7, and as it was enemy territory they were bound to bring up more men. Whoever you are up against, I can tell you, odds like that aren't fun."

But the men are undaunted by the challenge and face it with a refreshing "matter of factness." Yet as the *Manchester Guardian* points out, the film's weakness is that the enemy is "impossibly instead of credibly cowardly," the Italians behaving "with less valour than sheep show towards a sheep-dog."[14]

In films such as *San Demetrio, London* and *Nine Men*, the emphasis had been on the camaraderie and teamwork of ordinary people in adversity. This is also the theme of the 1944 classic *The Way Ahead*, which tells the story of how a group of civilians plucked from "Civvy Street" are molded into a tough and effective fighting unit. *The Way Ahead* is an example of what Raymond Durgnat called the "omnibus genre." As he put it, "Since service life unites people from different backgrounds, their separate stories find not only a common purpose, but a common interest."[15]

But here the unity and cooperation of these soldiers is far from apparent at the outset. For these new recruits are largely disgruntled at leaving behind their civilian lives. Private Davenport (Raymond Huntley), traveling with his junior employee, declares it thoughtless that the two men should be selected together in the same unit despite their differentiated status. He laments the "unsanitary" living conditions, while Private Brewer (Stanley Holloway) is scathing about the "terrible" food.

Private Stainer (Jimmy Hanley) deplores the army for being "full of people who want to make you suffer because you're no good at polishing buttons." He declares himself "independent" and cannot fathom how civilians can be placed under the control of tough army sergeants. When the men first meet up, they share their reservations about the army, appearing to share Davenport's observation that their present predicament is tragic.

The civilians' first encounter with army life is an intense period of training under Sergeant Fletcher (William Hartnell). Fletcher is a tough, no-nonsense figure who believes in drill and discipline, but his approach is resented by the men. Two recruits, Stainer and Lloyd, stage a revolt in the middle of an important military exercise. This act of subversion is a turning point in the film, for it leads to a sharp rebuke from Lieutenant Jim Perry (David Niven).

Far from disciplining the men, he talks proudly of the regiment's history and the famous battles they have fought. The central value of this regiment is that men have always fought for each other with a common sense of purpose. The lecture has the desired effect, and the men begin to show pride in their performances, rejecting their previous self-centeredness and individualism.

The men are now posted to fight in Tunisia and travel as part of the convoy for the Allied landings in North Africa. Their spirit and resolve is put to the test when their ship is torpedoed and they have to work together to put out the fire. Having dealt with this crisis, the soldiers must now win "hearts and minds" among the locals in Tunisia, something that is far from easy. A Tunisian café owner (Peter Ustinov) is reluctant to put them up, as he is a sworn pacifist who believes the war is a distant concern.

Yet he is won over by that most English of institutions—sport. As the men are playing darts one evening, some local Arabs take a strong interest. Then the café owner joins in, showing off his prowess by scoring a bull's-eye. The game has brought different nationalities together and helped break culturally sensitive barriers. Later, as the Germans advance towards the town, the café owner rejects his pacifism and helps fight against the enemy.

This film is about a "People's Army" which has learned to become an effective unit in the most trying of circumstances. The army has blended people of different social backgrounds without submerging their individuality and good humor. The film is therefore forward looking, seeing the war's social leveling as an opportunity for greater equality in the future. The critics generally praised the film and saluted it as a tribute to the infantry. It was also Trevor Howard's first film, making him a star of the screen as well as the stage.

RAF

Alexander Korda had planned a film from before the start of hostilities about how Britain could repel a German air attack. There was cooperation from the Air Ministry, and once war started, the MOI gave it their seal of approval.

The Lion Has Wings (1939), produced in only six weeks, is a simplistic and, at times, crude piece of wartime propaganda. It is imbued with messages about the values and character that define England, and how these will equip the people for the momentous task ahead. Though not yet adjusted to the "People's War," it appeals to the idea of a solidly united, patriotic community.

The film shows many facets of British life: the rural, the industrial and the modern. At the outset the camera pans across beautiful swathes of countryside, with its sleepy villages and churchyards evoking the spirit of a bygone age. "This is Britain, where we believe in freedom." The audience is reminded that for eight centuries the nation has "opposed every dictator who arose and tried to enslave Europe."

Next we see the fruits of industrial Britain where hospitals nurture babies with compassion, and schools provide progressive and tolerant education. But the wider reach of the state has not displaced the traditional British tolerance for individual differences, particularly in the nation's love of sports and recreation.

By contrast, Germany is characterized by herd uniformity. From seeing people using their leisure time playfully in England, the scene cuts to a Nazi rally in Germany. The audience is asked whether it is better to be led by a jackbooted tyrant who requires an armed escort or a king who walks freely among his subjects. In the former case, individuals live at the behest of a baying mob who behave in a robotic and brutal manner.

The next section of the film looks at the state of British readiness for conflict. We are given a rollercoaster ride around British factories and observe a formidable array of offensive power: fighters, bombers, bullets, guns, shells and anti-aircraft guns are all part of the dazzling selection of weaponry to repel the invader. These scenes show the English being roused to action in time to face the enemy. They also reinforce the spirit of common unity and cooperation among the British workforce, symbolic of the common spirit of the British people.

The film ends with how a future Battle of Britain may pan out. In one sense the mythologized portrait of the Battle is anticipated. Dashing pilots, anxious to down the Luftwaffe, are the latter day chivalrous knights of the air, engaging in aerial jousts with the enemy over the skies of southern England. The pilots are all young white males who are eager, confident and daring. The film interestingly anticipates the importance of Fighter Command and the role of coastal watchers.

But in one sense the depiction of battle reflects a degree of overconfidence. In a German raid on a British site, the Nazi pilots are foiled by barrage balloons and have to turn back, unable to complete their mission. In 1940–1, many British citizens found out, to their cost, how ineffective this line of defense really was against high-level German bombers.

The British love of jovial humor, even in adversity, is apparent throughout. One man chalks a message on a bomb saying "One for Adolf," while the voiceover says that these fighters make jokes despite having poor odds for survival.

The film also features an allegorical parallel between the Armada of 1588 and contemporary events. In a scene borrowed from Korda's *Fire Over England*, Elizabeth I sounds a defiant tone in the face of an invasion threat. She declares, "Pluck up your hearts, by your peace and camp and valour in the field we shall shortly have a famous victory." We see the glorious ships stationed in the Channel, which are ready and waiting for Philip II's armada. Immediately we cut to contemporary events, but instead of ships, we now see the modern representatives of defense—aircraft. This is history as propaganda, a stirring depiction of past glories designed to improve current morale.

Merle Oberon's closing peroration exhorts the audience to "fight for what we believe in." This is summed up as "truth and beauty and fair play and kindness." It is a very English list of traits in a film where the English are shown to be fun-loving and peaceful. Nonetheless, *The Times* declared that this was "emphatically an instrument of war."[16] Michael Powell was less impressed and more self critical. He later admitted that some "stagy episodes were rather embarrassing" and contributed to an overall "outrageous piece of propaganda."[17]

The First of the Few (U.S.: *Spitfire*), made in 1942, was a biopic of the designer of the Spitfire, R. J. Mitchell. The film won plaudits from contemporary reviewers for its contribution to raising morale:

> It is a work of the greatest possible value to the national value, because of its inspiring theme, and the inspiration and encouragement it will afford to every man and woman engaged in the war effort.[18]

The film seemed to justify the accolade, for, behind *Mrs. Miniver*, it was the most successful picture at the British box office in 1942. Churchill played a significant role in getting the film off the ground. He provided Howard with access to military airfields and RAF pilots while also allowing the famous "few" epithet to be used in the film's title.

The two characters R. J. Mitchell and Geoffrey Crisp (modeled on Jeffrey Quill) played important roles in the Battle of Britain. Until his death in 1937, Mitchell worked flat out to produce a revolutionary plane which would outclass all others, including the German Messerschmitt. Quill tested all the variants of the Spitfire and helped troubleshoot various design problems. He later became a test pilot and had the distinction of shooting down two enemy aircraft. Leslie Howard offers a sympathetic portrait of Mitchell, while David Niven gives an assured performance as Crisp.

The film starts in the summer of 1940. The camera descends from the clouds onto a map of Europe, showing the tide of Nazi conquests. One country after another is turned black as Hitler's army rolls eastwards. The spread of Nazism is likened almost to a plague that extinguishes freedom, hope and vigor. We then hear a voiceover of American reporters stating that Britain faces mortal peril, and that "apart from its courage, it has nothing to fight." Next we switch to Zero Day, September 15, 1940, the decisive day of the Battle of Britain. A control room is under bombardment, with its inhabitants showing typical English phlegm and resilience. At this stage Crisp starts to talk about Mitchell's contribution to Britain's current defense capabilities, and the many trials and tribulations he faced over 20 years.

Mitchell's plans require money and backing, making it inevitable that he will encounter bureaucratic objections and red tape. He is duly rebuffed by officials, bureaucrats and colleagues who think his designs will not work and may prove too expensive. Nonetheless, Mitchell has a drive and determination which spurs him on. He believes in his own destiny, something he reveals to his wife when he admits that he could not get a job unconnected with airplanes. To do that would be "giving up something I was meant to do ... almost as if I were doing something wrong." The view is shared by Crisp, who is impeccably played by Niven. Despite setbacks, including a plane crash, Crisp tells Mitchell to carry on regardless: "I know you hold a tremendous future in your hands—something for England, for the whole world maybe, and you can't pack up now, you can't stop whatever the cost."

There are times when Mitchell's efforts make him a symbol of opposition to appeasement. On a visit to Germany in 1933 he hears the terrifying Nazi philosophy first hand and realizes that it will involve the creation of a powerful German air force. When he arrives back in Britain, the prevailing mood is one of complacency and appeasement, with "Trust Baldwin" posters hanging from windows. He persists and is at last given financial backing by Vickers and Rolls-Royce. According to Crisp, Mitchell's triumph was one of a "farsighted individual over a nearsighted government." He also relies on a generous benefactor, Lady Houston, whose favorite rallying cry is "Down with the government. Wake up England!"

As Mitchell's work progresses, his health deteriorates. He sees a doctor, who warns him that if he continues to overwork he will die within a year. Spurred on by renewed official interest, he carries on his exhausting schedule, unafraid of death. As he puts it, "We've all got to pack up some time or other, it is not when we pack up that matters but what we do when we're here." He is utterly resigned to his fate, his sole concern being the defense of Britain in an impending war. As in *Pimpernel Smith*, the protagonist is a committed and courageous man of principle rather than a daydreaming boffin. He is an intellectual prepared to sacrifice himself for greater principles and just causes. As the Spitfires descend into the heavens at the end, we know that Mitchell is deservedly eulogized as the "first of the few."

There is a heavy dose of myth-making in the film. According to his son Gordon, R. J. Mitchell may never have gone to Germany, as the film character did, nor did he have to go to the great ministries to build a single-seater fighter. The cause of Mitchell's death is also changed in the film from rectal cancer (in real life) to overwork. This chimes nicely with the theme of individual sacrifice for the sake of duty.

The Big Blockade (1942) much resembles *Ships with Wings* and *Convoy* in the explicit nature of its propaganda, its lack of realism and its caricatured depiction of the enemy. Charles Frend, who had worked with Balcon at MGM-British, was brought in to direct a documentary-style film about the British economic blockade of Germany. The second half of the picture deals with the role of Bomber Command.

At the start, the Minister of Economic Warfare, Hugh Dalton, explains that "fighting is one side of war," but another weapon, the blockade of Germany, reduces her ability to hurt Britain. Then in a series of episodes, some involving documentary footage, we chart how the naval blockade is strangling the German war effort. The film has a semi-comic theme throughout, using mockery and self-effacing irony to ridicule German pretensions to superiority.

In an early scene, Leslie Banks, playing an English commercial traveler, has a conversation with a Nazi sympathizer, Schneider (Frank Cellier). Banks tells Schneider that the English position worsens every day. Anticipating that he will be deluged with Nazi propaganda, Banks says that the deterioration is no doubt the result of the British government's provocative policy of encircling the Reich.

Responding to the claim that Germany would not lose a second war, Banks replies that he was also under the impression that Germany had not been defeated in the previous war, "merely stabbed in the back by Jews or something." The scene emphasizes the fact that humor is really the Englishman's secret weapon, and that its key ingredient, self-effacing irony, is invisible to foreigners. Humor remains the most redoubtable bulwark against tyranny, its very individuality striking a blow against authoritarian power.

A number of scenes now set out to mock Schneider and any idea that Germany can survive in this war. When we next catch up with the German, he is sitting in a train compartment with a Russian, specially sent to Germany to assess the German economy under blockade. The Russian is peeved that he has had to change trains 18 times, explaining that this is the result of British bombers targeting the rail infrastructure and industrial centers.

As if to demonstrate, an air raid follows, which strikes at an ersatz rubber factory and an oil refinery. Schneider is then offered meatless sandwiches and non-alcoholic lager, reminding the audience that the blockade is drastically reducing material comfort. Nonetheless, Schneider clings obstinately to the deluded belief that all will be well, fitting perfectly the stereotype of the deferential and unthinking German citizen. Schneider's character is an obvious but amusing caricature.

British red tape and bureaucracy are used at the expense of a German official who is desperate for the blockade to be lifted. After a ship bound for Germany is stopped in Malta, the official demands that the barrier be removed. He is told to put his request in writing to the Admiral Superintendent's office by filling out a special form. By the end of the instruction, the official hangs up the phone. What is especially amusing is that a German, who normally gets his way through coercion, is now held back by that seemingly harmless bugbear of Englanders: red tape.

Finally we receive a visual lesson in warfare by following a Bomber Command operation. The film shows the fighter squads in a favorable light as the targets chosen are non-civilian, and the men operate with relative impunity. In reality, Arthur (Bomber) Harris, the Commander in Chief of Bomber Command, had authorized a policy of saturation bombing targeting civilian cities in 1942. Not surprisingly, this policy did not feature in British wartime films.

One of the film's major contributions to British wartime propaganda was to suggest complete unity between not only branches of the armed forces (RAF and Navy) but also the civil service and the press. In the film, they operate in unison on the basis of a carefully coordinated policy, and there are few signs of discord.

The movie itself rests on false historical assumptions. In 1940 the Ministry of Economic Warfare believed that Hitler lacked the manufacturing capacity and raw materials to continue in the war for more than another 10 months.[19] Nonetheless, after the difficult months of the Blitz, the public would have had little problem seeing Britain "dishing it out" as well as taking it.

Overall, *The Big Blockade* cannot be considered one of the finest achievements of British wartime propaganda. Despite its mix of documentary and comic interludes, there is too much caricature and bluff optimism for the film to be taken seriously.

Though more a romantic melodrama than a film about the RAF, *Dangerous Moonlight* (U.S.: *Suicide Squadron*), made in 1941, deserves to be mentioned here. Directed by Brian Desmond Hurst, it focuses on Stefan Radetzky (Anton Walbrook), a Polish composer and concert pianist who flees his native country for America after the German invasion in 1939, only to arrive in Britain the following year where he enlists in the RAF. The central theme is the choice one has to make between romantic love and a sense of duty, between desire and obligation. In this case, he is prepared to leave his wife out of a sense of patriotism and the need to "do his bit" for his struggling countrymen. The film is chiefly remembered today for Richard Addinsell's stirring "Warsaw Concerto," and for its beautiful merging of music and scenes of bombing.

If *In Which We Serve* and *The Way Ahead* offered the definitive tribute to the navy and army, the 1945 production *The Way to the Stars* (U.S.: *Johnny in the Clouds*) did the same for the air force. The result of a creative collaboration between Anatole de Grunwald and Anthony Asquith, who had worked together on *The Demi Paradise* (among other movies), the film offers a poignant tribute to the fighter pilots who sacrificed their lives during the war. It is also a stirring tribute to the spirit of Anglo-American cooperation, which had already figured in Hollywood's *Forever and a Day* (1943).

The film, told in flashback, looks back at key events at an airfield when pilots of the British and American air forces lived and worked together. At the beginning we see the airfield in a derelict state, with empty hangers, disused buildings and a barren crew room. As the camera pans over this forgotten place, we come across some names scrolled on a wall, evidence of the young lives snatched away during the war. There is already a deep sense of nostalgia and a lingering sadness for the dead.

But this drama is less about aerial combat and more about the emotional lives of the airmen. With deep sensitivity, the film explores how people deal with loss during wartime and dwells on the need to maintain hope despite the imminence of death. Flight Lieutenant David Archdale (Michael Redgrave) reacts to the loss of pilots by finding solace in poetry, and one poem in particular, "Missing," which sums up the need for stoicism and restraint when handling loss. When David takes to the air for the last time, he leaves behind his lucky cigarette lighter. The camera then focuses on the lighter, but when it is picked up, it is Peter Penrose (John Mills) who holds it. We instantly know, without further commentary, that David has become another wartime casualty. As Drazin comments in relation to this film, the pilots "use banter and euphemism to shut away their pain.... So much meaning lay in the unsaid."[20]

When Penrose breaks the news to David's widow, Toddy Asherson (Rosamund John), there is an absence of emotionalism. Using characteristic understatement, Penrose describes the death as a "bad show," and Toddy accepts this. There are pauses, glances and uncomfortable silences, which convey the reality of death, and which seem to have a rhythm and cadence all their own. This is the familiar form of restraint that was so quintessentially English for an audience in 1945. As another historian puts it, "There is no flag waving, no soupy soundtrack music, no over-the-top emotionalism."[21]

Yet this film is not purely about a longing for the dead. When breaking the news to Toddy, Penrose feels profound emotional unease and ends his own relationship with Iris (Renée Asherson), fearing that he will make her a widow too. Toddy persuades him to propose, assuring him that war should not sever romantic attachments.

The film also pays tribute to the fact that despite their stereotypical social

Michael Redgrave, Basil Radford and John Mills in the definitive wartime tribute to the RAF. *The Way to the Stars* (1945) offers the most stirring and eloquent reflection on human loss in the entire genre (United Artists, Photofest).

differences, a cohesive Anglo-American unity was formed. Initially the presence of loud-mouthed, uncouth American fighters is resented by the local community, their brash and arrogant demeanor a far cry from demure English manners. Flying Officer Parsons (David Tomlinson) and boisterous American Lieutenant Joe Frizelli (Bonar Colleano) enjoy impersonating the other side's quirks in a dismissive fashion.

Yet gradually each unit adjusts to the other with the realization that they have more in common than they might imagine. By the end of the film they are successfully carrying out joint raids on the enemy, and even Joe, the loudest of the foreign contingent, has learned to imitate English manners. At the end both groups are equally rowdy, leaving one observer to comment, "There's nothing to choose between you." Michael Redgrave saluted a movie that "commemorated a way of life that was vanishing while the film was being made." He also rather amusingly commented that his own part in the picture was so short that the film could be dubbed "One of our actors is missing."[22] *The Way to the Stars* remains one of the most stirring and eloquent reflections on human loss in the entire genre.

Chapter 6

Cloak and Dagger: The Victory of the Amateur

British interest in spy fiction had been growing from the late nineteenth century onwards and would reach fever pitch in the years before the First World War. A deep suspicion of foreign powers, stoked up by the cheap press, ensured that the public was receptive to novels about the machinations of foreign powers. The prolific writer and journalist William Le Queux was perhaps the most prolific exponent, penning the best-selling anti–German invasion novels *The Great War in England* and *The Invasion of 1910*.

In Ernest Childers' influential 1903 novel *The Riddle of the Sands*, two yachtsmen sailing around the German coastline stumble upon a German plan for an invasion of Britain. These amateur spies manage to foil the plans, but the book serves as a warning against military complacency. John Buchan came to dominate the genre with a series of adventure novels, the most celebrated of which was *The Thirty-Nine Steps*. This was also the era of Arthur Conan Doyle's Sherlock Holmes and Baroness Orczy's *The Scarlet Pimpernel*, the classic novel about a British spy during the French Revolution.

In the 1930s, Alfred Hitchcock popularized the espionage genre with a series of impressive thrillers: *The Man Who Knew Too Much* (1934), *The Thirty-Nine Steps* (1935), *Sabotage* (1936) and *The Lady Vanishes* (1938). All featured the director's trademark techniques, such as the use of close-ups and clever camera positions. In these four films a convention of sorts was established for the British spy genre. Plucky English innocents helped outwit enemies whose sinister designs were threatening British liberties. They evinced a quiet, modest patriotism without obvious flag waving. These were amateur spies with little training or professional expertise, but what they lacked in technical prowess they more than made up for in tenacity. In other words, they had to *muddle through* in a very English sense, often against technically superior adversaries.

With the upheaval of the Phoney War, espionage films were again popular and fell into two categories: madcap espionage comedies and spy thrillers. Light-hearted comedy capers exploited the zany talents of Arthur Askey (*Back Room Boy* and *Bees in Paradise*), George Formby (*Let George Do It, Get Cracking, Spare a Copper*), Will Hay (*The Black Sheep of Whitehall* and *The Goose Steps Out*), Arthur Lucan (*Old Mother Riley Joins Up*), Robertson Hare (*Women Aren't Angels*), Tommy Trinder (*Sailors Three*), and Gert and Daisy (Elsie and Doris Waters) in a trio of wartime comedies.

These films had a largely anarchic quality, borrowing much from the music hall tradition, and resembled a Boys' Own adventure in which fifth columnists, spies and other assorted villains received their comeuppance at the hands of English amateurs. They were light-hearted, low-key vehicles for entertainment, with their English heroes possessing just enough phlegm, pluck and good humor to defeat the enemy. More importantly, they were also vehicles for comic relief. In the words of Michael Balcon, they "provided some respite for a public that had known nothing but bad news for a long time."[1]

In a typical Hay comedy, *The Goose Steps Out*, the comedian plays a dual role, both a schoolmaster teaching modern languages and a German spy for whom he is mistaken. After the real spy is captured by the British, Hay goes to Germany so he can impersonate the spy and obtain details of a secret bomb. The humor is somewhat slapstick, with numerous gags at the expense of the enemy. The Germans are largely characterized as predictable, unsympathetic, cold, humorless and regimented.

In one hilarious scene, Hay is training a group of German students who are wholly ignorant of English mores. He teaches them a typical English greeting, which is the insulting reverse of Churchill's V sign. To Hay's amusement, the students insult their own leader's portrait, while the film simultaneously mocks German stupidity and sheep-like conformity. The humor is typically English: cheeky, at times irreverent, and ironic. Hay succeeds against the Germans in spite of being bumbling and incompetent, surviving only because he can muddle through against the odds.

The same light-hearted and slapstick humor is found in another Hay comedy, *Sailors Three*. After a drunken night out, three British sailors accidentally stumble on board an enemy ship that they have been assigned to scuttle. For some brief moments the hapless trio try to blend in with German naval exercises before their cover is blown.

The trio conceives an improbable plan to capture the ship of more than 60 men, an idea made the more implausible by the previous night's reckless escapade. Nonetheless, the mighty Germans are humbled once again by English pluck and Dunkirk spirit, with the enemy's superior force exposed as a sham. It is guile rather than sophisticated plans that helps the English to victory. The Germans are predictable caricatures: robotic, clumsy, stupid and humorless.

But the war was also used as a backdrop for more conventional espionage dramas. *Bulldog Sees It Through* (1940) is a small scale Harold Huth production using a Bulldog Drummond–like figure to expose Nazi agents and foil an attack on an arms factory. There were also straightforward detective films, such as *Inspector Hornleigh Goes to It* (1941), in which Hornleigh joins the army in a bold effort to unmask German spies. *Contraband, Night Train to Munich, They Met in the Dark, Pimpernel Smith* and *The Adventures of Tartu* all involved exciting stories of spying and counter-espionage, and featured a galaxy of top British talent. The leading actors included Rex Harrison, Robert Donat and James Mason, upper-class heroes who were a far remove from the ethos of the People's War. Most are amateur rather than professional spies.

Carol Reed's *Night Train to Munich* (1940) has often been compared to Hitchcock's *The Lady Vanishes*. As both films were written by Frank Launder and Sidney Gilliat, this is hardly surprising, and Reed's film thus follows the 1930s conventions for a thriller-comedy. The movie was originally going to be called "Gestapo," but Reed felt this was no longer appropriate once the war had started. He felt it "wrong to make something so heavy at such a time."[2]

The plot is simple enough: a Czech munitions scientist, Axel Bomasch (James Harcourt), escapes from Prague to London on the eve of the Nazi takeover. His daughter Anna (Margaret Lockwood) is not so lucky and is placed in a concentration camp. In the camp she becomes friendly with another inmate, Karl Marsen (Paul Henreid), who is actually a Nazi agent. They escape the camp and arrive in England where she is re-united with her father, who is under the care of a British intelligence officer, Randall (Rex Harrison). Marsen tracks Anna, and later he and his agents capture both father and daughter, returning them to Germany.

Determined to free the pair, Randall arrives in Germany in disguise as an army major. He persuades the authorities to take them to Munich by train where he can interrogate Anna. On the train he meets up with two old pals, Caldicott and Charters (Naunton Wayne and Basil Radford). By the time the Nazis discover Harrison's real identity, he has come up with a plan to outwit his captors. Together with his two pals, they flee the Nazis and escape over the Swiss border after a final shootout.

The Germans vary from cerebral figures, such as Marsen (Paul Henreid), to one-dimensional characters who behave with predictable Teutonic savagery. The English characters, by contrast, mostly conform to Phoney War, class-bound stereotype. The heroes are upper-class gentlemen, epitomized by the suave and debonair Harrison, and the comic duo of Childers and Caldicott.

Wayne Naunton and Basil Radford took starring roles as Childers and Caldicott in the film adaptation of the radio show *The Crook's Tour* (1941). The pair, while traveling around the Middle East, visit a bar in Baghdad where they are mistaken for spies by German agents. They are handed a gramophone record, ostensibly a collection of songs by singer La Palermo, but which actually contains instructions from German intelligence. After they leave, the real spies turn up at the bar, and then a desperate chase ensues to retrieve the record from the Englishmen.

On one occasion after another, the intrepid English duo survive assassination attempts as they travel across Europe. Eventually they hand the record to a man they think is a British "cricketer" but who is actually working for German intelligence, while La Palermo, who tipped them off, is abducted by the German agents. Caldicott and Charters are themselves captured but manage a madcap escape and return to England, where they help foil an attack on an oil installation. They make an eccentric duo, a witty pair of English amateurs with a deep love of cricket who are unwittingly caught up in wartime espionage. It is their eccentricity and insouciance that gives this film a comic touch. But it remains a relative unknown among British wartime films.

Contraband (U.S.: *Blackout*), a slightly dated but nevertheless amusing 1940 production starring Conrad Veidt, belongs firmly in the spy subgenre. In the film, Veidt plays the captain of a Danish ship which is stopped by the British authorities for carrying suspected contraband. After cooperating with the authorities, Veidt discovers that some boarding passes have been stolen by two passengers, Mr. Pigeon and Miss Sorensen, and promptly follows them both to London. When the captain arrives, he and Sorensen are kidnapped by German spies, and it transpires that Sorensen is actually a British agent investigating how Germans use neutral ships to transport goods. Eventually he tracks down the German spies after a hair-raising chase through London.

On one level, *Contraband* is just a rather crude attempt at propaganda, highlighting the important work of British contraband control in the early stages of the war. When Veidt's ship is stopped, he is given a lecture about the role of neutrals in war: "You see, the unfortunate thing about war is that neutrals sometimes have to suffer. They may be carrying goods for our enemies, and we have to see that they don't. I know it means inconvenience and delay, but we think that our way is a better one than putting a torpedo in you."

But this is no ordinary attempt at propaganda. Veidt defies authority on a number of occasions, ignoring the blackout regulations and overpowering the military authorities in order to track down the spies more effectively. Despite this apparent lack of respect for authority, Veidt is very much the hero neutral. He is resourceful in tracking down enemy spies and shows pluckiness in evading his captors. Then there are the flashes of English humor, such as when he uses a bust of Chamberlain to attack a German spy before declaring, "They always said he was tough." In real life, Conrad Veidt was passionately opposed to National Socialism, and his left-wing views and pro–Semitic sympathies were anathema to the Nazis.

Like *Contraband*, *They Met in the Dark* (1943) is an espionage thriller with a light-hearted romantic subplot. This one involves not one but two intrepid spies, each of whom tries to uncover a Nazi spy ring in an attempt to prove their innocence. Richard Heritage (James Mason) has been dismissed from the navy for disobedience after his failure to follow instructions led to the sinking of a merchant ship. In the course of trying to uncover the fifth columnists that he blames for changing his instructions, he arrives at a cottage which is being used by Nazi spies. He bumps into Laura Verity (Joyce Howard) who has already uncovered a dead body there, leading her to assume that Heritage is the murderer. She calls the police, but they dismiss her allegation as absurd, charging her with timewasting.

With both now determined to prove their innocence, they unravel clues that lead them to a dance academy, in reality a front for Nazi spies and fifth columnists. Here innocent women have been recruited to meet naval officers and extract vital information from them, one of whom had earlier manipulated Heritage's orders at the start of the film. While evading capture by the police and the spies, both these heroes succeed in unmasking the ring and preventing the further loss of British merchant ships. The film, which owes much to the plot of *The Thirty-Nine Steps*, remains entertaining and suspenseful throughout. In particular, Otto Heller's intriguing black and white cinematography is worth mentioning. Mason would later star in *Hotel Reserve* (1944), a spy film dealing with espionage prior to the war.

Espionage dramas, perhaps by their nature, were elitist. These films suggested that the Germans could be fought by suave intellectuals or charming men, and thus they said little about the experience of the common man. Another film that shares this characteristic is the 1941 *Pimpernel Smith* (U.S.: *Mister V*), a fantasy based on Orczy's *The Scarlet Pimpernel*. The film was a tour de force for Leslie Howard, who was producer, director and actor. Howard was ideally suited for the lead role, having already starred in Korda's 1935 version of *The Scarlet Pimpernel*. But more important were the very English qualities of character and temperament that he possessed.

In many of his roles, such as Professor Higgins in *Pygmalion*, Howard provided a more romantic portrait of the intellectual, making him seem both human, fallible and ultimately endearing.[3] Howard embodied many of the traits of which the English were especially fond—a gentle, almost dreamily romantic charisma, a cultured but insouciant manner, tolerance and a sense of compassion. Above all, he possessed a quintessential English humor that was ironic, understated and self-effacing. Like Robert Donat, Howard was the epitome of the debonair gentleman.

He was also a proud patriot with a deep love of English culture and civilization. Shortly before the outbreak of war, Howard returned to the U.K. after several years in Hollywood, determined to play his part for the Allied cause. Throughout the war he broadcast regularly to the United States and the Empire, becoming one of the most famous anti–Nazi propagandists around the world. He was naturally held in contempt by the Nazis, who understood Howard's value to the Allied cause.[4]

Though a fantasy, *Pimpernel Smith* is firmly rooted in the ideological dimension of the war. We are told at the outset that it is "based on the exploits of a number of courageous men who were and still are risking their lives daily to aid those unfortunate people of many nationalities who are being persecuted and exterminated by the Nazis."

Professor Horatio Smith (Howard) is one of these courageous few, a somewhat absent-minded but amiable academic who worships a statue of Aphrodite. Yet far from being a detached bookworm, he has an alter ego, a dashing and courageous "shadow" who rescues people from the clutches of persecution. The men that Horatio Smith rescues are scientists, doctors, artists and writers, a cultured elite which, as he sees it, is "essential for the survival of civilization." This reinforces one of the film's central ideological tenets—that the natural enemies of the Nazis are men of high culture and erudition.

In one of his most daring operations he disguises himself as a scarecrow overlooking a field in which prisoners are being beaten and humiliated by a German guard. In order to deter the men from stopping work, the guard shoots the scarecrow and promises to do the same to the men. The camera then focuses close up on the scarecrow, and we see a trickle of blood dropping down its arm.

The film is heavily allegorical, drawing not just on the primal myth of a hero fighting monsters but on specific Christian sources. In the scene above, the analogy with the crucifixion and Christian martyrdom is inescapable.

Yet Smith demonstrates a very English modesty when confronted with tales of his exploits. He dismisses suggestions of heroic bravery and is embarrassed at his students' hero worship. He tells his students, when they discover his dual identity, that he is just a "singularly weak person who invariably gives way to his impulses."

The decency, tolerance and good humor of Professor Smith is contrasted with the brutal savagery of Nazism, centered on the figure of the Gestapo officer Von Graum (Francis Sullivan). Von Graum worships "power and strength and violence," and believes it will "rule the world" and crush all opposition. By contrast, Smith confesses to a hatred of violence, believing that it is "so uncivilized." Yet he also recognizes that one must take up arms in the struggle against fascism, whatever the personal costs may be.

The film ridicules not just the German jackboot mentality but their lack of humor. In one scene, Von Graum is struggling to work out the English sense of humor, which, he has been assured, is a secret weapon. He plows through volumes of P.G. Wodehouse, Punch, Edward Lear and Lewis Carroll, and comes to the conclusion that they are all unfunny. The English, he believes, have no secret weapon. This is deliciously ironic, for Howard uses his "secret weapon" to merciless effect.

Particularly amusing is the conversation between the Professor and Von Graum at the British Embassy in which the two men discuss Shakespeare. Von Graum insists that he was a German writer, and that proof has been found to this effect. Without disagreeing, the Professor replies that at least the English translations are "most remarkable." Later, he visits a concentration camp disguised as an American journalist. The Americans, he says, are fools for thinking camp inmates unhappy. Americans only pretend to be democrats, he adds, whereas they are actually 100 percent national socialists.

Leslie Howard as the romantic intellectual, carefree but patriotic, in *Pimpernel Smith* (1941). Howard is trying out England's "secret weapon" on the hapless Von Graum (Francis L. Sullivan) (United Artists, Photofest).

Lurking beneath these light-hearted asides is a man of serious moral purpose. Finding himself trapped in a railway station with Von Graum about to shoot him, Smith tells the German that his creed of violence "will never rule the world," and that "those who have demoralized and corrupted a nation are doomed." These are the words of a man of action rather than an aloof academic. The film was generally well received, becoming one of the box office successes of the year.[5] Though essentially a thriller, this film shares the sub-genre's ideology.

A very different type of spy hero appears in *The Adventures of Tartu* (U.S.: *Sabotage Agent*), made in 1943. Robert Donat stars as Captain Terence Stevenson, a trained British chemist who happens to be fluent in German and Romanian. He is parachuted into Romania where he assumes the identity of Jan Tartu, a member of the pro–Nazi Iron Guard. His task is to sabotage a factory in occupied Czechoslovakia where an important new poison gas is being manufactured. Before he can do that, he has to persuade the Nazis that he detests the Czechs, while at the same time assuring the Czech underground that he is not betraying their interests.

Towards the end, his identity as a British double agent is unmasked, and he has to outwit the Gestapo, with the help of the underground, in order to complete his mission. With its constant bluff and double bluff, and the shifting allegiances of its actors (Valerie Hobson co-stars as a Nazi collaborator and Czech patriot), this is anything but a conventional spy story.

Robert Donat lacks the natural wit and intelligence of Howard's Pimpernel, but his role is no less effective. Like Rex Harrison in *Night Train to Munich*, Donat manages to combine a debonair manner with decisiveness, though without Harrison's upper-class bearings. Also, the sexual chemistry between him and Valerie Hobson is exhilarating.

One disturbing feature of the film is its refusal to hide the darker aspects of Nazi occupation. On two occasions, Czech factory workers are summarily shot after being caught in attempted sabotage, while the native population is subjected to cruel taunts and arbitrary violence. As Robert Murphy puts it, these impart to the film "a dark stain of meanness and misery."[6] But the movie is also an effective tribute to the fortitude of the Czech underground, whose most famous operation was the assassination of Reinhard Heydrich in 1942.

One of the more unusual wartime thrillers in this cycle is *Warn That Man*, a 1943 production based on a play by Vernon Sylvaine, and starring Finlay Currie and Raymond Lovell. In narrative terms, it bears some similarities to *The Eagle Has Landed* in that it deals with a plot to kidnap Winston Churchill. Ludwig Hausemann, a German stage actor with an impeccable English accent, is approached by a German agent with an audacious plan: to parachute him into England and take over a stately home where he will kidnap and impersonate the owner.

The plan succeeds, and Hausemann begins to impersonate the owner, Lord Buckley, with Lovell playing a dual role. The spies plan to abduct Churchill, a regular visitor to the house, so that they can escort him to Germany in triumph. But a group of guests turn up unexpectedly and begin to suspect that all is not what it seems. When they come across the Earl's niece, who had been forced to hide inside the house since Hausemann's arrival, the full plot is revealed. Together, the group use all their guile and ingenuity to outwit the Nazis and send a last minute warning to the Prime Minister who is nearing the house. The film is marred by some fairly wooden performances and a somewhat unlikely plot. But it is enlivened by Gordon Harker's Cockney wit, which seems to embody the fighting spirit and unconquerable humor of the typical underdog.

Wartime spy melodramas are largely characterized by their having male protagonists. One notable exception is *Yellow Canary*, a 1943 feature directed by Herbert Wilcox and starring Anna Neagle. This is by no means a straightforward espionage thriller because the identities of the characters are not as they seem, and the film is full of twists and surprises. Neagle plays Sally Maitland, a London socialite notorious for her pro–Nazi views. She boards a ship bound for Canada and receives the attentions of two men, a "Polish" officer, Jan Orlock (Albert Lieven), and a British man, Jim Garrick (Richard Greene). While cool towards Garrick, she begins to warm to Orlock, and a romantic subplot develops.

When she arrives in Halifax, she meets Orlock's mother, and it soon becomes clear that the two have differences of opinion over foreign policy. It later transpires that Orlock is a fanatical Nazi who has been trailing Maitland from the start, desperate to recruit her for covert wartime activities. But unknown to him, Maitland is actually working for British intelligence, and her affections are but a ruse to infiltrate Orlock's Canadian spy ring. She discovers a Nazi plot to destroy the port of Halifax, but as she is divulging this information to British intelligence, she is shot by Orlock. In a somewhat contrived ending, we discover that the bullet has been intercepted by a cigarette case given to her by Orlock, and she emerges unscathed at the end, with the Nazis rounded up by Garrick.

Anna Neagle was well used to playing stoical and patriotic characters from her roles in *Nell Gwynn*, *Nurse Edith Cavell* and *Victoria the Great*. She typified a very British sense of resolve and determination from her portrayal of real-life heroines thrown into situations of grave difficulty. Here she exemplifies these qualities to create a convincing spy, and, on the whole, the production shares in the ideological consensus of the other espionage melodramas.

Chapter 7

Heroic Johnny Foreigner: Resistance and the Triumph of the Underdog

For the anti-fascist powers, 1940 appeared to be a bleak year. Hitler's armies had overrun Western Europe with apparent ease, adding France, Belgium and Holland to their previous conquests in Central and Eastern Europe. Of the major Continental powers, Britain stood alone against the might of Nazi Germany, with Churchill's bulldog tenacity symbolizing the spirit of his country's resistance. In his inspiring speeches to the nation he had vowed never to surrender to tyranny while promising that he would settle for nothing less than "victory at all costs." By all accounts, these were morale boosting pieces of oratory that have become legendary in the annals of military leadership.

But even Churchill knew that his options for defeating Germany were limited. Despite her imperial resources, and her naval and aerial might, Britain lacked the means to inflict defeat on Hitler. The evacuation from Dunkirk was a reminder of the perilous state of the military, and of Britain's overstretched financial resources. The strategy for defeating Hitler rested on aerial power and the belief that Germany's economy would collapse as a result of the British blockade.

Moreover, it was assumed that the peoples of Europe would never submit to enemy occupation and would rise up accordingly against their oppressors. This belief led Churchill to set up the Special Operations Executive (SOE) in July 1940, tasked with "setting Europe ablaze." The SOE was a British secret service that was designed to aid resistance movements in enemy territory, using sabotage and intelligence gathering to thwart the Axis powers. It would go on to have a number of notable successes, such as the successful disruption of the Nazi atomic bomb project in Norway and the assassination of Reinhard Heydrich in 1942. By the end of the war, the SOE had helped raise morale in Europe and provided beleaguered nations a ray of hope for the future.[1]

A number of wartime films celebrated the spirit of resistance among the occupied peoples of Europe. More often than not they involved the projection of English character traits onto other nationalities, showing how courage, self-sacrifice and the underdog mentality were not a monopoly of any one people.

The Boulting Brothers' *Pastor Hall* (1940), based on a play by Ernst Toller, was one of the first war films to celebrate the spirit of opposition within Nazi Germany. It is based on the true story of Martin Niemoller, a German Lutheran pastor who publicly condemned the Nazi control of the church and spent nearly a decade in concentration camps. The film draws a stark contrast between a small rural German community, imbued with tolerance and generosity, and the fanatical and sadistic Nazi movement.

The community is led by an unassuming apolitical pacifist, Pastor Hall, played by the outstanding Wilfrid Lawson. In his opening exchanges with a Nazi stormtrooper, Marius Goring, Hall delivers a quietly spoken rebuke to the Nazi philosophy. He extols the virtues of his local villagers and declares that none of them are enemies, including the local Jews. Later a Nazi official confronts him about his Scripture lessons, insisting that they conform to party lines.

While these attempts at ideological indoctrination make little impression on him, the Pastor is roused to anger by some incidents in his village. First there is a ferocious attack on a local Jew, then a villager's son is murdered in the Night of the Long Knives, and finally a teenage girl (Lina) is raped at a German labor camp.

The villagers themselves resort to spying on each other and gossiping, their own collective character tainted by Nazi influence. The pastor declares, "People aren't like they used to be, they've become bitter and cruel." When Lina kills herself rather than face her villagers' cruel taunts, Pastor Hall decides to speak out against the evils of Nazism.

He is arrested and sent to a concentration camp, where he witnesses acts of unspeakable barbarity. The camp scenes nonetheless lack genuine realism and authenticity, though this is hardly surprising. In 1940, knowledge of wartime conditions in the concentration camps was somewhat sketchy, and scenes of extreme violence would have dissatisfied the censors. Later, Hall escapes from the camp, thanks to the efforts of Heinrich Degan (Bernard Miles), but characteristically refuses to end his denunciation of Nazism. He delivers a final sermon in his church, proclaiming his Christian humanity in the face of overwhelming evil.

Pastor Hall is a low-budget production lacking dizzying technical expertise and is reliant on sets. While the English voices are often ill suited to the German characters, the film is lifted by Lawson's bravura performance. Robert

Murphy's assessment of Lawson remains apt: "He handles the role with great sensitivity and restraint and turns what might have been sentimental propaganda into a moving testament to human dignity and bravery."[2] Though made on a small scale, *Pastor Hall* remains a highly effective piece of anti–Nazi propaganda.

Freedom Radio (U.S.: *A Voice in the Night*), made in 1941, continues the theme of resistance and internal dissent in Germany. As with *Pimpernel Smith*, the hero is a cultivated intellectual who courageously puts his beliefs into practice. Clive Brook plays a doctor whose visceral disgust with Nazism leads him to set up an underground radio station. His wife, however, has ingratiated herself into the regime, having been promoted to director of pageantry. As a Nazi sympathizer, she believes that her husband's opposition to the regime is tantamount to treason.

After enlisting the help of another committed dissenter, Brook starts his anti–Nazi broadcasts, much to the consternation of German officials. His resistance activities continue as the number of German listeners to his broadcasts grow, and they climax when he sabotages a Nazi rally that his wife has organized. After the invasion of Poland, she has a Damascene conversion and joins her husband in a remote location for another of his broadcasts. But the Nazis discover their hideout and shoot the couple. Just as the Nazi officials believe that they have crushed the spirit of rebellion, another dissenting broadcast can be heard on the airwaves, suggesting that Brook has awoken a latent spirit of resistance in Germany.

The film depicts the Nazis as fundamentally indecent, and, as in so many movies, this is announced at the start by the storming of a church. The priest had asked his congregation to pray for the victims of Nazi misrule. He is subsequently manhandled by a German officer and then killed. Brook, who witnesses this episode, is roused from his previous indifference and condemns "blind obedience to a rule of force and terrorism." Far from simply obeying orders, officers enjoy carrying out their duties.

His conversion to anti–Nazism is shown through a series of images of the previous six years of tyranny. Jewish shops are smashed, opponents are ruthlessly beaten, and thugs run rampant through the streets. We know little of Brook's previous involvement with the regime, and so his sudden conversion might seem a little unrealistic. The film also suffers from miscasting, particular the upper-class Brook as a Viennese doctor. As Louis McNeice argues, "The typical Englishman, especially if he has an Oxford accent, is not cut out to be a Gauleiter."[3]

The movie epitomizes the distinction between good and bad Germans. The film's premise is that Nazis are simply Germans who have been polluted with the wrong propaganda, and that if they can only see sense, they will resist the regime and rise up for freedom and dignity. If they choose to acquiesce to a brutal dictatorship, they will be unable to escape the moral consequences. As Brook says in his final broadcast, "For this thing rests with you, you cannot escape responsibility by blaming it on your leaders, if you allow this thing to happen, the blame is yours and you will earn the loathing of posterity, you gave this man his power...." As Drazin comments, "At a time when Nazis portrayed on the screen were invariably gross caricatures of evil, it provided an intelligent insight into how decent people could become seduced by fascism."[4]

Two notable films are set in France, "the locus classicus of resistance stories."[5] The 1943 feature *Tomorrow We Live* (U.S.: *At Dawn We Die*) is set entirely in France and deals with the moral quandaries faced by ordinary citizens in deciding whether to collaborate with or resist the Nazi occupiers. Jean Baptiste (John Clements) is a youthful French idealist who seeks sanctuary with the local Mayor and his daughter. They are renowned for collaborating with the enemy, but, unknown to the Germans and the French townspeople, they are actually leading the local resistance movement.

Baptiste joins the cause and helps Allied soldiers escape by boat back to England. But as the acts of resistance intensify, including an audacious attack on a German train, the SS are called in to deal brutally with the locals. After two Germans are killed, an order is given to round up 50 French hostages, all of whom are shot for refusing to cooperate with the investigation.

The film celebrates the spirit of patriotic self-sacrifice shown by the townspeople. But unlike some other entries in this genre, it does not take this sentiment for granted. Faced with the choice of cooperating with the Nazis or facing a firing squad, one local is determined to save his skin. But he is reprimanded by the mayor, who rallies his countrymen not to put their own individual lives before the life of their country. In a final moving scene, the hostages are led to their deaths, heads unbowed, while proudly singing "La Marsailleise." It is a final dignified act of resistance to Nazi tyranny.

Secret Mission (1942) stars James Mason as a Free French resistance officer, Raoul de Carnot, who, together with three companions, engages in a clandestine operation to locate a German military installation. In typical English fashion, they outwit the Germans using pluck and ingenuity rather than brutal Teutonic efficiency. Utilizing false papers supplied them by a pretend Vichyite, Monsieur Fayolle, Peter Garnett (Hugh Williams) and Red Gowan (Roland Culver) enter the secret German HQ masquerading as champagne salesmen. While inside they manage to take photographs of a local German hanger before making their exit. After being unmasked as frauds, the men are hunted by the Nazis and manage to evade capture on several occasions. The Nazis are outwitted again when they release an American prisoner to men who are disguised as German officers but are actually members of the resistance.

At the end, British parachutists, alerted by a signal from the saboteurs, descend from the air and storm the German hanger, destroying it in the process. Despite its credible cast, the story itself defies credibility—but in a sense that ignores the film's main message: Ruthless efficiency and firepower are no match for guile and quick thinking.

Unlike some other movies in this cycle, the hero's patriotic sense of duty does not go unquestioned. When de Carnot arrives at his sister's house, he is told that his spying activities for "his new masters, the English" are not welcome. This may seem in retrospect to be a rather Anglophobic sentiment that was out of tune with the spirit of the times. In reality, Anglo-French relations had been strained following the attack on the French fleet at Oran in July 1940.

De Carnot's sister, Violette, begs him to remain in France: "Surely your work is here, to nurse the land until the Germans are kicked out." Raoul retorts that it is precisely by fighting with the Free French and their British allies that he can help liberate the land that he loves. But his choice of defeating tyranny over family life (the greater family over the lesser one) represents the ultimate sacrifice, for he is later shot and killed by the Nazis. In her grief, Violette lashes out at her brother's companions, blaming them for his death. But later she is reconciled to the cause and agrees to help her brother's comrades.

Violette risks her life by defiantly tuning in to a banned radio station. Monsieur Fayolle takes a gamble by supplying false identity papers, and a priest tells Mason, on his death bed, to be proud of his resistance work with the Free French. This is the defiant courage so championed by the SOE.

One of Our Aircraft Is Missing (1942), which celebrates the wartime alliance between Britain and Holland, was a well received Powell and Pressburger production. The film deals with a British bomber crew who are forced to bail out of their RAF Vickers bomber near the Zuider Zee in Nazi-occupied Holland. They enlist the help of the Dutch resistance, who enable them to find shelter as well as suitable disguises. Eventually they are helped to the border where they are able to make their escape across the North Sea back to Britain. The film represents the plot structure of *49th Parallel* but in reverse. In that film a group of Nazi agents, stranded in neutral America, squabble among themselves and are killed or captured by the end. Here the British work together (and work with the Dutch) to affect a successful escape.

The very English characteristics of the crew—heroic resistance and refusal to surrender, fearless courage, tolerance, light-hearted humor and readiness for self-sacrifice—are reflected in their Dutch hosts. Despite having little food and no luxuries, the Dutch still "think and hope and fight." Dutch resistance is epitomized in the motto "The sea is a common enemy and against a common enemy, we must unite." Later the men find another Dutch motto, written 300 years ago when the House of Orange drove the Spanish out of the Netherlands:

"We can take it." This, of course, was very much the Blitz mentality, and it is left to Bernard Miles to comment that "we don't seem to have progressed much." The film cements the ideological and religious links between the Protestant Dutch and English, and binds them together in resistance to the Nazis.

The movie has a decidedly realist air. It has no asynchronous sound, and a faithful attempt is made to recreate the Dutch landscape. Powell writes in his biography, "I had decided on complete naturalism. There would be only the natural sounds of a country at war. It was not a documentary; it was a detached narrative, told from the inside, of what it is like to be a pawn in the game of total war."[6]

The Silver Fleet (1943), a stirring tale of wartime courage and raw patriotism, is another Powell/Pressburger production set in Nazi-occupied Holland. But this story, unlike many others, unfolds through the diaries of the film's lead character, Jaap Van Leyden (Ralph Richardson). Van Leyden co-owns a shipyard that makes submarines for the Dutch navy. Following the occupation, he is coerced into working for the Nazis and is branded a Quisling by his friends. But he is determined to harm Nazi interests and finds inspiration when he overhears a school teacher telling her pupils about Piet Hein, the Dutch naval hero who captured Spain's silver fleet.

Using Piet Hein as his *nom de guerre*, Van Leyden sets about organizing a resistance network to sabotage the submarines in his yard, despite outwardly complying with Nazi officials. The first Nazi submarine is captured by the Dutch crew and sails to England. The Nazis increase security and impose draconian punishments, though Van Leyden persuades them to show more leniency. Finally he sabotages the second submarine, with Nazi officials—and himself—on board. At the end his rousing words remind listeners of the sacrifices needed in this war:

> As long as Dutchmen live in Holland I shall be here. Because I was one of the seeds from which Freedom grew again. I shall not die! Does a seed die when it is buried in the earth? Has the wind died when it ceases to blow? Are the waves dead when the sea is calm? The truth is that a nation will only live as long as it has people ready to die.

Resistance films largely centered on France, Belgium and Holland, nations that were closest to Britain herself. However, prior to Germany's invasion of Western Europe, the Nazis had launched Operation Weserübung in April 1940, the invasion of Norway. The 1942 *The Day Will Dawn* (U.S.: *The Avengers*) pays tribute to the valiant Norwegian people forced to live under the terrible yoke of Nazi occupation. Set almost entirely in Norway, the film revolves around a British journalist, Colin Metcalfe (Hugh Williams), before and after the German occupation.

At the outset we are told: "Terror rules in Europe. The people are chained. Yet their souls do not submit. This film is made in the faith that those who batter down the prison gates from without will find brave allies among the prisoners within."

The Day Will Dawn is interesting because it deals with the high political struggles in the early stages of the war. At the start we observe a discussion among journalists about the September 2, 1939, debate in Parliament. There is an implicit attack on Neville Chamberlain for his decision to delay a declaration of war on Germany. Later the same journalists report the famous debate of May 7 and 8, 1940, with one quoting an extract from a speech by Leo Amery that helped seal Chamberlain's fall from office. Later Metcalfe shows his approval of Churchill's maiden speech (blood, toil, tears and sweat) as prime minister.

The film's less than subtle political ideology supports not just Churchill but the range of austerity measures that his government brought in. Metcalfe's editor spells out how the Battle of the Atlantic will be won: "We've got to ... damn well learn to eat less, wear less and generally learn to go without."

The Norwegians as a whole are presented as a loyal, defiant and patriotic people who cherish freedom as much as the British. In one early scene in a Norwegian bar, Metcalfe meets local people who engage in a rendition of "Rule Britannia." They are overheard by German sympathizers, one of whom menacingly throws a bottle in their direction. A brawl ensues, with injuries to both sides, but the pro–British sympathy of the locals is unmistakable. At the end, eight Norwegians are rounded up and told they will be shot for harboring a spy. They accept their fate with equanimity, while Metcalfe tells the Nazi captors that millions more of their countrymen will rise up against Nazi occupation with the same unswerving courage.

The Norwegians' stout resistance to tyranny is typified by Olaf, a Norwegian seaman whose daughter, played by Deborah Kerr, falls in love with Metcalfe. Olaf is possessed of a very English sense of honor and duty. He is arrested for distributing banned copies of an anti–Nazi speech given by the Norwegian king, and risks his life to help Metcalfe locate a U-boat base. After his arrest, Olaf's daughter laments her father's loss of liberty in words that sound positively Nelsonian: "Can you not think what it means to a seaman never to be free, never to hear the wind or sail in the fjords?"

The Germans are depicted with the usual caricature, though there is one interesting moment of humor at their expense. A German officer (Francis Sullivan) reveals his distaste for the Norwegian naval command, who, he claims, model themselves on the British navy. Sullivan says he is purging them of "antique notions of chivalry," such as "picking up survivors." This is a humorous backhanded compliment to the British as well as marking out the enemy's fundamental inhumanity.

While most films in the resistance cycle focused on Nazi-occupied Europe, *49th Parallel* (U.S.: *The Invaders*) is unique in that it is set in Canada. In January 1940 the MOI had called for a film that would deal with "the history of the growth of freedom," and which would refer to "the American parallel." This would appeal to "United States audiences."[7] At the same time, Powell and Pressburger wanted to produce a picture on Canada's entry into the war and, after meeting Kenneth Clark, went on a location trip to Canada to work out a suitable story. Wherever the creative impetus emerged, this is certainly a gripping and, at times, visually impressive production.

The film opens with a sequence showing us the vast undefended U.S.–Canadian border, the 49th parallel. Along this border there is no "chain of forts, or deep flowing river, or mountain range," but a "line drawn by men upon a map nearly a century ago, accepted with a handshake and kept ever since." For these two giant bastions of democracy, the world's longest undefended border is governed by bonds of amity and an inviolable sense of trust. For the Nazi enemy, on the other hand, the borders of other states afford an opportunity for naked conquest and aggression.

The film unusually follows the exploits of a group of Nazis, led by Lieutenant Hirth (Eric Portman), who travel through Canada after their U-boat becomes stranded. Realizing they might face internment, they seek refuge in the still-neutral U.S. According to one contemporary review, the film's difficulty is that "the natural heroes of its adventures are the campaigning Nazis."[8] But any initial empathy quickly evaporates when the crew's ideological motivations are laid bare. As the film progresses, we perceive a clear contrast between the ruthlessness and amorality of the Nazis, and the peaceful, cultured and law abiding communities with whom they come into contact.

Johnnie (Laurence Olivier), a Canadian who is skeptical about Nazi atrocities, thinks that the German government is no different to any other. Expressing nationalist sentiments, he thinks French Canada should have nothing to do with defending Poland. But he is soon disabused of his pacifist sentiments when he witnesses the brutal killing of an Eskimo at the hands of the Nazis.

Johnnie uses humor to mock Nazi pretensions, displaying the stereotypical English fondness for ironic wit. The Nazis tell Johnnie that they will guarantee freedom and liberation for the oppressed French Canadians who are living under the "tyranny" of British rule. Johnnie retorts by asking if this is the same freedom afforded to the poor civilians of Poland and occupied France. Johnnie is light-hearted and genial, the Nazis are mechanical and brutally efficient. The previously pacifistic Johnnie now tries to alert the authorities by radio, only to be shot for his efforts.

When the Nazis arrive at a Hutterite settlement they sense a chance for comradeship; this is, after all, a German community. But these industrious people are decent-minded Germans who dislike their former country's new regime. They are a pious and welcoming group who believe in egalitarian values. Indeed, their whole social existence is based on the unwritten rules of Englishness: they value individuality, freedom, spontaneity, simple pleasures, and a growing distrust of authoritarianism. In many ways, the community is cemented by their labor, which is defined by common purpose and not social hierarchy. It is a perfect microcosm of how labor ought to be organized under the pressures of wartime contingencies.

These values so alienate Hirth that he is forced to expound to a Hutterite on the *Fuhrerprinzip*, the leadership principle that binds the German people to their leader. His fanatical belief in blind loyalty and subservience to dictatorship is met with incredulity from the Hutterites.

It is perhaps inevitable that the Nazis meet an Englishman on their travels. Philip Armstrong Scott (Leslie Howard) is a civilized and genteel aesthete who has come to a remote part of Canada to study the Native Americans. His carefree manner infuriates the Nazis, and they view his indifference to war as a sign of decadence. Scott invites the Nazis into his tent, showing off his love of art and quoting from Thomas Mann, an author whose works were banned by the Nazis. Scorning Scott's love of high culture, Hirth and Lohrmann (John Chandos) seize the treasures and commit some to the flames.

Scott typifies the eccentric British art lover, a man obsessed with hobbies who wants nothing more than a quiet life. But he is roused from his slumber after the indecent treatment of his beloved art works. Scott escapes from the tent and confronts Lohrmann, who is in a cave. Advancing towards him, he faces four shots, one of which wounds him, before pouncing on his prey and beating him. "He had a fair chance. One armed superman against one unarmed decadent democrat." At the end, Hirth too receives his comeuppance, at the hands of a wayward Canadian soldier with little time for the Nazi fanatic.

Portman reprised the role of a Nazi on the run in *Squadron Leader X* (1942). In that film he plays a Luftwaffe pilot who is instructed to bomb a Belgian town before bailing out in RAF uniform and trying to convince the local population that the British are responsible for bombing raids. He is mistaken (understandably) for a British pilot and spirited out of the country by the local resistance, only to arrive in the U.K. a little later. There he finds himself hunted both by British intelligence and furious Gestapo officials; but unlike in *49th Parallel*, he manages to escape the country by stealing a British plane. As he flies over the English Channel, however, he is again mistaken for a British pilot and shot down by the Luftwaffe. This film offers a backhanded compliment to MI6 by suggesting that German games of bluff are hopelessly ill-conceived and cack-handed.

Ealing's 1943 *Undercover* (U.S.: *Underground Guerrillas*) completes the picture of resistance films, this time focusing on the Balkans. The movie explores the valiant struggle of two Yugoslav brothers in their fight against Nazi occupation. Milosh Petrovitch (John Clements) leads a guerrilla movement from the hills, carrying out deadly acts of subversion against enemy targets and becoming a top target himself. The other, Dr. Stevan Petrovitch (Stephen Murray), cooperates with the occupiers but uses this apparent goodwill as cover for his own act of resistance.

The German occupation is every bit as brutal as in other resistance films. A young boy reads out a German leaflet which promises that the Nazis will liberate his country. A moment later we see the results of this "liberation" as German bombers wreak havoc from the air and kill the innocent. The Nazis inflict collective punishment on the innocent, with the governor promising to massacre 100 civilians for every German killed. A group of school children are shot for helping their schoolteacher escape custody.

Yet none of this dims the spirit of the hardy and courageous Yugoslavs. They are a nation enthused by tradition, religion and custom, a people conditioned to peace but willing to fight for their freedoms in war. Together they show a spirit of resolve and defiance in resisting occupation. As Anna Petrovitch (Milosh's wife) tells her brutal Nazi interrogators, "We had other conquerors as powerful and ruthless as you. We beat them in the end."

The film was not without some political controversy. It was originally titled *Chetnic*, the name of the guerrilla forces attached to the Serb general Draza Mihailovic, and the movie had the backing of the emigre Yugoslav government. But as Michael Balcon recalls, when Churchill switched support from the royalist Mihailovic to the communist Tito, the film's title changed accordingly and the script had to be altered.[9]

What animates the resistance films is the simple principle that despite facing the daunting military might of their enemy, the occupied peoples of Europe will never succumb to tyranny. Their dogged resistance, ingenuity and determination can win the day. In other words, the struggles of the Continent's oppressed peoples are a powerful reminder that the virtues inspiring the British to victory are shared by their allies.

Chapter 8

History and Heritage as Propaganda

Not all wartime propaganda dealt explicitly with military events or with the dramas of the home front. Some films adopted a more subtle approach, exploiting the rich tapestry of English heritage and history in order to make political points of contemporary relevance.

Historical subjects had featured prominently in British cinema of the 1930s. The cycle was best represented by costume dramas that revolved around the monarchy, the most famous of which was Korda's *The Private Life of Henry VIII*. That film was dominated by the imperious Charles Laughton in the title role and introduced new stars of the future—Robert Donat, Merle Oberon, Elsa Lanchester and Wendy Barrie. The movie was a huge commercial success, winning numerous accolades and spawning new ventures.

In 1934 Herbert Wilcox made *Nell Gwyn*, an amusing production that starred Anna Neagle as Charles II's bawdy mistress. It is full of amusing double entendres, sexual innuendos and displays of cleavage, but there is a serious point underlying it about the king's innate decency and patriotism. These films were followed by *Tudor Rose* and 2 hagiographical productions that paid tribute to Queen Victoria (*Victoria the Great* and *Sixty Glorious Years*). Also noteworthy is *Fire Over England*, with Flora Robson playing the part of Elizabeth I during the time of the Spanish Armada.

Aside from stirring an interest in the English past, these pictures were tapping into a deep popular reverence for the monarchy. The films about Victoria emphasized her role as the "mother of the nation," her belief in public service and her pivotal role as head of the British Empire. The effect of these movies was to imagine a glorious past that was dominated by heroic, larger than life characters, a counterpoint to the climate of international uncertainty prevailing in the 1930s.

At the same time, these films illustrated that there were lessons to be drawn from our past. Values held dear by 20th century Britons were indelibly etched in the nation's past. Thus, in *Sixty Glorious Years* (1938), made the same year as the Munich conference, the Queen is shown opposing any surrender to aggression, and her robust stance is very much a mirror of contemporary anti–Chamberlainite sentiment. It helped that the picture was partly scripted by Sir Robert Vansittart, a trenchant critic of Nazism and appeasement.[1] Elizabeth I in *Fire Over England* is represented as the mystical embodiment of national virtue, a symbol of truth and justice in contrast to her malevolent Spanish foe. The message is that the contemporary nation needs leaders of similar mettle when facing equally potent threats to security. Pierre Sorlin is right when he argues that it would "repay our interest to analyze historical films" because "we have a chance of finding a view of the present embedded within a picture of the past."[2]

The romantic embellishment of history was turned into morale-boosting propaganda during the war years. Two historical biopics, *The Young Mr. Pitt* and *The Prime Minister*, offered a paean to two nineteenth century British statesmen and war leaders, William Pitt the younger and Benjamin Disraeli.

Britain's greatest combat hero, Nelson, features in the lavish costume drama *Lady Hamilton*, while *Henry V* offered a literary adaptation of Shakespeare's famous hero. Within these visions of the past are clear messages for a wartime audience: the need for strong leadership, self-sacrifice and duty, and staunch opposition to tyranny in all its forms. The past is held up as a mirror for the present, reminding us of the timeless nature of English character.

But the heritage cycle also includes films that attempt to capture the essence of English character by burrowing deep into the heart of the rural landscape. Three of the more unusual heritage films are *This England*, *A Canterbury Tale* and *Tawny Pipit*, all set in idyllic countryside and quaint villages. They have a slightly whimsical and eccentric quality, playing on the English love of tradition, freedom and individuality. Yet their deep reverence for the past is unmistakable.

Biopics

The Young Mr. Pitt (1942) celebrates the courage and self-sacrifice of William Pitt the younger. The film gives us a historical tour of the key events of the Pitt administration—the French Revolution and the rise of Napoleon, the battle of the Nile, and the victories of Nelson—all of which are woven into a narrative of Pitt's own personal triumphs and defeats.

Pitt's rise to greatness is shown as far from inevitable. At the outset, the young prime minister is pilloried in the House of Commons by an uncomprehending mob of aloof aristocrats. Their puerile outburst stands in stark contrast to the sober, mild-mannered leader they are attacking. Next he is physically attacked by a mob and forced to defend himself with the help of his loyal colleagues, William Wilberforce and the boxer Dan Mendoza. But after winning a general election, he outwits his opponents and sets about a program of domestic and naval reform.

Pitt's fortunes are transformed by events in France, as first the revolution forces the overthrow of the *ancien regime*, and then terror spreads throughout the country. When Pitt denounces the French wars of conquest across Europe, he is cheered by his fellow Parliamentarians. Napoleon, played by a young Herbert Lom, is depicted as a ruthless tyrant intent on the subjugation of Europe. And it is Pitt's genius to recognize that "a nation of armed fanatics led by an arch fanatic" cannot be defeated by "half measures and half hearted completions." Such is the man's devotion to defeating France that he puts the national interest ahead of his own health.

Nonetheless, Pitt's fortunes fluctuate as the peace party's calls for neutrality become increasingly urgent. Fickle crowds, which once cheered the prime minister, are now angry and indignant at high taxation and other restrictions on liberty. He is forced to resign following a defeat on land, but later, with Napoleon's forces massing across the Channel, he once again returns to lead the nation. On one level the film is a simple exercise in historical self congratulation. Pitt the Younger is the heroic leader who bravely defies Napoleonic tyranny, though the movie is marred by a rather flattering, one-dimensional portrait. On another level it is a blatant piece of cinematic propaganda, attempting to mold history to present-day concerns by revealing the timeless nature of English character.

Director Carol Reed draws significant parallels between Pitt and Churchill. Both are derided as warmongers in their own time, Pitt by Fox and Churchill by Chamberlain. Both receive national vindication but only after the failure of appeasement. Both come to power at a time of dire national emergency and after humiliating setbacks—Pitt (initially) after the loss of the American colonies and Churchill after the Narvik fiasco. Both stubbornly reject peace terms and remain convinced that their enemy must be destroyed.

Like Churchill, who had to see off domestic foes (within the Tory party) as well as Hitler, Pitt was confronted by enemies at home as well as Napoleon. Both men rally the nation through dark times and lead by example—in Pitt's case, to the detriment of his health. And both men are forced to rally their nations alone and while their enemy controls mainland Europe. Pitt's rousing defense of the war with France has an indisputably Churchillian echo:

> It is security against a danger which, in degree and in extent, was never equalled, a danger which threatens all nations of the earth. Now we face that danger alone. But we shall meet it undaunted, determined to stand or fall by the laws, liberties and religion of our country.

Donat's sensitive performance as Pitt is a tour de force, while Robert Morley gives a convincing display as his arch nemesis, Fox. Nonetheless the film is marred by offering a simplistic, hagiographic portrayal of the lead character. Pitt and his enemies appear in black and white when shades of grey and chiaroscuro would be more convincing. The public are depicted as fickle and simple minded, spouting lines that are often predictable and unsophisticated. Mindful of the film's flaws, and in particular its historical inaccuracies, Raymond Durgnat commented scathingly, "'It butchers the past to fit the present."[3]

Another British leader, Benjamin Disraeli, emerges as his country's national savior in Thorold Dickinson's 1941 film *The Prime Minister*. The film's general themes are the importance of duty and self-sacrifice, the supremacy of British values (guided by the nation's monarch), and the futility of appeasement. As the narrative of Disraeli's career unfolds, these values become paramount and are shown to have parallels with contemporary wartime events.

In the early part of the picture the young Disraeli is mocked and jeered by hostile MPs during his maiden speech. His struggle for acceptance and his eventual triumph certainly offer an instructive parallel with Churchill's struggles in Parliament in the 1930s. Gradually Disraeli wins over his critics and emerges as a man of the people, in contrast to his more backward looking peers. He sides with the Chartists and their democratic cause, declaring that "a new spirit is awake in England, the spirit of youth."

Disraeli's Churchillian stubbornness and courage are vital in the second half of the film when he becomes prime minister. He addresses the Cabinet about the dangers of a hegemonic Germany and the growing Russian threat to the Balkans, warning of a coming domination of the East. Hearing calls for appeasement among his ministers, he offers this thundering denunciation: "Peace can be purchased at too great a price." In a monologue that Churchill himself would have been proud of, Disraeli declares:

> I know these dictators, these men of blood and iron.... Their god is power. The virtues we hold dear they call weaknesses and what we love they despise. They hold themselves a race apart, divinely ordained to rule the world to the exclusion of all others. That is a form of madness that must eventually destroy the world or be destroyed. It cannot be appeased by soft words or good neighbourliness. All civilized methods of approach to international agreements are signs of weakness to these men. They recognize one argument and one argument alone: force.

Disraeli and his opposing ministers are Victorian mouthpieces for the raging debate over appeasement in the 1930s. But so too is Queen Victoria, who reminds Disraeli that his resignation will leave the British Empire in mortal peril. The film elevates the monarch to a position of supreme importance to both nation and Empire.

Yet there are strong elements here of simplistic characterization and caricature. Bismarck is depicted as a dark and menacing figure with sinister designs to dominate Europe. Disraeli's domestic opponents mouth rather unsophisticated views on foreign policy, making them pawns in the contemporary struggle over said policy. As William Whitebait observes, this movie "smooths corners ... gives character a face-lift, and this is what every historical film secretly aims at."[4] *Picturegoer and Film Weekly* offered a similar viewpoint: "We frequently accuse American producers of distorting facts in pictures dealing with English history, but apparently our own movie moguls can be equally misleading judging by this biographical film of Disraeli's life." Nonetheless, it acknowledged the parallel drawn "between events then and those that are occurring today."[5]

Two American made films, *Sea Hawk* and *Lady Hamilton*, highlighted the role of Britain's naval heroes in defeating Continental tyranny. *Sea Hawk* was a lavish Warner Brothers production starring the quintessential action-adventure hero, Errol Flynn. The picture highlighted the heroic role of Elizabeth I at the time of the Armada and suggested a stirring parallel between the sixteenth century and modern times. Flynn was a dashing and suave performer, and in films such as *Captain Blood*, *The Charge of the Light Brigade* and *The Adventures of Robin Hood* was cast as a swashbuckling defender of justice. In this movie, Flynn plays Geoffrey Thorpe, a character modeled on Sir Francis Drake, who plunders Spanish ships in order to build an English fleet against the Armada.

Elizabeth I remains unconvinced by the Spanish threat and is advised by Lord Wolfingham to use diplomacy. But Wolfingham is a traitor, acting on behalf of Phillip II, and at the end of the film he is killed by Thorpe in a climactic swordfight. By picture's end the Queen has sent her fleet to meet the Armada, convinced that the armed threat from Spain is real after all.

Throughout the film we discern the clearest parallels with the modern age. Philip II is Europe's sixteenth-century Hitler, a man drunk on power and with a tyrannical thirst for Continental domination. "With England conquered," he declares, "nothing can stand in our way." At the end of the movie the Queen gives a rousing speech of Churchillian defiance that espouses the universal rights of mankind:

> When the ruthless ambitions of one man threaten to engulf the world, it becomes the solemn obligation of all free men to affirm that the earth belongs not to any one man but to all men, and that freedom is the deed and title to the soil on which we exist.

Lady Hamilton (also known as *That Hamilton Woman*), made in 1941, is a lavish historical drama that draws clear links between Britain's past and present struggles. It was produced by the Hungarian born Alexander Korda, whose previous output included a number of highly patriotic films, such as *The Private Life of Henry VIII* (1933), *Sanders of the River* (1935) and *The Four Feathers* (1939). Korda's production sees Laurence Olivier paired with the sparkling Vivien Leigh as the ill-fated, star-crossed lovers Admiral Nelson and Emma Hamilton. Their romantic liaisons are told in flashback by an aged Lady Hamilton, who in late life has been slung into a debtor's prison in Calais.

The film draws stirring parallels between Nelson's combat heroics and Britain's military feats in 1940. In an early scene the great admiral shows frustration with the complacency of the Neapolitan people and their monarch. He warns the king that "as long as these madmen (i.e., the French) have their armies on land, no country in Europe is free." He goes on: "If you value your freedom, stir yourself." But Naples remains decadent, with Lady Hamilton and her husband, Sir William Hamilton (Alan Mowbray), living in opulent surroundings. When the city falls, Nelson bemoans its loss, describing it as "a little kingdom miles away in the Mediterranean," just as Czechoslovakia was "a far away country of which we know little."

His battles against Napoleon, and his triumphs, mirror those of Britain in its finest hour. He is a foe of appeasement who tells the House of Lords in his maiden speech that, though a man of peace, he would not "for the sake of any peace consent to sacrifice one jot of England's honor." This is a clear swipe at those who, even at the height of the Second World War, still believed in a compromise peace with Hitler. The weapons with which he intends to defend his country are a small number of ships, the 18th century version of "the few" being owed so much by the many. They are all that stand in the way of a Napoleonic conquest of Britain.

But unlike the Churchill of popular legend, Nelson is presented as a flawed hero, a man who succumbs to personal lust in contrast to his wife's undying loyalty. The romantic scenes between the lovers (married in real life) are energized by the pair's sexual chemistry, with Leigh's effervescence matched only by Olivier's stern intensity. This is both romantic melodrama and historical propaganda at its best.

The film was a clear favorite with Churchill, who reportedly saw it no fewer than 11 times. Nonetheless, it fared less well with some critics. The legendary Caroline Lejeune was less than impressed: "It is my impression that the film would have been a better job if it had stuck more to this man Nelson and bothered less about that woman Hamilton. These are not days when we have much patience for looking at history through the eyes of a trollop."[6]

As a paean to British military resolve, this was at first glance a brave film to make. For the prevailing mood in Hollywood, at least prior to America's own involvement in the war effort, was to maintain a form of cinematic neutrality. This was partly in keeping with the prevailing sentiment of isolationism that was shared by German-Americans and by various pressure groups that wanted the U.S. to stay out of a European conflict. Nonetheless, the censors raised few objections to the script. The adulterous liaison between Lord Nelson and Lady Hamilton did raise eyebrows, however, for the film appeared to condone such extra-marital relations. Thus, in the released version, Lady Hamilton suffers for her misdemeanors by being exiled from England and forced to live on the streets of Calais in rags.

No English writer has stirred the imagination or summoned up visceral emotions better than Shakespeare. His *Henry V* is a paean to the courageous fifteenth-century monarch who led his army to victory at the Battle of Agincourt. It is also a triumphant piece of patriotic literature with a rousing call to arms from a king to his soldiers on the eve of battle. Thus the contemporary parallels to the Second World War, and the D-Day landings in particular, are evident straightaway in this 1944 adaptation. Indeed, the title caption contains this dedication: "To the Commandos and Airborne troops of Great Britain—the spirit of whose ancestors it has been humbly attempted to recapture in some ensuing scenes—this picture is dedicated."

The centerpiece of the film is the spectacular Anglo-French battle sequence. It is a visual spectacle of stunning splendor, which features intercutting between shots of charging French knights and English archers with their longbows, all accompanied by William Walton's stirring score. At the heart of the action is Olivier, whose peerless performance as the king was one of its most notable features. Olivier combines a debonair and sensitive manner with a brand of sexually alluring vigor and masculinity. It is a triumphant fusion of qualities.

As James Chapman points out, "The low-angle shots of Henry isolate him, enhancing his status as leader."[7] The king exhorts his followers to ever greater feats of courage, appealing in particular to their status as underdogs. Hence his famous words in the Crispin speech, "If we are mark'd to die, we are enow to do our country loss; and if to live, the fewer men, the greater share of honor." There is an echo of the Blitz spirit here and a reminder of how Churchill exhorted his countrymen to show determination and courage in the face of the Nazi onslaught. But King Henry, like Churchill, is also a man of the people who communicates with them on a personal level. Hence his now legendary descriptions of his warriors as a "happy few" and a "band of brothers."

But while the message of *Henry V* echoes the contemporary struggle against Continental foes, it is also an important heritage film in its own right.

Caroline Lejeune was right to proclaim it "a salute to high adventure: a kind of boyish exaltation of man's grim work."[8] Olivier received a special Academy Award for his "Outstanding Production Achievement as Actor, Producer and Director in bringing *Henry V* to the screen."

The biopics of the era feature a cavalcade of male figures. The exception was *They Flew Alone* (U.S.: *Wings and the Woman*), a heroic portrait of champion aviator Amy Johnson. Johnson became a global celebrity when she became the first woman to make a solo flight from England to Australia in 1931. Johnson's life, as portrayed by Anna Neagle, typifies all those qualities of resolve, endurance, patriotism and courage which are found in the historical biopics. To achieve greatness she has to overcome all manner of adversity, including a schoolteacher who decries her individuality and female ambition.

Thus her individual achievement is seen as a force for liberation—not just for other women but for all those stifled by others. She also endures the perils of long-distance flying but faces each new challenge with an unquenchable resolve. Her pioneering spirit is matched by Jim Mollison, a Scottish aviator whom she eventually marries. But his heavy drinking takes its toll on their marriage, and they are divorced. When war breaks out she joins the ATA (Air Transport Auxiliary), but she dies in a flying accident in 1941. At the end, Johnson's image fills the screen while the audience is reminded about the enduring need to win the freedom of the skies.

The Heritage Cycle

This England (1941) surveys the grand sweep of English history through the life of a typical English rural community, the village of Clevely. We start in the present with an American outsider, played by Constance Cummings, arriving in the village. After witnessing an air raid in which the villagers behave with impressive phlegm, she meets two inhabitants who narrate the story of the village, selecting four episodes from the past. She hears about the villagers' communal solidarity in 1086 as the Norman Conquest swept the country, next how the village coped during the Spanish Armada of 1588, then how they survived the threat of a Napoleonic invasion, and finally their resilience during the First World War. What kept this community alive was a sense of social solidarity and harmony, people pulling together to face external threats regardless of their position in the rural hierarchy. It offers a somewhat rosy picture of social solidarity which, while not unrealistic in 1940, seemed scarcely credible during those earlier eras. It is a rather crude piece of propaganda, with the kind of clichéd lines and theatrical performances that are to be found in *The Lion Has Wings*. Nonetheless, it evokes the spirit of England's rural communities and uses history, albeit a simplistic version, to hammer home its point.

A Canterbury Tale (1944) was one of the most aesthetically ambitious but least appreciated of the Powell and Pressburger productions. It is a mystical and sometimes mystifying fable, but one with a clear philosophical message for wartime Britain. As Powell explained, "The whole idea was to examine the values for which we were fighting ... we felt the moral issues of the war were almost as exciting as the war that was being fought."[9]

In *A Canterbury Tale*, those values ultimately reside in the land itself, in tranquil rural communities with quaint churches and craftsmen, in a countryside that was so lovingly described by Chaucer, Milton and Shakespeare. The film has a conservative ethos, harking back to an imagined glorious past in which reside England's abiding and most cherished values.

At the beginning we see medieval pilgrims traveling towards Canterbury on the Pilgrim's Way. Six centuries later we are informed that little has changed except that the town is now host to "another kind of pilgrim" as a U.S. tank rolls across the countryside. This sets the scene for the arrival of three more pilgrims, one an American serviceman, Bob Johnson (played by a real U.S. sergeant, John Sweet), a British sergeant (Dennis Price), and an English volunteer for the Land Army, Alison (Sheila Sim).

On their arrival in Chilingbourne, a nearby village in Kent, Alison is attacked by "the glueman," a nocturnal pest who pours glue into the hair of women who befriend servicemen. The trio spends much of the film trying to discern the identity of this local nuisance, only to discover that it is the town's highly respected magistrate, Thomas Culpepper (Eric Portman). Culpepper admits that he carries out these attacks partly to deter men from having affairs, but also because he wants the men to attend his local history lectures instead of being distracted by the opposite sex.

Culpepper's misdemeanors are less important than the journey of discovery made by the three explorers. For in their own way they discover something of England's pastoral beauty and quaint ways.

Initially we see Alison as the embodiment of urban modernity. She has worked in a London department store, and when she starts work on the farm she is mocked for not knowing simple rural terms. Her fellow farm workers are simple folk whose entire working lives have been spent in their profession. Yet she adapts willingly to the new role, revealing her love of gardens and the countryside. Later she is transfixed by the haunting beauty of Canterbury Cathedral, imagining that she hears the sound of horses' hooves. Culpepper admits he has underestimated her, moderating his somewhat misogynistic views.

Johnson appears to embody soulless materialism and the endless pursuit of leisure. A loud-mouthed character, he reveals to Culpepper that on a visit to Salisbury he had enjoyed going to the cinema rather than more historic cultural attractions. He cannot understand England's quaint customs and her obsessive tea drinking. Yet his experience of rural life leaves him spiritually regenerated, admitting that the army had only taken care of his body. He, too, is overpowered by Canterbury Cathedral, the embodiment of England's religious heritage. By the end, each pilgrim has received a blessing.

For Culpepper the past breathes through the landscape. At his lecture he urges his listeners to get close to nature, for this is how they can connect with their medieval ancestors from six centuries ago: "They climbed Chilingbourne Hill just as you did, they sweated and paused for breath just as you did today. And when you see the bluebells in the spring and the wild thyme and the broom and the heather you are only seeing what their eyes saw...."

Though his activities as the glueman mark him as an unstable eccentric, his motives seem sincere enough. Like a missionary, he feels he has to educate the savages and "do his duty" by transmitting a love of the country to others.

Eric Portman was ideally suited to the role of the glueman. He had a cold and ominous persona which gave his performances a sinister and disarming intensity. His most famous wartime role was in *49th Parallel*, playing a stranded Nazi U-boat commander with a chilling devotion to the Nazi cause. After the war Portman would establish a reputation for portraying dark, complex figures, often carrying terrible secrets. Yet he was equally adept at playing the officer type, as in *One of Our Aircraft Is Missing* and *The Colditz Story*.

For all its aesthetic qualities, *A Canterbury Tale* was not a box office success and received poor reviews, with Lionel Collier labeling it a "meandering and sometimes quite inexplicable" picture.[10] Caroline Lejeune was equally unimpressed, particularly with the character of the Glueman: "This fellow may be a mystagogue, with the love of England in his blood, but he is also plainly a crackpot of a rather unpleasant type with bees in his bonnet and blue-bottles in the belfrey."[11]

Another heritage film that evokes the spirit of the English countryside is the little known *Tawny Pipit* (1944), written and directed by Bernard Miles and Charles Saunders. This whimsical, Ealing-style production centers on the imaginary town of Lipsbury Lea, an idyllic rural retreat with charming cottages, quaint country lanes and captivating views.

During a countryside jaunt, a fighter pilot and his nurse stumble across a pair of rare nesting birds, the Tawny Pipits, which have only once before bred in Britain. They alert the local community, who, led by their redoubtable local squire, Colonel Barton-Barrington (Bernard Miles), agree to offer the birds sanctuary. The rest of the film features the villagers' attempts to protect the birds from a variety of predators: poachers who want to steal the birds'

Eric Portman with Sheila Sim in Powell and Pressburger's mystical *A Canterbury Tale* **(1944). With his dark and menacing persona, Portman was ideally suited to play the mysterious "Glueman" (Eagle-Lion, Photofest).**

valuable eggs, the army who want to carry out maneuvers on the field, and bureaucrats at the Ministry of Agriculture who want to plough up the land for the war effort. In each case the villagers manage to outwit their opponents, who, in turn, come to see the error of their ways.

The villagers' efforts serve as a metaphor for the wider war effort. The defense of the birds from their rapacious enemies is on par with Britain's valiant struggle against fascism. And the villagers' fondness for the Pipits and their love of animals reflect other national characteristics that differentiate the English from their Continental foes. As Barton-Barrington tells the villagers:

> This love of animals and of nature has always been part and parcel of the British way of life. Now we've welcomed to our country thousands of foreigners at one time or another—French, Dutch, Poles, Czechs and so on—and a lot of them are jolly decent people, and anyway they can't help being foreigners. Well that's what these little pipits are, you see, and we're jolly well going to see to it that they get fair play or we shall want to know the reason why ... in my opinion the big difference between ourselves and the Hun is that the Hun doesn't know the meaning of playing the game, he never did and he never will.

As with *The Demi Paradise*, a visiting Russian extols British values in *Tawny Pipit*. A female Red Army soldier praises the spirit of Anglo-Russian wartime solidarity and offers a paean to her nation's rural values: "It is a rich land, full of growing. It is our home.... We shall fight to the last."

Like in *A Canterbury Tale*, England's unspoiled countryside forms the backdrop to the film's dramatic events. But the connection between land, the creatures that nestle in it and national values is more straightforward in *Tawny Pipit*. In a powerful final sequence we see the villagers giving thanks for the survival of the Pipits by singing the hymn "All Things Bright and Beautiful." But as they sing, Jimmy's plane flies over the church and soars high above the fields. The image conveys the interconnectedness between the war effort, in which Jimmy still plays a part, and the values for which it is being fought, values that reside in the land and its community.

Chapter 9

The Postwar Interlude: War Films 1945–1950

After six years of traumatic conflict, Britain emerged from the Second World War a weaker and much less prosperous nation. More than 450,000 people had died, including at least 60,000 citizens in the Blitz. Her major export and domestic industries had been shattered, she was heavily in debt and her shipping had been reduced by nearly one third. In 1947–8 she suffered an economic crisis marked by fuel shortages, a balance of payments deficit and the devaluation of sterling. In the years to come, Britain would be forced to cede the remainder of her Empire as the relentless tide of nationalism swept through the Asian sub-continent and most of Africa. From this postwar denouement would come an irrepressible narrative of national decline and decadence that would last for decades.

Nonetheless, she had been part of an Allied triumvirate that was responsible for the outright defeat of totalitarianism. She could claim, unlike the USSR and the USA, to have fought against Nazism for the entire duration of the war, and to have stood alone against Hitler in 1940–1, something that would become an enduring source of national pride.

Moreover, there were social achievements to be proud of too. It was widely believed that the collective experience of war through the Blitz, evacuation and rationing had forged a new national identity. The war appeared to have broken down class barriers and created a genuine sense of social solidarity. This was the famous "myth of the Blitz," as Angus Calder described it, which gave rise to the prevailing ethos of social democracy in wartime cinema.

The postwar years appeared to provide fertile ground for maintaining this wartime social consensus. The new Labor government, led by Clement Attlee, had pledged to create a "cradle to the grave" welfare state with fairness for all, not just the privileged few. Between 1945 and 1950, Britain's key industries were nationalized, and a system of state-subsidized healthcare was created. This new political experiment was designed to eradicate poverty, unemployment and hunger, the trio of ills that had plagued the British working man in the prewar years. This was the "New Jerusalem" to which the governing classes now aspired.

Amid this political revolution, there appeared to be an overwhelming nostalgia for the war's community spirit, and a growing belief that, if the British people were not careful, it could be irretrievably lost in peacetime. There were many positive experiences of wartime camaderie, with the experience of army life having brought routine, structure and a sense of purpose to everyday activity. It also brought a sense of male companionship, intensified by groups of men living in confined quarters while facing common dangers. But all this had to be set against the tedium and disappointment of postwar civilian life. One historian writes of civvies seeming "listless, preoccupied and aimless," and this was no doubt exacerbated by the monotonous tasks they were now doing.[1] Hence, there was a need for social unity and cooperation, rather than the class divisions of the prewar years.

One film that sought to convey the need for class cooperation was *Landfall* (1949). Here an upper–middle-class RAF pilot, Rick (Michael Denison), falls in love with a working-class barmaid, Mona (Patricia Plunkett), creating social tensions that are evident to them both. But when he is unjustly accused of sinking a British vessel, after he believed it to be a German one, he is charged with neglect and transferred to the north of the country. Mona meanwhile fights for his cause, producing evidence that the vessel he destroyed was actually a U-boat. She helps clear his name and later they get married, revealing that cooperation and even romance between different classes is possible after the war.

No film cycle better expressed the postwar yearning for social unity than the whimsical Ealing comedies of the late 1940s and 1950s. In *Hue and Cry* (1947) an intrepid group of schoolchildren foils a master criminal gang in London who were using their comic to communicate with each other. Cooperation and solidarity triumph in *The Titfield Thunderbolt* (1953) when a local community defies attempts by the all-powerful British Rail to close down a section of its rural branch line. In *Passport to Pimlico* (1949) a small community defies the heavy-handed bureaucracy of Whitehall and fights for its claim to independence. Finally, in *Whisky Galore* (1949) the inhabitants of a small island in the Outer Hebrides work together to prevent an illicit cargo of whisky from falling into the hands of the English.

These are the victories of small communities over the big forces (bureaucracy, unrestrained capitalism, greed) that threaten to derail the prospects for a stable postwar society. In *Seven Days to Noon* (1950) there is a similar nostalgia for the spirit of wartime cooperation. In that celebrated film we see the population of London being evacuated in an orderly fashion after a rogue scientist threatens to detonate a nuclear weapon in the city.

But these were not war films as such. In fact, the period from 1945 through 1950 is sometimes assumed to be the "doldrums moment" between the golden age of the war and the '50s revival, a period when few war films were made. The British people, it is argued, demanded escapism in the aftermath of the bloodiest conflict in history. This would be true were it not for the fact that in these five years there were actually a considerable number of World War II movies, though modest in comparison to the following decade. There were espionage thrillers, melodramas about the POW experience and the SOE, productions dealing with the creation of radar and the battle of Arnhem, films that questioned postwar Anglo-German relations, and a cycle of "ex-servicemen" movies.

One issue addressed by postwar British war cinema was how veterans had failed to come to terms with peacetime and tried instead to enjoy the fruits of criminal enterprise. In *Night Beat* (1948), a British crime drama directed by Harold Huth, two wartime comrades join the police when peace is declared. But while one remains honest and law abiding, the other becomes associated with spivs and racketeers. *The Flamingo Affair* (1948) features an ex-commando captain, Dick Tarleton (Denis Webb), who, disillusioned with civilian life after being demobbed, becomes involved in a dangerous web of intrigue and crime via a glittering femme fatale.

Cavalcanti's *They Made Me a Fugitive* (1947) stars Trevor Howard as a disillusioned and drunk ex–RAF officer who falls in with a gang led by a vicious working-class criminal, Narcy (Griffith Jones). Morgan is then framed for killing a policeman, receiving a 15-year sentence, but he later escapes in a desperate bid to clear his name and confront Narcy. In *Cage of Gold* (1950) a young artist (Jean Simmons) realizes too late that the ex–RAF officer (David Farrar) that she fell in love with (and who made her pregnant) is a rogue. Believing him to be dead, she re-marries, but her first husband returns and starts blackmailing her and her husband. *The Intruder* (1953) sees Jack Hawkins, the former commander of a tank regiment, being burgled by a man who used to be under his command. Hawkins tries to uncover what happened to the man after the war that might have turned him to a life of crime.

Lance Comfort's *Silent Dust* (1949) features another returning serviceman who falls into criminality and deception, particularly regarding his own family. It is an intriguing story of betrayal and cowardice. When Simon Rawley (Nigel Patrick) is reported killed towards the end of the war, his blind father Robert decides to build a sports pavilion in his son's memory, ignoring requests from his neighbor (Lord Crandon) to dedicate it to all the local men who lost their lives in the conflict. Shortly before the grand opening, Robert surprises an intruder on his property who turns out to be Simon, though it is Angela, Simon's ex-wife, not Robert, that recognizes him.

It transpires that far from dying a heroic death on the battlefield, Simon was a deserter who elaborately faked his own death. Since the war he has been a black marketer, and now he has returned to extort money from his family. When Robert finally realizes that his son is in his house, he confronts him, and in the ensuing climax Simon falls to his death from a balcony. In a fitting conclusion, Robert changes the dedication to suit Crandon's wishes. The conflict between a sense of family loyalty and the wider loyalty to the community's fallen is resolved when Simon's perfidy is revealed.

The implication in all these films is that war provided a sense of purpose and belonging that is now badly missing in peacetime. In reality, this reflected a very real and growing problem of postwar criminality. After 1945, some 20,000 deserters went on the loose in Britain and, without hope of gainful employment, simply swelled the growing ranks of the black market.

However, one film provides a welcome counterpoint to this disturbing narrative of fallen men. In Powell and Pressburger's 1949 BAFTA-nominated *Small Back Room* (U.S.: *Hour of Glory*), based on the novel by Nigel Balchin, a man overcomes his self-destructive urges to work for the betterment of his country. David Farrar plays the part of Sammy Rice, a bomb disposal expert working for a backroom team in London during the Second World War. Rice is an embittered man due to his contempt for an incompetent military establishment and the crippling personal pain he suffers from an artificial foot. He has turned to alcohol to lessen the pain, but this has only brought on bouts of self-destructive behavior and put an abrupt end to his relationship with Susan (Kathleen Byron).

Rice is then called in by Captain Stuart (Michael Gough) to deal with booby-trapped explosive devices dropped by Nazi bombers. Despite being in a drunken state, after his girlfriend has walked out on him, Rice seizes the chance for redemption and successfully defuses a bomb that had been left on Chesil Beach. At the end he is re-united with Susan. Farrar's battle against an alcohol addiction is memorably conveyed in one surreal sequence. Alone in his flat one evening, he undergoes a delusional episode in which a bottle of whisky comes to dominate the entire room. Clever lighting and intricate camera angles combine with a haunting score to convey a terrifying sense of claustrophobia.

While some productions looked at the role of the outsider in British society, others explored Britain's fractious relations with the nations of postwar Europe. Ealing's *Frieda* (1947) tackles one of the thorniest of social problems courageously—namely, whether it is possible to forgive Germans after the horrors of World War II. In the film an RAF officer, Robert (David Farrar), marries a young German girl, Frieda, played by Mai Zetterling, who had enabled him to escape from a prisoner of war camp.

When they arrive at his home town they both face the unrelenting hostility of the local population, particularly Robert's unforgiving aunt, played convincingly by Flora Robson. In one memorable scene, Frieda experiences humiliation when she visits a cinema that is screening horrific images from the concentration camps. Matters are made worse for her when her Polish brother, a passionate Nazi, turns up in London and alleges that his sister shares his views. Driven to the brink of suicide, she is saved at the last by Robert after he had initially believed the allegations. In a wider sense, the film explores whether bitterness and recriminations will give way to Anglo-German cooperation, or whether the hatred induced by two world wars will hold sway.

There is no such moral quandary in *Portrait from Life* (1948), a film in which a British officer travels through displaced persons camps in Germany in search of Hildegarde (Mai Zetterling), a young girl whose portrait he has seen in London. He finds her living with a Nazi, played skillfully by Herbert Lom, who has exploited the girl's amnesia in order to give him cover for his own tarnished identity. In reality, the girl's father is a Jewish professor living in London who is desperate to see if she is still alive. Here we are dealing with an innocent child forced into an identity change by her unfeeling "guardians," and no issues about forgiveness or redemption arise.

Another film which explores postwar attitudes is the highly theatrical *The Lost People* (1949), a British production with a clearly didactic message about the need for tolerance and goodwill between nations. Two British soldiers hold a hostile group of displaced people from separate nations in a German theater. The group is torn apart by national rivalries (Pole and Russian, Serb and Croat) which compound the wartime tragedy that has already befallen them. The only thing that unites them, albeit temporarily, is the fear that they may collectively succumb to a bout of bubonic plague.

The film emphasizes the need for disparate peoples to unite in the face of a common threat rather than risk their mutual destruction from petty rivalries. The movie relies on studio sets and dialogue, giving this production a somewhat stagey feel. Nonetheless, in its humanist approach to the problems of postwar Europe, it is effective, even if its tendency to be didactic may be wearisome to some viewers.

The little known Anglo-Dutch production *But Not in Vain* (1948) deals with the moral dilemmas of patriotism and resistance. Jan Alting (Raymond Lovell) is a leading member of the Dutch underground who has taken it upon himself to shelter people wanted by the Nazi authorities, among them a Jewish couple. He comes into conflict with his son, a collaborator with the German authorities, who demands that his father turn over to the Nazis those he is sheltering. Jan realizes he has to choose between abandoning them or sacrificing his son, between family and national loyalties.

The theme of bluff and resistance would feature regularly throughout the 1950s, often in a POW setting in which superior German might had to be countered by native British wit. *The Captive Heart* (1946) establishes some of the conventions of this subgenre and is given added authenticity by being partially filmed in an ex-naval German prisoner of war camp. Michael Redgrave plays the role of a Czech soldier (Captain Karel Hasek) who, after escaping from a concentration camp, assumes the identity of a dead British soldier. After being captured again, he ends up in a POW camp where he must maintain this new identity, outwitting both the Nazis and suspicious British soldiers who suspect that he is an imposter.

To maintain the pretence he decides to write to the dead soldier's widow, who, in turn, is led to believe that her husband has fallen back in love with her after a shaky period in their marriage. When they meet up in Britain, following his repatriation, she realizes that she has fallen in love with the man who she wrongly believed to be her husband.

The film combines a story of survival against the odds with an endearing romantic subplot. But the picture also offers a highly sanitized view of life as a POW, a key feature of such later films as *The Wooden Horse* and *Stalag 17*. Convivial relations are established with a number of German guards, and in one scene Basil Radford and a camp guard share friendly banter with an ease and familiarity that seems highly contrived. Nonetheless, the scenes of soldierly camaraderie are convincing enough.

But the film is also a testament to the English stiff upper lip and the paramount importance of stoicism. Throughout the movie Karel is forced to adopt the mannerisms of fellow British soldiers, together with their unfailing sense of duty. Karel imbibes their determination and restraint as a survival mechanism, both in adopting his fake persona and when he has to injure his hand in order to disguise his handwriting. Stoicism is what helps keep British soldiers alive, and it is also essential for Karel. As Boyce puts it, "The film suggests that Britishness is not something inborn, but claimed, believed, and lived out just as the British soldiers transform their prison into a little piece of Britain."[2] The connotations of the stiff upper lip, of duty, self-deprecating humor and emotional restraint are also central to Redgrave's persona and would be used to great effect in *The Sea Shall Not Have Them* and *The Dam Busters*.

While *The Captive Heart* deals with outsmarting the Germans in a POW setting, *Night Boat to Dublin* (1946) offers the same—but according to a more conventional formula. In this film, which echoes wartime spy melodramas, British undercover intelligence officers get the better of German agents in order to capture a high-profile scientist who is inadvertently feeding them information. Here the stakes could not be higher, because the Swedish scientist, Professor Hansen (Martin Miller), is an expert in atomic weapons research and is therefore of extraordinary value to the Nazis. However, the film is marred by its overly complicated plot and its occasionally bizarre twists and turns, though the performances from Robert Newton (as Captain David Grant) and a chilling cameo from Herbert Lom as a Nazi make it watchable.

Ealing's *Against the Wind* (1948) offers a more straightforward war drama set amid the operations of the Special Operations Executive. The title is taken from some lines from Byron: "Yet freedom! Yet thy banner, torn but flying, Streams like the thunderstorm against the wind." A group of individuals with differing backgrounds is put through a rigorous training program by the SOE in order to carry out sabotage in Nazi-occupied Belgium. Once their program is complete, they are parachuted behind enemy lines where their missions include the destruction of an important Nazi record office and the rescue of an SOE agent from custody. The film also features an Irish double agent, Jack Warner, who is promptly executed in cold blood when evidence of his treacherous activities comes to light.

Against the Wind features a memorable performance from Simone Signoret as a hard-nosed saboteur who puts duty above sentiment. Producer Michael Balcon was certainly impressed with her, lauding her "fine intelligence, warmth and compassion," and describing her as a "wonderful actress" and "great woman."[3]

Yet the film was not a box office success and failed to receive the critical acclaim that Ealing might have expected. A *New York Times* critic lamented how the movie contained "contrived melodrama" and "a minimum of the truth behind the sabotage of World War II." This was somewhat unfair, as Tibby Clarke, author of the screenplay, had gathered "true incidents from people who had served in the Belgian resistance."[4] Perhaps the film, which lacks nothing in excitement and drama, suffered more from bad timing.

Finally, some films dealt more directly with the war years. *School for Secrets* is a cinematic paean to the "boffin," specifically to a select group of scientists who assisted the RAF during the Second World War by developing radar. The men, who include Ralph Richardson, David Tomlinson, Raymond Huntley and John Laurie, are brought together just as war is starting and work in secrecy to put this vital weapon in the hands of Britain's fighting forces. We see the success of their efforts reflected in the RAF's growing prowess in 1940, with the film using documentary footage effectively.

These men are upper–middle-class intellectuals who are initially skeptical about working in such a practical environment. But far from being aloof academians, they are men guided by a sense of duty. They temporarily set aside their academic careers, as well as their family lives, for the sake of aiding their country. When one of the scientists, Mr. Watlington (Tomlinson) dies during an experimental run in a bomber, the others accept the loss with equanimity but regard the invention as a fitting tribute to his memory. For its part, this film justly honors those who helped to achieve an important technological breakthough.

Yet despite the large number of World War II–related pictures immediately after the war, the true heyday of the patriotic war film would have to wait until the following decade.

Chapter 10

Obsessive Nostalgia: The British War Films of the 1950s

In 1958 the *New Statesman*'s film critic, William Whitebait, offered this reflection on the British people's fondness for the war genre: "A dozen years after World War II we find ourselves in the really quite desperate situation of being not sick of war but hideously in love with it."[1] He had a point, for war films had been the most popular of the decade. Four major war productions, *The Cruel Sea*, *The Dam Busters*, *Reach for the Sky*, and *Sink the Bismarck!* were the top box-office attractions of their year, while David Lean's masterpiece *The Bridge on the River Kwai* was a huge global success, winning seven Academy Awards in 1957. The most popular British actors of the period, including Jack Hawkins, John Mills, Kenneth More, Richard Attenborough and Dirk Bogarde, were the backbone of the war genre.

Many films, such as *Cockleshell Heroes*, *Above Us the Waves* and *Sink the Bismarck!*, offer reconstructions of significant naval victories in which a small group of intrepid men battle the odds to win the day. Films about the land war are rarer, though *They Were Not Divided* stands out as an early paean to Anglo-American cooperation. However, the war in the East is well represented by films such as *The Purple Plain*, *A Town Like Alice*, *The Camp on Blood Island* and the multi–Oscar winning *The Bridge on the River Kwai*. Adventure is provided by POW films such as *Albert RN*, *The Wooden Horse* and *Colditz Story*, while the important wartime role of the SOE is highlighted in *Odette*, *Carve Her Name with Pride* and *Ill Met by Moonlight*.

War movies were therefore an important component of the 1950s, a decade that witnessed a dramatic fall in cinema admissions from 1,365,000,000 in 1951 to 500,000,000 by 1960, fuelled by the advent of television and the closure of many cinemas. To understand why the wartime genre persisted throughout the decade, perhaps more than any other genre, some historical context is necessary.

The 1950s saw a shift from a period of national austerity to one of consumption and affluence. This coincided with the transition from a welfarist government to the Conservatives, who promised to "set the people free." During the 1950s incomes rose and taxes fell, while the old vestiges of wartime government control, including ration books, identity cards and credit restrictions, were gradually swept away. The period of affluence was reflected in a greater demand for consumer goods, given the increased purchasing power of the working class.

The drift towards greater consumer and individual choice, and away from community values, made it increasingly "difficult to represent the nation as a tight lipped knowable community" in the late 1940s and early 1950s.[2] This had implications for British national identity, a construct that increasingly relied on the perception of a largely united nation. Perhaps this offers one interpretation for the nostalgic overdrive in the war movies. Those films were trying to recapture that mythic golden age when individual aspiration and selfishness were subservient to a nationwide community spirit. As T. S. Eliot wrote: "It is often assumed that the unity of wartime should be preserved in time of peace.... People often express regret that the same unity, self sacrifice and fraternity which prevail in an emergency, cannot survive the emergency itself."[3]

Ironically, this was also a time when the military was still a highly visible presence in British life. Two million British men entered the forces as part of national service, an institution whose emphasis on discipline only added to the ethos of a settled social order in Britain. Until 1955, the country was presided over by the avuncular Churchill, a towering symbol of the old order and, for some, of the important class hierarchies that existed before the war.

The desire to relive a period that was fondly remembered for its rosy picture of national unity could only have been enhanced by the increasingly shaky prospects for international peace and security. The 1950s were times of deep international uncertainty. The Cold War had ushered in an atomic age in which warring nations faced the very real threat of mutual annihilation. The testing of the H-bomb in the early 1950s, a weapon capable of laying waste to entire cities, only reinforced the deep uncertainties about what a new war would herald. Britain in particular was very much on the front line during the Cold War, and its American bases made it a target for Russian bombers. As Philip Taylor put it: "Set against the backdrop of cold war, the traumas of decolonisation and the threat of atomic annihilation ... the second world war became the object of what may be described as a cinematic historiography that often said more about the post-war period than it did about the war itself."[4]

The nuclear age brought added cynicism about the conduct of war. War would no longer be represented by the gentlemanly pursuit of the enemy. It was now a matter of cold and impersonal science, of remotely pressing buttons that would decide the fate of peoples and nations. But films about the last war could at least represent the conflict differently. They could reveal a war of clear moral boundaries which was conducted, so we imagined, in a more civilized fashion. As Whitebait puts it, the British tendency was to "creep back to the lacerating comfort of last time." The effect of the nostalgia was to create "an imaginary present in which we can go on enjoying our finest hours."[5]

The reliance on "our finest hour" arguably helped lull anxieties and uncertainties about the Cold War. It allowed us an easy way to "hark back to that mythic time when (it was believed) the British people stood alone but together, bravely faced adversity of the most fearsome type, and bested it."[6] All this suggests a certain nostalgia for the war itself (itself a British trait), as well as the values that were believed to have underpinned final victory.

There were arguably other sources of insecurity. West Germany in the 1950s was economically and industrially resurgent, and the country had begun to re-arm. For many, this was a reminder that German militarism had not been fully defeated and remained a threat. The need to defend insular British life from the threat of European hegemony was becoming a major concern for many. A number of war films picture the indecency of "the Hun," with the Teutonic threat failing to quash true British spirit. The films perhaps remind us to stay wary of the Continental threat that Britain had largely helped defeat.

Amid these fears and concerns, it is understandable that filmmakers wished to invoke the idea of a stable and united nation with a confident sense of its own identity. Indeed, for most of the decade the wartime national image of gentlemanly conduct, stoicism, duty and irrepressible humor stayed largely intact.

On celluloid, these qualities were represented by the gentlemanly officer, a masculine personage whose stoic fortitude, courage and tolerance came to symbolize the wider nation. He was a military paterfamilias, a responsible father figure for the younger recruits whose occasional reckless behavior had to be curbed. The war films of the 1950s are almost all dominated by the officer class, with working-class characters playing a subordinate but supportive role. Women, too, are excluded, at least from positions of real influence and responsibility. They largely play supportive roles, either as loyal wives or patient girlfriends awaiting the safe return of their men.

If one British actor exemplifies the gentleman-officer in the 1950s, it is Jack Hawkins. With his rasping voice and steady demeanor, he embodies a virile and gritty masculinity that is always reliable and reassuring. He is tight-lipped and self-controlled, the essence of British sang froid, though in some of his films he offers flashes of charm and sensitivity. He has a paternalistic role in *Angels One Five, Malta Story* and, above all, in *The Cruel Sea*, perhaps his most famous film. In a very real sense, the apotheosis of Jack Hawkins' career as a dependable father figure mirrors the high point of the British national image.

John Mills epitomized a classless type of decent Englishman, a dependable figure of integrity, grit and determination. His performances showed an ability to transcend class and status, revealing that he could play both gentleman officer and working-class Tommy with equal conviction. After appearing in a number of wartime classics (*In Which We Serve, This Happy Breed, A Way to the Stars*), he would go on to play a naval commander in *Above Us the Waves*, a clapped-out military officer in *Ice Cold in Alex* and a corporal in *Dunkirk*.

Trevor Howard was another popular figure of this era. In his film roles Howard had established himself as a thoroughly decent, typical Englishman, often assuming positions of authority in an imperial or military role. He was highly efficient and understanding, but at times craggy and world weary in disposition. Having appeared in some key wartime classics (*The Way Ahead, The Way to the Stars*), he co-starred in *Odette* (1950), where he played an SOE agent, as well as *The Cockleshell Heroes* (1955).

John Gregson is a less familiar mainstay of this genre in the 1950s. He was usually cast as a mild-mannered, dependable English character, the epitome of middle-class manners and good humor. He would go on to play roles in several British war films of the 1950s, including *Angels One Five* (Septic Baird), *Above Us the Waves* (Lieutenant Alec Duffy), *The Battle of the River Plate* (Captain Bell) and *Sea of Sand* (Captain Williams).

The war films of the 1950s are divided into subgenres, with service films predominant, though the cinematic representation of the Far East war, and the war of subversion and deception, is also discussed.

War in the Air

Angels One Five is a reverential tribute to "the few" and the first film of the decade to center on the Battle of Britain. But rather than showing the aerial battles themselves, as would later be the case in *Battle of Britain*, this movie focuses on the camaraderie of the pilots and the mechanics of the control room. This gives the film a touch of historical accuracy. Even though "the few" had been immortalized as gallant knights of the air, the battle was won by a strategy of sending small groups of fighters into the air, using information from radar and ground control, and launching raids on the Luftwaffe. There is an emphasis on teamwork, rather than individual derring do, in the film.

The new pilot officer "Septic" Baird (John Gregson) would love nothing more than to engage in heroic combat with the Germans. But his arrival at Pimpernel Squadron's airfield is marked by disaster when he crash lands his plane in order to avoid a collision with another pilot. Tiger Small (Jack Hawkins) duly admonishes him with the words, "We have no time for personal jamborees." Septic is told that he cannot fly until his neck injuries have healed, and that he will have to serve in the less glamorous control room instead.

During a raid, Septic goes up in the air and appears to redeem himself when he shoots down an enemy aircraft. However, when he inadvertently leaves his radio set on transmit, endangering other pilots, he is again demoted to more menial duties. Eventually he returns to combat action but is fatally wounded while shooting down an enemy aircraft. The courage of the fighters is accentuated by the odds stacked against them. Small is told the realistic odds against a British success are 6-to-1 against, but he is then instantly reassured that "we can cope with that." When the underground bunker is about to be bombed by the enemy, Hawkins admits, "This is where we learn to take it." Learning to take it was a key motto of the Blitz, and that mentality has been transferred to the air force.

Mrs. Clinton shares this sense of courageous endurance. Asked by Hawkins to leave her house in order to avoid civilian casualties, she replies that she is "going nowhere." She shows just the staunch determination and resilience that Small expects from his squadron and leads him to label her a "remarkable woman."

The heroism here is suitably restrained, with death conveyed through metaphor and understatement. One pilot never returns, though all we see is his empty beer glass; another pilot's death is simply "rotten luck." Shortly before Septic's fatal air crash, he tells Tiger on the radio that their planned return foot race will have to be "postponed indefinitely." Two elderly women, surveying the wreckage of their house after a raid, proclaim, "Wasn't so much of a little house, was it." As elsewhere, understatement is a key device for concealing emotion.

If the film revolves around the officers, there are also allusions to the People's War. The Clintons, whose house is at the end of the airfield, do their bit for the squadron by leaving their lights on to guide incoming planes. Mrs. Clinton is a wartime "lady of the lamp," caring not just for the incoming pilots but working at the hospital for sick and wounded soldiers. They too suffer privation when their home is partially destroyed in an air raid. Nonetheless, the Clintons continue to light a candle in a room of their house to enable the pilots to land.

Sir Douglas Bader later said, "I went to the film with my tongue in my cheek. I came out amazed. I can't fault it in any detail."[7] Yet some of the mainstream reviewers were rather less impressed. *The Manchester Guardian* reviewer declared, "One day, surely, one of our great directors ... will take up this great, nostalgic and deeply poignant subject and will turn it to fuller and more daring account."[8] Writing in the *New Statesman*, William Whitebait pointed to the film's "passion for understatement," which undermined "the excitement and psychological tension that such a film should engender."[9] This picture, like most British war movies, shows little by way of thrilling action sequences or military maneuvers, preferring instead to concentrate on character studies and relationships. This was a drawback for Leonard Mosley of the *Daily Express*: "One big grumble, The Battle of Britain was won in the air. Couldn't we have seen more of the actual dogfights?"[10]

Films about Bomber Command were few and far between in Britain, but the 1953 *Appointment in London* (U.S.: *Raiders in the Sky*) is one notable example. Wing Commander Tim Mason, played by Dirk Bogarde, is obsessed with completing 90 missions before he is grounded. Such is his determination that he ignores advice that he is risking his health and even ends up disobeying orders when he takes to the air for his final mission.

On that occasion he climbs on board a plane piloted by Flight Lieutenant Bill Brown (Bill Kerr) after another pilot suffers a near fatal accident. Though Mason faces a court martial for insubordination, he redeems himself by taking control of the mission when it would otherwise have ended in disaster. The bombing raid towards the end of the film is notable for its realism, though, understandably, it does not depict events at ground level.

Far from denigrating Mason's individualist streak, the film seems to laud his single-minded determination and obsessive quest to "do his duty." Bogarde plays the role with skill and sensitivity, and his debonair manner allows for a radically different treatment of masculinity. As is typical with these films, there is a low-key romantic subplot, with Mason falling in love with war widow Eve Canyon (Dinah Sheridan).

In *Reach for the Sky* (1956) the hero undergoes redemption in war for an earlier act of recklessness which came at great personal cost. The film is a biopic of the controversial World War II fighter ace Sir Douglas Bader. In real life, Bader (played in the film by Kenneth More) was a living legend, a symbol of defiance in adversity and indomitable courage. He was also a cocksure and immensely self-confident figure who enjoyed clashing with authority. He had shown tremendous bravery and willpower by surviving a horrific air crash in 1931 in which he lost both his legs. Despite his injuries, he went on to become a fighter ace in the Battle of Britain, reputedly shooting down 22 German fighters before being forced to bail out over occupied France. Imprisoned by the Germans, he attempted several unsuccessful escapes from POW camps, and at the end of the war led a victory fly-past in London.

The film largely focuses on Bader's battle for survival and mobility after his crash. While he is lying on a hospital bed he overhears two nurses saying that he is dying. In typically defiant and resolute mood, he thinks to himself, "We'll see." After only a short time with his new tin legs, he insists on trying to walk on his own, much to the amazement of his doctors. Bader cares little that every man in the past with a similar impediment has had to use a stick, insisting he will not do similarly. He thinks of himself as possessing a unique will power that makes him rise above mere mortals. He goes through the pain barrier to start walking again, so determined is he to get back inside a plane.

Bader shows the same superhuman strength of mind when he assumes command of five squadrons at the height of the Blitz. His great skills of leadership and his sense of determination have an enormous effect on his men, some of whom initially regarded him as a limp passenger. In the voiceover we learn that the "pilots looked on him [Bader] as a superman," and he had a reassuring "breezy confidence." His men felt him to be "invulnerable," and his presence "shielded those who flew with him." This was the romantic myth of the great knight of the air, a somewhat different ethos to that in *Angels One Five*. Indeed, as Mackenzie says, "If *Angels One Five* had been about the Few, *Reach for the Sky* was about the One."[11] The message is clear. Bader's superhuman courage and conspicuous displays of valor are just the tonic for a crisis-laden Britain in 1940.

Kenneth More was the perfect choice for the role of Douglas Bader. Over a number of years he had built up a persona as a somewhat pugnacious and self-confident character, carefree yet utterly reliable. In the words of one critic, he "projected a matter-of-fact heroism or an ability to get the job done."[12] He played the defiant Lionel Fallaize in *Appointment with Venus* (1951) before making a name for himself as the brash and boisterous advertising salesman Ambrose Claverhouse in *Genevieve* (1953). His jovial performance as Grimsdyke in *Doctor in the House* (1954) solidified his reputation, and he went on to become a major box office attraction throughout the 1950s.

In his autobiography, *More or Less*, Kenneth More explained his attraction to the role of Douglas Bader: "I was convinced I was the only actor who could play this part properly.... I wanted this part, not just because I felt I could do full justice to it, but because it was an embodiment of my own belief that courage, faith and determination can overcome all obstacles."[13]

He certainly prepared well for the part, not only meeting Bader in person but seeking advice from experts in the rehabilitation of amputees. The result is a highly believable performance, and it remains More's most famous role. Bader himself was less impressed by the film and refused to cooperate in its production, citing historical inaccuracies in the script. He would later come to mellow his views.[14]

An altogether different aspect of the aerial war was portrayed in *The Dam Busters*, perhaps the most iconic British war film of the 1950s. It deals with the legendary assault on the Mohne Dam in Germany by Squadron 617, using its famous "bouncing bomb," and features a stirring score by Eric Coates. The film is effectively structured in two parts, the first half showing the progression of the bouncing bomb from an experimental stage to a workable weapon of war, and the second the lead up to the raid itself. The film is interspersed with documentary footage of the bomb, as well as some special effects of fairly dubious quality.

Barnes Wallis, played with great sensitivity by Michael Redgrave, combines ingenuity with a willingness to muddle through in adversity. Like R. J. Mitchell, he is a patriotic man driven to defend his country, and he pursues his invention with a single-mindedness verging on obsession. Before the bouncing bomb is approved, he undergoes all manner of privations and disappoint-

Richard Todd as Guy Gibson surveying the damage brought upon German dams by the bouncing bomb. *The Dam Busters* (1955) remains perhaps the most iconic British war film of the period (Warner Bros Pictures, Photofest).

ments. He neglects food and sleep, battles against Whitehall red tape and witnesses the failure of the initial bomb tests. But he remains obdurate, for, as he explains to his wife, "When you believe in a thing as much as I've believed in this there really isn't any other work until you've seen it through." As well as being single-minded, he is also possessed of a certain very English eccentricity. He is in many ways the perfect amateur, possessed of an engaging, almost childlike enthusiasm for his project.

In the film, disappointment, loss and death are treated with a familiar refrain and understatement. When Wing Commander Guy Gibson (Richard Todd), who commands the mission, learns that his dog has been run over in a car accident, he shows little emotion. In a decisive break with sentimental affection, Gibson throws the dog collar in the bin, a sign that his relationship with the dog is now but a distant memory. The deaths of the airmen are suggested by telling visual images—a letter home that will now be dispatched to the next of kin, a clock wound up accurately but whose owner will never see it, and empty tables in the breakfast room following the raid.

Wallis' heroism, like that of Gibson, is subtle and unassuming. Upon hearing that the operation had been a success, his only thought is for the high number of fatalities sustained. Wallis expresses doubts about its moral validity, saying that the death of fifty-six men may have been too high a price to pay for the operation. "If I'd known it was going to be like this, I'd never have started it," he says. Gibson offers words of consolation, telling Wallis that if the men had known they were not to return, none would have dropped out. This touching moment is a poignant reminder of the tremendous sacrifice that these operations entailed.

In many ways, this is *the* archetypal British war film that encapsulates the ideological underpinning of all films in the genre. It is an exhilarating testament to the virtues of Englishness (endless pluck, an amateurish ability to improvise, unrestrained duty and sang froid) that enabled the nation as a whole to endure the war. It received generally fine reviews from critics. The *Financial Times* praised the film's "restraint and painstaking documentary thoroughness," while the *News of the World*'s Peter Burnup declared that the film climbed "to clouds of glory which befit the RAF itself."[15]

War at Sea

A number of pictures reveled in British naval achievement during the war years, with some displaying a quite jarring realism and sensitivity. Most famous perhaps is *The Cruel Sea*, a memorable production from 1953 which never spares its audience the horrors and moral quandaries of the U-boat war.

The film is imbued with an authentic grittiness and harrowing realism that is typical of many an Ealing production. Adapted from a best-selling novel by Nicholas Monsarrat, the movie tells the story of two wartime officers, Captain Ericson (Jack Hawkins) and his second in command, Lockhart (Donald Sinden), and their lives on board the ship *Compass Rose*.

From the outset we view the war as a bleak and deadly affair played out against an utterly inhospitable environment. In the initial voiceover we are told that the men are the "heroes," the ships are the "heroines" and the only enemy is "the sea, the cruel sea that man has made more cruel."

Ericson admits that the war has had a dehumanizing effect on him. The Battle of the Atlantic was like a "private war," and "if you were in it, you knew how to keep watch on filthy nights, how to go without sleep, how to bury the dead and how to die without wasting anyone's time." While the voiceover is being played, you see the process of burial at sea take place, almost

Jack Hawkins on *Compass Rose*, surveying the "Cruel Sea" in the 1953 film of the same name. With his rugged looks, stiff upper lip and rasping voice, Hawkins was the archetypal British officer (Ealing, Photofest).

as if it has become a routine. Images such as these appear to suggest that *The Cruel Sea* was the earliest anti-war statement of the 1950s. But as Durgnat points out, "It is precisely the horrors of war which give heroism its meaning."[16]

Towards the end Ericson declares, "Whereas before there was understanding people and making allowances, now there is simply "killing the enemy." His cynicism stems from an earlier incident, the most famous in the film, when he orders depth charges to be lowered into the ocean to destroy a U-boat, even though he knows that they will also kill several British sailors in the water awaiting rescue.[17]

Hawkins is accused of being a "bloody murderer," and he later breaks down in front of Lockhart. However, at no point is it suggested that the Captain committed an error of judgment. He believes that this is one of those things you have to do, and you then "say your prayers at the end." Nobody "murdered" the men, but it was instead "the whole bloody war" that created an unfortunate moral dilemma resulting in the death of innocents. Far from being an "anti-war" moment, this scene reminds us that Ericson has a warm and sympathetic side beneath his stiff upper lip.

The pain of loss is conveyed with the usual emotional restraint. Typical of this is the touching scene in which Petty Officer Tallow (Bruce Seton) finds out that his sister has been killed in a bombing raid on her street. Far from showing visible grief, Tallow is silent as he wanders, rather bewildered, into the local army center. Again, when told his sister has died, there is little show of despair or sadness, merely a calm but rather shocked expression.

The same silence greets the news of the sinking of *Compass Rose*. Lockhart's girlfriend has a demeanor of almost complete resignation. And characteristically, her inner turmoil is left unexpressed and repressed as she immediately resumes her duties at the operations center. The ship's fate is simply "bad luck," a rather cold understatement given the circumstances.

In *The Cruel Sea*, as in *Angels One Five*, Hawkins is a rugged and battle-hardened leader of men, a solid no-nonsense figure of authority with a sympathetic side. His powerful male physique, which exuded "stiffly backboned English middle-class manhood," allowed him to come across as a paternalistic figure of reliability and assurance.[18] Interestingly, Hawkins himself did not appreciate his stiff upper lip characterization. He once wrote, "I am an emotional man and I can do other things than sticking out my over-blown jaw."[19]

In a film which explores questions about English masculinity, women are very much in the background. Ericson's wife is mentioned but never seen, while Lockhart downplays romantic involvement with his girlfriend, Julie Hallam (Virginia McKenna). This is a movie in which men form emotional attachments to each other and to their ships, rather than to the opposite sex. When

Hawkins later mused that he had acquired "a reputation of being able to make better love to a battleship than to a woman," he probably had this film in mind.[20]

The Sea Shall Not Have Them, based on a novel by John Harris, deals with the work of the air sea rescue service and shares the documentary feel of *For Those in Peril*. It is a gritty exploration of war at sea and of survival against the odds, though its lack of emphasis on "officer heroes" differentiates it from other films of the period.

At the outset, a British bomber is shot out of the sky by a German plane, leaving the four men on board, including Air Commodore Waltby (Michael Redgrave) and Flight Sergeant Mackay (Dirk Bogarde), to board a dinghy. Redgrave's briefcase contains top secret blueprints for new German weapons, and thus his survival and rescue are paramount. The action switches continually from the dinghy to a rescue vessel, commanded by the irascible Nigel Patrick, which eventually finds the men and brings them home.

The men's plight at sea is highlighted vividly. They endure Arctic conditions, stormy weather and near starvation as they cling to life. Even when close to rescue they are forced to evade a floating mine and sustained bombardment from German coastal batteries. Their survival against the odds is a testament to the men's resilience.

During their ordeal they are sustained by flashes of humor, songs and a bottle of brandy. Redgrave is the model of stoical self-control, helping to exercise a calming influence on the occasionally hysterical Bogarde. But though his rank and manners give him superior status, he is not in control of the dinghy. He demands to be treated as one of the crew and even reminds the Sergeant that his father was a porter in Luton. In this sense, the film shares in the social democratic ethos of the People's War.

In aesthetic terms, *The Sea Shall Not Have Them* is scarcely one of the most successful naval dramas. Unlike *In Which We Serve*, the film uses few imaginative or stylistic devices, and the plot and dialogue are somewhat conventional. The critics offered mixed reviews, with Derek Granger, writing in the *Financial Times*, complaining about "stiff, upper lippery depicted in a style somewhere between Biggles, Henty and Beau Geste."[21] V. Graham, for the *Spectator*, added: "One wishes that these particular men were less cold and more interesting."[22]

Noël Coward, after noting the film's two leading (homosexual) stars, is said to have remarked of the title, "I don't see why not. Everyone else has."[23] On a more scathing note, Brian McFarlane suggested the film could be retitled *The Sea Is Welcome to Them*.[24]

It was only natural that a number of war films would celebrate specific naval victories and specialist operations. *Above Us the Waves* and *The Cock-*

leshell Heroes are two relatively modest productions that examine small-scale but heroic victories by a group of highly trained men.

Above Us the Waves tells the true story of the attack by midget submarines on the German battleship *Tirpitz*. At the beginning we learn, using documentary footage, that Britain's survival depends on the convoy system. But the *Tirpitz*'s position in a Norwegian fjord is aiding German U-boats in the Battle of the Atlantic. Commander Fraser (John Mills) conceives of a plan to destroy the battleship using human torpedoes, an idea that is initially resisted by the Navy.

But after a dummy trial is successful, the operation goes ahead. Fraser leads a group of men in an initial attack on the *Tirpitz*, but their attempts to enter the Straits are frustrated. They end up in neutral Sweden, from where they are subsequently flown back to Scotland. They are briefed on an updated plan which involves an attack using midget submarines to blow up the *Tirpitz*, but this time with the men inside the vessels.

In the tense second half of the film we follow the crews as they attempt (in two cases successfully) to attach mines to the *Tirpitz*. However, these crews are then intercepted and taken on board the German ship, where they anxiously wait to see if they will survive the blast. Shortly after these mines detonate, the third submarine explodes as it attempts to surface.

The movie lacks the obvious visual splendor of other naval productions, but there are nonetheless moments of genuine tension. The climax, when the third submarine is destroyed, is a poignant reminder of wartime sacrifice, and the reaction of the survivors as they sail slowly past the wreckage is suitably restrained. For the *Daily Worker*, this was a "nostalgic reminder of the days of the last war when individual initiative and bravery still counted for something."[25]

Cockleshell Heroes is a tribute to the Royal Marine Commandos who carried out Operation Frankton in 1942. The plan involved a small group of Marines paddling to Bordeaux after being dropped by submarine 75 miles away, and then planting limpet mines on a number of important German ships. Despite suffering numerous setbacks, the operation was successful, with a large number of ships suffering mysterious explosions, according to the Germans. Sadly, only two men survived the operation, with most of the others shot by the Germans under Hitler's "commando order."

Major Stringer (Jose Ferrer) is put in charge of recruiting the commandos, but his unorthodox methods are frowned upon by his second in command, the bad tempered and cynical Sergeant Hugh Thompson (Trevor Howard). Most of the film deals with the training and preparation of volunteers, often with amusing moments, and the only real tension comes from the confrontation between Stringer and Thompson over the former's methods.

It is only in the last third that the operation unfolds, and here the film builds genuine drama and excitement. The Marines face long odds, and as their numbers are depleted they must evade capture from the marauding Germans. It is a testament to English pluck and ingenuity that the operation even partially succeeds, given that the raid is carried out in heavily defended enemy territory. When two of the men are interrogated by the Germans they refuse to divulge information and respond instead with sardonic wit, one scrawling "Rule Britannia" on his questionnaire.

During the war, many service films shared in the social democratic ethos by showing groups of civilians being molded into a cohesive unit. This formula is also used in *The Gift Horse* (U.S.: *Glory at Sea*), made in 1952. Trevor Howard plays a cussed disciplinarian, Lieutenant-Commander Fraser, who captains one of the 50 American destroyers loaned to Britain in 1940. Things go badly when Fraser adopts an authoritarian approach to the men under his command, breeding inevitable resentment. Many of the civvies, exemplified by trade unionist "Dripper" Daniels (Richard Attenborough), are insubordinate and surly. But Fraser also confronts his own demons, as eight years previously he was held responsible for a naval collision that forced his retirement to civilian life.

As the war progresses he turns inexperienced civilians into an effective fighting unit before leading them on a mission to destroy a dock in France that is being used by the Germans. Sadly, the mission necessitates the destruction of the ship and the capture of its crew. Such self-sacrifice allows Fraser to achieve some form of heroic redemption for past misdemeanors (a formula also used in *Ships with Wings*). He had earlier heard that his son, who enlisted in the navy months earlier, had been killed on active service. He receives the news with equanimity and restraint, remaining a model of stoicism for his men.

Naval dramas tended to emphasize important British victories at sea with dramatic and exciting reconstructions. *The Battle of the River Plate* (U.S.: *Pursuit of the Graf Spee*), a 1956 Powell and Pressburger production, deals with the naval battle in December 1939 between Royal Navy cruisers and the formidable German pocket battleship *Graf Spee*.

This film celebrates the gallantry of both the Royal Navy commanders who won the battle and Captain Langsdorff, the latter scuttling his ship rather than face the humiliation of defeat. Powell and Pressburger refuse to caricature the Germans, a noticeable feature of their *The Life and Death of Colonel Blimp*. Thus, Captain Hans Langsdorff (Peter Finch) is a humane figure who develops a bond with Captain Dove of the British merchant vessel *Africa Shell*. Though not generally considered one of the better Powell/Pressburger films, it was nonetheless their most commercially successful production. Howard would go on to star in *The Key* (1958), an unusual and somewhat macabre production in which a voluptuous female (Sophia Loren) shelters a succession of lovers, all of them world weary tugboat captains whose lives are cut short by the perils of war.

War on Land

In the 1950s films about the land war were less numerous than those dealing with the navy and air force. Nonetheless, the decade's first major conflict film was about the army, and it very much set the tone for later combat movies. *They Were Not Divided* (1950), directed by Terence Young, is dominated by upper-class officers who mold their NCOs into thoroughly decent chaps. The "chaps" in question—an Englishman, Philip Hamilton (Edward Underdown), an American called David Morgan (Ralph Clanton), and the Irishman Smoke O'Connor (Michael Brennan)—are called to serve in the Guards Armoured Division.

Together they undergo the rigors of strict military training before joining a tank regiment that takes center stage in the liberation of Europe. At this point a fairly insipid production is enlivened by authentic battle sequences, including some spectacular real footage of tank warfare. This gives the film an air of semi-documentary realism that can also be found in *The Cruel Sea* and *Sea of Sand*.

The men take part in key Allied operations, such as Operation Market Garden, the Battle of the Bulge and finally the Ardennes offensive. Sadly, the British and American officers die in an explosion, and at the end they are buried next to each other. In a slightly contrived final moment, the flags adorning their graves lean towards each other, symbolizing the eternal bonds between the two allied nations. Nonetheless, it is a fitting motif, for the film celebrates the great transnational sacrifices that were necessary to defeat Hitler. The movie is also noteworthy for a splendid cameo from Michael Trubshawe as a no-nonsense major.

Though less famous than the desert film *Ice Cold in Alex*, the 1958 *Sea of Sand* (U.S.: *Desert Patrol*) deserves to be considered a minor classic, with its lavish cinematography, poignant performances and terrific action sequences. The film pits the intrepid members of the Long-Range Desert Squadron against the perils of both the German forces and the Sahara desert. Their mission is to go behind enemy lines and destroy an important German fuel dump, thus impeding the enemy's advance into Egypt just as the 8th Army attacks El Alamein. But the squadron are attacked by the Luftwaffe and German tanks, suffering grievous casualties in the process. The raid goes successfully until they are discovered by the Germans, and then a thrilling chase ensues across the desert. The men are determined to reach Cairo after discovering that the

Germans have tank squadrons at the depots, which will be used in the battle to come.

Despite its rather conventional plot, the film eschews the simplistic heroics of earlier productions. Despite their courageous display against the enemy, some of the men are openly cynical about the privations and loneliness of army life, an attitude epitomized by the defiant Brody (Richard Attenborough). Yet he is no coward. He pleads in vain with Captain Cotton (Michael Craig) to stay with the injured Blanco (Percy Herbert) after the vehicle they are traveling in breaks down in the sand.

The scene where Blanco is left to await certain death is truly poignant. Taking up position with a rifle, he listens to the radio while staring longingly at a photo of his loved ones. As the Germans approach, he opens fire in the hope that he can inflict casualties on the enemy and protect the rest of the party. His death soon follows before the camera closes in touchingly again on his family photograph. Nothing better proves the old adage that in war men die for their friends, not their country. Yet in this film, as in so many others, death brings a familiar emotional refrain—an absence of histrionics, and an enduring stoicism and resignation.

In this sense, *Sea of Sand* is typical of its decade in celebrating the warmth of human comradeship and raw courage in the face of adversity. John Gregson, who made memorable appearances in *Angels One Five* and *Above Us the Waves*, puts in a creditable performance as Captain Williams, while Richard Attenborough plays the part of a rule-breaking driver to perfection. Attenborough, often cast as the spiv/criminal type, was less impressed by the part. "I was cast as a minor variation on the same bloody character I seemed condemned to play forever."[26]

War in the Far East

In the 1950s a spate of films dealt with the war in the Far East. Given that Britain suffered a series of crushing defeats in 1941 and 1942 to the Japanese, it was hardly surprising that the films centered on POW dramas rather than military engagements. This was an advantage in that it sidestepped questions of poor military performance (Churchill had described the fall of Singapore as the worst disaster in British history), and concentrated instead on the bravery and stoicism of the prisoners. *The Camp on Blood Island* and *The Bridge on the River Kwai* (discussed in the next chapter) are set in POW camps, while the characters in *A Town Like Alice*, *The Wind Cannot Read* and *Yesterday's Enemy* are merely prisoners of the Japanese.

Despite its leading Hollywood star and Technicolor cinematography, Robert Parish's *The Purple Plain* (1954) has a very British sense of understated heroism. Captain Forrester (Gregory Peck) is a Canadian RAF pilot who is tormented by the death of his wife in an air raid. He is fuelled by an instinct for self-destruction, but begins to recover some emotional stability when he meets and falls in love with a Burmese woman, Anna (Win Min Than).

After his plane crashes while on a routine mission in Burma, Forrester and his fellow passengers, Flight Lieutenant Blore (Maurice Denham) and the injured navigator Carrington (Lyndon Brook), traverse the Burmese plains in order to reach safety. Peck has to contend not just with the unremittingly hostile environment (the scorching heat of the Burmese summer and the rocky terrain) but the sniping from Blore, who thinks that Forrester is mentally unbalanced.

For the most part, *The Purple Plain* does not deal with the horrors of Japanese cruelty or the war in the Far East. Instead it focuses on a grim struggle for survival against the odds. Peck brings his usually trademark integrity to a demanding role, giving his character real depth and intensity.

On a similar theme, *A Town Like Alice* (1956) features a group of British women forced by the Japanese to trek across Malaya in search of a POW camp. Led by the indomitable Jean Paget (Virginia McKenna), the women endure scorching sub-tropical temperatures, torrential rain and the hazards of swamp territory.

The trek is futile, as none of the POW camps are prepared to accept the women. Some of the women and children die in the terrible conditions, yet Paget's spirit remains undaunted. Later she meets an Australian man, Sergeant Joe Harman (Peter Finch), who is working for the Japanese. They fall in love, but he is later sentenced to death by the camp guards after striking a Japanese officer. His captors spare him from death when they recognize his fortitude and bravery, though Paget does not discover this until the end of the film.

Eventually the women reach a Malay village where they remain until the end of the war. The villagers show them some kindness when they realize that the newcomers are self-sufficient and willing to work hard for the community. There is no simple dichotomy in the film between cruel Easterners and noble Westerners, a point reinforced by the humane behavior of the last Japanese sergeant left in charge of the women. Recognizing their ordeal over many months, he takes pity on the women, but he too is weakened by the rigors of the trek. Before he dies he tearfully reveals a photograph of his family, showing that he is just as capable of human emotions as they are.

Courage here is quiet and restrained. The women and children maintain a cheerful and tolerant disposition despite their intense ordeal, and this very naturalism lends the film credibility. There is little passion or hysteria, just a very English attempt to maintain dignity and calm under appalling circumstances. As a contemporary reviewer put it, "It is a moving story because it seems so very close to the real truth of such an ordeal."[27]

The film is a powerful tribute to human endurance in the face of senseless inhumanity. McKenna, who played the part of the cool, calm and utterly courageous Englishwoman to perfection, rightly won a BAFTA award for her performance. However, the film was withdrawn from the Cannes Film Festival so as not to offend Japanese viewers, leading Finch to describe the festival as a "joke" and a "racket."[28]

By contrast, there is nothing restrained about the Hammer production *The Camp on Blood Island* (1958). Condemned at the time for its unforgiving portrait of the enemy, as well as its graphic violence, the film portrays the efforts of POWs not to reveal to their captors that the Japanese government has surrendered to the Allies. Throughout we witness the appalling treatment of the camp inmates. In a notable reversion to caricature, the Japanese are humorless, sadistic brutes who revel in humiliating and torturing their prisoners. Unlike *The Bridge on the River Kwai* and *Yesterday's Enemy*, the commander here lacks any human qualities. He and his soldiers behave robotically and without mercy.

Yet the scenes of bloodshed, which include a man being beheaded, were too much for some contemporary critics. For the renowned Caroline Lejeune, the film was nothing short of an abomination, while a reviewer in *The Times* accused the producers of "re-awakening feelings of hatred and the desire for revenge."[29] Hammer's attempt to restore its reputation would be the less graphic and more successful *Yesterday's Enemy*. Hammer's *The Secret of Blood Island* (1964) was a loose sequel to *Camp on Blood Island*.

Bluff, Double Bluff and the POW Movie

In the 1950s the POW genre was well represented by *Albert RN*, *The Colditz Story* and *The Wooden Horse*. All these films celebrated the pluck and ingenuity of British prisoners who managed to outwit their German captors in audacious escapes.

The Wooden Horse (1950) set the scene for the POW subgenre and, like *The Colditz Story* and *Albert RN*, was based on real-life events. In the film, a small group of officers plot an escape from Stalag Luft III, a German POW camp. After their initial plan runs into difficulties, they think up an inventive solution: under the watchful eyes of the German guards, a tunnel is built under a wooden vaulting horse that is brought out into the yard for daily gymnastics. It is amusing that sport—that most English of hobbies—is the vehicle for outsmarting Teutonic efficiency. The plan is carried out methodically, as if it was a military operation, and eventually two men, Peter (Leo Genn) and John (Anthony Steel), manage to escape to Lubeck and then on to Denmark. Incredible as the plot seems, it was based on a real-life POW escape.

As is inevitable in a film dominated by English officers, the accents and delivery belong to the upper-middle class, making this a throwback to class conscious productions like *Ships with Wings*. But these men work well as a team, despite occasional arguments over mess duties, and are sustained by their spirited and often humorous defiance of their captors.

In Lewis Gilbert's 1953 *Albert RN* (also known as *Break to Freedom*), the vehicle for escape is a cleverly constructed dummy (Albert) who "marches" with the men while a real prisoner flees the camp undetected. But the film is not just an opportunity for high jinks and a bit of derring-do at the Germans' expense. It has a darker edge, represented in particular by the behavior of the scheming Captain Schultz (Anton Diffring), who shoots a prisoner in cold blood. Gilbert would go on to direct a number of key films from this period, including *The Sea Shall Not Have Them*, *Reach for the Sky* and *Carve Her Name with Pride*.

POW films brought together different nationalities in their heroic bid for freedom. Here we see a number of prisoners, including John Mills (third from right), Theodore Bikel (far right) and Lionel Jeffries (fourth from right, others unidentified) under the watchful eye of a Nazi guard in *The Colditz Story* (1955) (Distribution Corporation of America, Photofest).

Similar themes can be found in *The Colditz Story* (1955), starring John Mills and Eric Portman. This is another true story of a daring escape by British POWs from the notorious Sonderlager (special camp) Colditz in Saxony. Colditz was situated by a rocky outcrop above a river, making it appear an ideal site for a maximum security prison.

The camp is home to a variety of nationalities, with French, Polish, Dutch and British officers all intermingling. But their camaraderie is sorely tested when the first British escape attempt clashes with Polish escape plans, leading to their detection by German guards. The clear message is that if each nationality works separately from the others, their plans are unlikely to bear fruit. Colonel Richmond (Eric Portman) suggests that they cooperate, and by the end of the film some "home runs" (successful escapes) have been made by different nationalities.

In *The Colditz Story*, the British frequently use humor as a stereotypical weapon of choice against their adversaries and as a means of dealing with captivity. As a result, according to one critic, "The Colditz story is not a grim one."[30] By contrast, their German captors, typified by the frightening Kommandant (Frederick Valt), are depicted in a somewhat caricatured fashion: brutal, robotic and humorless creatures whose sole concern is to issue violent threats if prisoners escape.

Andy Medhurst believes that the film is "just a backdrop for masculine high jinks, a stirring story of strength and ingenuity."[31] But there are more serious moments, particularly when Richmond confronts MacMcGill (Christopher Rhodes) about his escape plan. Richmond warns Mac that while the plan is faultless, he will jeopardize the mission because of his large size and belligerent attitude, advising him to pull out for the sake of others.

A somewhat deflated Mac withdraws but later vaults over the fence in an ill-advised bid for freedom. He is shot by the Nazis, and his death adds a somber touch that is missing from *The Wooden Horse*. For the *Observer*, *The Colditz Story* combined "discipline with adventure; audacity with vigilance; and dignity in adversity with schoolboy derring-do."[32]

Danger Within (U.S.: *Breakout*), made in 1959, is the last of the 1950s POW dramas and features an impressive array of British acting talent, including Richard Attenborough, Dennis Price, Bernard Lee and Richard Todd. But this film is differentiated from the earlier productions by being set in an Italian POW camp, and also because it features a successful mass breakout by 400 prisoners. In some ways, *Danger Within* has a much darker edge than films like *The Wooden Horse* and *The Colditz Story*. For one thing, it features a particularly sadistic camp commander, Capitano Benucci (Peter Arne), who revels in killing would-be escapees. But more sinister still is the presence of a British informer whose double dealing is directly responsible for the death of several inmates. The film shares the key elements of national character ideology: heroic underdogs outsmarting a merciless authority figure; pluckiness and ingenuity in organizing an improbable breakout; and the use of verbal wit to mock an uncomprehending enemy. It remains a highly watchable addition to the genre.

Films showing British ingenuity and amateurism at the expense of the Germans had featured throughout the Second World War. Three similar pictures stand out in the 1950s, the first a light-hearted comedy, and the next two reconstructions of real-life events.

The 1951 *Appointment with Venus* (U.S.: *Island Rescue*) is a modest, light-hearted production in which a plucky British outfit outwits a German occupation force. For a relatively unknown film it surprisingly features a stellar British cast, some of whom became regulars in 1950s war movies. Based on a novel by Jerrard Tickell, the film charts the unlikeliest of wartime missions: the rescue of a cow from under Nazi noses.

The picture starts by showing the German takeover of the Channel Islands, one of which is the fictional island of Armorel (possibly based on Sark). Officials at the Ministry of Agriculture discover that a prize pedigree cow, Venus, lives on the island and are determined to prevent it from falling into German hands. They duly ask the War Office to mount a rescue operation. The task is assigned to Major Valentine Morland (David Niven), ably assisted by the daughter of the island's suzerain, Nicola Fallaize (Glynis Johns).

After arriving on Armorel and locating Venus, they plan to hide her until they can be picked up by submarine and returned to England. Their plans are scuppered when German commander Weiss (George Coulouris) plans to have the cow shipped back to Germany after realizing just how valuable she is. The intrepid rescue squad now use all their guile and ingenuity to carry out the rescue operation. Falaize's brother Lionel (Kenneth More), a pacifist painter who enjoys defying German soldiers, agrees to paint another cow to make it resemble Venus. This ensures that the cow is eventually taken back to Britain, right under German noses.

The plot sounds farfetched, even farcical, but it would be wrong to classify the film as a simple comedy. Certainly it has its moments of whimsy, such as the scene in which a determined Lionel spirits Venus away from the Commander's back garden while Falaize desperately tries to engage the German in conversation.

But this is also a celebration of resistance and fortitude among the native Channel Islanders. As Johns tells the War Office before the start of the mission, "Armorel may be small, but they will do everything they can to resist the Germans." The people of Armorel are a proudly patriotic island people, fiercely protective of their liberties. Their quiet defiance is symbolized by More, whose role as a determined and courageous underdog is later replicated in *Reach for the Sky*.

Undoubtedly the most audacious Allied bluff of the Second World War was "Operation Mincemeat," depicted in Ronald Neame's *The Man Who Never Was* (1956). By the beginning of 1943, the Allies were in control of vast swathes of North Africa, and it was only a matter of time before they started the invasion of mainland Europe. The Nazis assumed (correctly) that the Allies would launch an amphibious assault on Sicily as a prelude to attacking Italy.

In order to fool the Germans into thinking that Greece and Sardinia were the intended targets, British intelligence came up with an ingenious plan. They took the dead body of a 34-year-old Welshman, Glyndwr Michael, and floated the corpse off the coast of Spain. Attached to the cadaver were top secret official documents, the most crucial of which was a letter from Sir General Nye to General Harold Alexander, purporting to outline plans for an imminent invasion of Greece.

The hope was that the Spanish authorities, who were only nominally neutral, would search the body and hand over the documents to German intelligence, with whom they enjoyed good relations. It was assumed that the Germans would be fooled into thinking that they had come upon a great prize of intelligence and, as a result, divert troops to Greece. In the event, Martin's body was duly picked up off the coast of Spain, and German intelligence was informed of the find. The documents were believed to be authentic, and subsequently the Germans diverted Panzer divisions to Greece.

Ewen Montagu, the brilliant naval intelligence officer who co-authored Operation Mincemeat, later wrote the book *The Man Who Never Was*, which was the basis for the film. It is, in fact, one of the most intriguing and suspenseful war movies of the '50s, eschewing violent battle scenes to concentrate fully on how the masterplan was carried out and nearly foiled.

The film celebrates the inventiveness of naval intelligence, not just that of Montagu, played sensitively by Clifton Webb, but of British "boffins" such as the Home Office pathologist, Sir Bernard Spilsbury, whose expertise is required in discovering whether the Germans had opened and re-sealed the envelope in Martin's briefcase. Like Barnes Wallis, Montagu also encounters his fair share of bureaucratic inertia and principled objections to his plan. At the outset he is told that the plan is "outrageous, disgusting, preposterous" before being told that it will be looked into. Unlike Spilsbury, he is an amateur strategist who relies on his inventiveness and cunning to outwit the enemy. His use of a dead body for intelligence purposes is undoubtedly morbid and gives the film a chilling edge which is lacking in other productions.

A less memorable film on a very similar theme was *I Was Monty's Double* (1958), directed by John Guillermin. The film recounts the improbable but

The body of "The Man Who Never Was" (1956) floats towards the Spanish coast en route to the Nazis. "Operation Mincemeat" was one of the most audacious British intelligence plots of World War II (Twentieth Century–Fox, Photofest).

true story of how an Australian actor was hired to impersonate General Montgomery in order to fool the Germans into miscalculating the location of the D-Day landings. Meyrick Clifton-James was employed by British intelligence officer Major Harvey (John Mills) to travel to Gibraltar, at the time a hotbed of German spies, where his presence would persuade the Germans that the Allies were planning a land assault somewhere in the Mediterranean. Operation Copperhead, as it became known, was a success because the British ensured that a Spanish officer (in reality a pro–Nazi spy) knew of Monty's movements, thus guaranteeing a flow of false information to the Germans.

The task is an uphill struggle. James, played by himself in the film, dismisses the whole idea as "fantastic" and doubts he can pull it off, despite Mills' constant reassurance. The idea is indeed fantastic; James' chief weapons are his acting ability and his uncanny resemblance to Monty. That he pulls off the eventual deception in front of adoring crowds is a tremendous feat of ingenuity.

As in *The Man Who Never Was*, the best laid plans run into difficulties. After a tip-off from a double agent, James' villa is raided, and he is captured by German forces. Realizing that "Monty" will be turned over to the enemy,

Harvey and a fellow officer kill and then impersonate the two Germans who were coming for him. James is then rescued in a breathtaking climax, well handled by Guillermin, though it involves a degree of artistic license. In reality, no such kidnapping took place because James spent the next few weeks in Cairo recuperating from his stressful endeavors.

The Two Headed Spy is a most unusual production in that it is almost entirely set in Germany, and its hero is a decorated German general. But General Schottland, played by Jack Hawkins, is actually Alex Scotland, a British agent who has spent over 20 years in Germany on espionage missions.

He receives information about his missions from clock seller Cornaz (Felix Aylmer), who instructs him to pass on information about German battle plans to the British authorities. But after Cornaz comes under suspicion, he is arrested and tortured to death by the Gestapo, with Schottland forced to look on impassively. Nonetheless, Schottland's aide, Lieutenant Reinisch, has mounting suspicions about the general's behavior. Those suspicions are exacerbated when Schottland meets his next intelligence contact, the beautiful Lila (Gia Scala), a singer for whom Reinisch has affections. The general and Lila pretend to be in love while secretly passing vital military secrets to the Allies. Only later their strong feelings for each other are made clear. The suspicious Reinisch shoots Lila after she attempts to escape the country and then confronts the general in his luxurious apartment. Schottland shoots his adversary and then tries to flee Berlin before the Gestapo catch up with him. After being met by Allied troops, he returns to London, a free man.

The film does suffer from the fact that every German figure, including Hitler, speaks English with an implausible German accent. Hawkins combines his trademark restraint and resilience with impeccable ingenuity, though it is his very Englishness that makes it hard to accept him as a credible "Nazi" figure.

Resistance and the SOE

During the Second World War, British studios produced a number of morale boosting films in the resistance subgenre. For obvious reasons, none could tell the story of the clandestine work of the Special Operations Executive (SOE), formed by Churchill in July 1940 to conduct sabotage in Europe behind enemy lines. After the war, its work came under the spotlight through a number of films: *Odette, Ill Met by Moonlight, Carve Her Name with Pride* and *Operation Amsterdam*.

Odette Sansom, the daughter of a French war hero, was trained by the SOE and sent into France in 1942 to work with the French Resistance. She met up with her contact, Peter Churchill, and acted as his courier and fund raiser. Later they were betrayed by a double agent, and after her arrest, Odette faced torture in Paris' Fresnes prison. She convinced the Germans that she and Churchill were married and that he was the Prime Minister's nephew. Although condemned to death and sent to Ravensbruck, she was never shot and at the end of the war persuaded the camp guards to drive her to Allied lines in the West.

Odette (1950) offers a deserved paean to the eponymous heroine's undoubted bravery. Anna Neagle was Britain's biggest box office draw in the year she made *Odette*, and her passivity in the face of torture and imprisonment is both powerful and poignant. Trevor Howard too felt a sense of responsibility in taking the part of Peter Churchill. He would later say, "The war was still fresh in the memory and although dear Anna had the leading role, I was playing someone who was a living hero, so that put a great responsibility on me which was not to be taken lightly."[33]

Virginia McKenna as the SOE heroine Violette Szabo in Nazi-occupied France. She is shown here with Maurice Ronet (Jacques) in *Carve Her Name with Pride* (1958) (Lopert Pictures Corporation, Photofest).

Neagle's performance, though impressive, seems less naturalistic than that of Virginia McKenna in *Carve Her Name with Pride* (1958). McKenna came to describe this film as "one of huge emotions" which demanded "total commitment to the real people we were interpreting," and the end result justified her thorough preparation.[34] The film, based on the book by R.J. Minney, celebrates the life and heroic sacrifice of Allied secret agent Violette Szabo.

Szabo, who is half French through her mother, is living in London during the Second World War. While visiting a military parade she meets a Frenchman, Etienne Szabo, with whom she has a whirlwind romance. Soon they are married, and while her husband is away on active service, Violette gives birth to their daughter, Tania.

After Etienne is killed at El Alamein, she is approached by the British government and asked to engage in espionage work in the south of France. She travels to Rouen where she meets up with the French Resistance but is forced to flee when the Nazis discover her identity. She returns for a second and more dangerous mission but is captured after a shoot-out with the Nazis. After refusing to divulge information about Resistance activities, she is transferred to Ravensbruck concentration camp, where she is executed in 1945.

Throughout the film, McKenna plays Szabo with compassion and sensitivity. She is an innocent and thoroughly ordinary suburban girl who risks her life for a noble cause. Yet the movie resists the temptation to create a black and white character portrait. Instead Szabo is seen to have doubts about the operation, torn between her loyalty to her young daughter and her patriotic zeal. Yet this very diffidence and self-doubt make her seem a highly credible and outstanding individual. As Isabel Quigly put it in *The Spectator*, "What is filmable is Violette Szabo's quality, her courage and the way it grew out of her very ordinary seeming self, gradually, without forcing, like a muscle exercised and toughened and developed over months."[35]

She displays iron courage in refusing to submit to her Nazi captors, despite suffering the worst ravages of sleep deprivation. Szabo becomes a physical wreck but remains undaunted about her fate, and faces a Nazi death squad with typically English stoicism. Odette Hallowes later said to the press, "Virginia has the same strong will, she could have been one of us. She has courage and a mind of her own."[36]

Powell and Pressburger's *Ill Met by Moonlight* (1957), their final collaborative project, is a stirring tale of pluck and adventure set in the Cretan landscape. It tells the true story of the kidnapping of General Kreipe, the Commander in Chief of German-occupied Crete, by SOE agents Patrick Leigh Fermor (Dirk Bogarde) and William Stanley Moss (David Oxby) in 1944. The band of intrepid kidnappers, after seizing their prey, drive through 22 roadblocks before ditching their car and heading for the hills. Here they must traverse rugged terrain and evade teams of marauding Germans before finally picking up a vessel that transports Kreipe to captivity in Egypt.

The desperate voyage across Crete is as much a battle of wits between Kreipe, who tries to bribe a Cretan youth into giving away their position to the Germans, and the partisans who are aware of his cunning. At the end he acknowledges that his captors, far from being bumbling amateurs, are hardened professionals who carried out a plan to perfection. In this sense, Kreipe fits the stereotype of the honorable and decent German soldier, a hallmark of other Powell/Pressburger productions.

For the most part, this lacks the gritty suspense and nail-biting excitement of other films in the genre. The *Monthly Film Bulletin* of the BFI wrote, not unfairly, "Any impression of actuality or of sharp conflict is missing, the direction relying mainly on a coating of naive boisterous humour and the personalities of the leading players."[37] This film is noteworthy for its beautiful landscapes and stirring score. Despite its faults, it does capture the spirit of an occupied people who are depicted as loyal, resourceful and patriotic.

One picture that highlights the work of the Dutch resistance movement is *Operation Amsterdam* (1959). This is an exciting, action-packed thriller in which two diamond experts, played by Peter Finch and Alexander Knox, travel to Holland to secure valuable stocks of industrial diamonds before they are seized by the Nazi occupiers. Helped by local girl Anna (Eva Bartok) and her father, they persuade the city's diamond dealers to part with their stocks, but as their stones are in a time-locked bank vault, the trio use saboteurs to break in. They escape to the coast, dodging both the local police and the furious air power of the Luftwaffe, before arriving at the Dutch coast. Anna, however, opts to stay in the country to help the national resistance. As in wartime resistance films such as *The Day with Dawn* and *The Silver Fleet*, *Operation Amsterdam* features a patriotic people who are prepared to resist tyranny and occupation.

Lewis Milestone's *They Who Dare* (1954) puts the people of Rhodes under the spotlight in a rare film about the Special Boat Service. The movie recounts how a small group of British naval commandos, working with two Greek naval officers and two guides, were sent on a mission to destroy German airfields on Rhodes. The idea was to reduce the threat from the Luftwaffe to British troops in Egypt prior to the battle of El Alamein.

In the opening scene, Lieutenant Graham (Dirk Bogarde) reveals that there will be twelve officers on a mission to destroy the airfields, facing some 30,000 enemy soldiers. "Good odds, even if we lose," he is told. Indeed, those odds seem daunting, almost insurmountable, as the entire island is crawling with German troops, the terrain is hazardous and the airfields are well defended. They arrive via submarine and move around the island at night via the mountains. The plan runs into trouble when one of the Greek guides decides to visit his family on the island, forcing the men to change their location and potentially jeopardizing the entire mission.

But they proceed after a touch of improvisation, and eventually infiltrate and destroy an airfield, albeit with the capture of a large number of men. Graham and Corcoran (Denholm Elliot) eventually escape the island, with Italian soldiers in hot pursuit.

In some ways the film questions the heroics of war. Graham admits to making mistakes during the operation and blames himself for the death of the men. Like Barnes Wallis in *The Dam Busters*, he cuts a somewhat forlorn figure by the end of the film, despite the operation's evident success. But while he loathes himself for what he believes to have been an earlier act of recklessness, he is reminded by one of the Greek captains to view his actions through the perspective of war. The picture is a reminder of the bitterly high cost of conflict, not that such operations are futile. It is altogether an impressive resistance film, with the islanders depicted as a resourceful people, and the Greek officers displaying the same stamina and bravery as their English counterparts.

Another national group that withstood an Axis onslaught, though without coming under occupation, was the Maltese. During the Second World War, Malta played a key role in the Allies' Mediterranean strategy, providing a vital base for intercepting Axis supplies (particularly oil) to North Africa. During 1941 and 1942, the island was repeatedly attacked from the air by both the Italian and German airforce, resulting in over 2,000 Maltese deaths and considerable damage to the island's infrastructure. Such was the islanders' fortitude that they were collectively awarded the George Cross for valor in 1942.

Their plight is vividly brought to life in *Malta Story*, a 1953 production starring Alec Guinness, Jack Hawkins and Muriel Pavlow. Flight Lieutenant Ross (Guinness), is an archaeologist traveling to Egypt who finds himself stranded on the island due to the intense bombing raids. He joins the RAF as a reconnaissance pilot and falls in love with a Maltese girl, Maria (Pavlow). Their romance is cut short when his plane is shot down during a vital mission.

This fictional story is interspersed with images of Malta living under enemy bombardment. Using a mixture of reconstruction and archive footage, the film presents harrowing images of mangled landscape, rubble-strewn streets and burning buildings, so that at times the film has a semi-documentary feel.

Yet the islanders are depicted as a hardy and stoical people who endure the very worst that the enemy can throw at them. After one bombing raid, groups of children come onto the streets and help adults repair bomb damage, maintaining a cheerful disposition despite the terror. Their plight and eventual survival provides a microcosm of Britain's own experience in 1940–1. Thus, at its heart the film is a tribute to the unyielding courage of the Maltese nation.

Aware that the island lacks defensive cover, one British soldier dismisses talk of the impending arrival of Spitfires. "There's been 50 Spitfires coming ever since I've been here, and all that's come is about 500 Gerries." These are the kind of cynical sentiments that would surface more frequently in later films of the 1950s, such as *Dunkirk*. But eventually the RAF also "dishes it out" by destroying convoys that were en route to Rommel's North African army.

The romantic scenes between Ross and Maria are kept low key, as if to emphasize the fragility of their emotional bonds in wartime. No one appreciates this better than Maria's mother. When Guinness asks her for permission to marry Maria, she points out that "war destroys many hopes, many plans." She is resigned to loss, having seen her husband perish in an air raid, and it is with resignation that she accepts that her son, who is guilty of spying for the enemy, will face execution at the hands of the British.

Guinness' death is handled with subtlety and restraint. Turning back from a vital reconnaissance mission, his plane is shot down by enemy aircraft and makes a rapid descent to earth. Maintaining his composure, and with typical English understatement, he simply says, "Ah, this is where it gets tricky." When radio contact is lost and it is clear that he has died, there are no emotional histrionics from Maria. At mission control there is stunned silence as she listens in forlorn hope.

The Ship That Died of Shame (U.S.: *PT Raiders*) from 1955 resists simplistic categorization. A dark and atmospheric thriller, it expresses nostalgia for wartime unity and moral integrity, sounding an ominous warning if those things are lost in peacetime. Combining Ealing's trademark combination of whimsy and important social commentary, it tells the story of how a trio of ex-servicemen fail to adjust to civilian life and become corrupted by engaging in smuggling and criminality. Like *The Cruel Sea*, the film involves a naval vessel, a motor torpedo boat ("the 1087"); but unlike *Compass Rose*, this one suffers a fall from grace at the hands of her British sailors.

At the start, a voiceover from Lieutenant-Commander Randall (George Baker) reminds us of one thing we know about ships—"that they are *not* alive. They are made of wood and metal, and nothing else: they don't have souls, they don't have wills of their own." But as the film progresses, this common sense judgment comes under relentless scrutiny.

After his boat building business collapses in peacetime, Randall is reunited with ex-serviceman Hoskins (Attenborough), who suggests buying the 1087 and using her for smuggling luxury goods. Randall buries his scruples and, together with Birdie (Bill Owen), joins the lucrative business. But Randall soon finds that Hoskins is conveying more dangerous goods: counterfeit money, guns and even a dangerous child killer. The ship's engine begins to break down repeatedly, "ashamed" of the uses to which it is being put. In the final scene, Hoskins is thrown overboard in stormy conditions, and Randall and Birdie escape, only to see the ship disappear forever beneath the waves.

George Perry said this film's attempt to mix conventional thriller and sentimental whimsy would seem "bewildering and absurd to the great mass of landlubbers."[38] A fair judgment perhaps, but the film's core ideological message is fairly clear. Whereas the war bonded the men and gave them (and the ship) a sense of moral purpose, their postwar criminality has destroyed both. The ship, representing the wider nation perhaps, is progressively destroyed by the corrupting influence of its smugglers, compensating for Hoskins' own lack of remorse. Its message seems to be that without the common purpose and the values that the war provided, social degradation would result.

The war films of the 1950s, until about 1957, were indeed harking back to a mythical golden age when the nation was united in adversity and a wartime consensus prevailed. Neil Rattigan suggests that whereas during the war years filmmakers "had been determined to show the British not losing the war," the 1950s provided "an opportunity, even a demand, to show the British actually winning it."[39] Certainly a number of films did show British victories, whether successful escape attempts by POWs, heroic attempts to dupe the Germans or significant naval victories. But even when the British were shown winning the war, there was a sense of restraint and a marked absence of histrionics or self-congratulation. The enemy was rarely shown being routed, as if the British were embarrassed to forego their status as the courageous underdogs. Indeed, attempts to demonize the enemy, as in *The Camp on Blood Island*, met with disdain.

Thus, in *The Cruel Sea*, U-boats were destroyed (there were two encountered by the ship), though the most memorable moment was Ericcson's moral dilemma in not sparing the lives of the stranded British sailors; the bouncing bomb did its work at the end of *The Dam Busters*, though the film concentrated more on how Redgrave reacted to the death toll of pilots; there were very few action sequences in *Reach for the Sky*, a film that centered on the heroic fortitude of Bader. British films of the 1950s were nostalgic for our victories in war, but particularly for those set of national characteristics (stoicism, duty, self-deprecating humor) that were thought to have helped us win it. As Rattigan himself put it so aptly, "Britannia with her back to the wall but refusing to give in is, to British eyes and minds, a much more appealing national image than Britannia out in the middle of the ring beating the living daylights out of a reeling opponent."[40]

Chapter 11

The Critique of Deference in the Aftermath of Suez

As we have seen, 1950s British war films reflected a strong degree of nostalgia for the social unity of the wartime years. They shared a largely patriotic narrative which regarded the war as a noble enterprise, and which reflected a larger narrative about national identity and character. But towards the end of the 1950s, some films began to make more subversive statements about the war and the behavior of its protagonists.

Films like *Dunkirk, Ice Cold in Alex* and *The Bridge on the River Kwai* reflected a growing climate of cynicism towards "high politics," war and the culture of deference embedded in the military. Their "heroes" no longer embodied the stoic ideals of gentlemanly conduct and emotional restraint. Instead they showed a gritty, at times harrowing, realism that was designed to reveal how men cracked under the pressure of combat. John Mills in *Ice Cold in Alex*, Stanley Baker in *Yesterday's Enemy* and Alex Guinness in *Bridge on the River Kwai* all play characters with psychological flaws or nervous dispositions; these are men "on the edge."

These films were made in the aftermath of the 1956 Suez crisis, a humiliating watershed moment in modern British history. British forces had been sent to Egypt to unseat Egyptian leader Gamal Nasser, following the latter's nationalization of the Suez Canal. But within days of the operation, Britain was diplomatically isolated at the U.N. and faced criticism from her closest ally, U.S. President Eisenhower. Following intense American pressure, British forces were withdrawn from Suez, but the domestic damage was severe. In Britain, an anti-war mood had built up, with much of the left-liberal press highly critical of the Suez operation. Marches and demonstrations were held across the country, the like of which would not be seen again until the Vietnam War. The country was polarized politically, while Anthony Eden's dishonesty in Parliament led many to question the authority of the political Establishment.

Suez showed clearly that Britain, far from being a military behemoth, was the junior partner in an increasingly shaky trans–Atlantic alliance. The British Empire was exposed as a paper tiger, with the mother country no longer able to project power abroad without American help. More importantly, it was no longer unthinkable to question deference to politicians or the military. This narrative of Britain in international decline, which was the product both of Suez and of decolonization, was mirrored by an awareness of Britain's growing weakness as an economic power.

These narratives, which would come to dominate popular culture in the 1960s with profound implications for national identity, were first seen in a wave of films made in the latter part of the 1950s. All began to question the heroic conventions of the war film, as well as the national character ideology that underpinned them. Though made in the late 1950s, they provide the starting point for a discussion about the "new wave" of anti-war films in the 1960s and 1970s.

The Bridge on the River Kwai (1957), adapted from the novel by Pierre Boulle, is perhaps the only true war epic of the 1950s and one of Britain's most successful films. Its production was plagued from the start: numerous actors turned down the lead role, among them Laurence Olivier, Charles Laughton and Ray Milland; there were problems with the choice of director; and numerous writers labored on the script. Nonetheless, the finished product earned rave reviews and numerous honors, including seven Academy Awards.

At the core of this compelling POW drama is the conflict between Colonel Nicholson, brilliantly played by Alec Guinness, and the camp commandant Saito (Sessue Hayakawa). The film reveals that these two protagonists, despite being on opposing sides, are actually driven by similar impulses. Both adhere to an inflexible code of military honor and are bound to their class.

The British prisoners are told that they must construct a railway to aid the Japanese war effort. Nicholson resists the order, insisting that officers must resist manual work under the Geneva Convention. The men are punished by being made to stand in the heat all day, with Saito reminding Nicholson that "this is war, this is not a game of cricket." But Nicholson's stubbornness allows him to win this contest of wills, leaving Saito distraught that the bridge will fall behind schedule.

But Guinness also believes that his men are best served by a diet of strict discipline and self-control. He comes to see the building of the bridge as a way of demonstrating British achievement and shows a ruthless efficiency that even the Japanese cannot match. The absurdity of his dedication lies not just in the willingness to help the enemy but in risking the lives of his men. Going on the sick list is condemned as "not military behavior," and he uses his influence to recruit the majority of sick soldiers.

In the second half of the film, a British commando unit led by an American escapee, Shears (William Holden), prepares a mission to destroy the bridge. The justifiably famous climax, almost Shakespearian in its tragedy, sees Nicholson try to thwart the explosion after alerting Saito to the wires leading to the bomb. Suddenly, Nicholson, realizing his folly and having been injured in an explosion, falls upon the detonator, blowing up the bridge in the process. It is then left to Major Clipton (James Donald) to pronounce his parting judgment on the whole affair: "Madness, madness."

Guinness embodies many of the virtues of the English masculine hero: a sense of duty, stoicism and self-sacrifice. However, they are subverted by an exercise in self-deceiving folly. Such is his misplaced sense of duty that Nicholson becomes an unwitting collaborator with the Japanese. He becomes so transfixed by the bridge that he fails to see its ultimate purpose in the war effort. In the words of Raymond Durgnat, "Guinness is the too brave Briton, upheld by an idealism which, in the end, blinds him to the world."[1]

The critic Ian Watt was probably right when he wrote:

Alec Guinness and Sessue Hayakawa spot wires connected to explosives in the unforgettable climax of David Lean's (1957) *The Bridge on the River Kwai* (Columbia, Photofest).

Nicholson's mastery of means and his complete, though unconscious, muddlement about ultimate ends, made him stand for our civilization in general.... Boulle's novel was really intended to show the destructive consequences that arise from the West's mastery of means but not ends."[2]

Lean himself described the film as "a painfully eloquent statement on the general folly and waste of war.[3]

The 1958 *Ice Cold in Alex* (U.S.: *Desert Attack*) is one of the most celebrated war movies of the 1950s and perhaps the most famous of the "desert" films. The campaign in North Africa had been the backdrop for only a small number of wartime productions, most noticeably Ealing's *Nine Men* (1943). But *Ice Cold in Alex* is unusual in that its heroes include a German spy, while the British character, Captain Anson (John Mills), is a flawed individual with a debilitating addiction to alcohol.

The film starts with the German attack on Tobruk in 1942. Anson, together with Sergeant Major Tom Pugh (Harry Andrews) and two nurses, evacuate their base and set off for Alexandria in an ambulance. On their journey they come across Van Der Poel (Anthony Quayle), who tells them he is a South African officer. Der Poel joins them on their trek, and together they encounter various natural and man-made obstacles. They encounter a minefield, their vehicle suffers damage to its suspension, and they are plagued by the hazards of the desert.

They also twice encounter units of the German Afrika Corps. Van Der Poel, a German speaker, persuades the Germans to let the group go, but this only raises suspicions about the South African and his mysterious "backpack." In fact, Anson discovers that Der Poel is carrying a radio transmitter, though he decides not to confront him about this.

When the South African becomes trapped in quicksand, they all help to save his life, and he reciprocates by helping lift the ambulance up a slope. Finally, they reach Alexandria, where Van Der Poel is arrested by the military police. However, he is spared from certain execution after being identified as a German officer, a deal arranged by Anson in grateful appreciation for the help he offered. Finally, Anson sits down to drink the ice cold lager that he promised himself in Libya. As he leaves, Van der Poel admits that the desert has been "the greater enemy."

It is tempting to view the film as a symbol of the *fin de siècle* disillusionment with British power. Anson is hardly the model of stoic restraint. He looks worn out and thoroughly disillusioned, his judgment clearly impaired by excessive alcohol. This represented a real character reversal for Mills, whose persona in earlier roles was that of a restrained, decent and honest soldier or officer, an utterly dependable figure whose composure under fire was legendary. He later admitted, with considerable glee, "It [the film] destroyed forever that ridiculous stiff upper lip image I had been stuck with."[4] By contrast, the German spy looks cool and unflappable, the model of English composure. Quayle would later describe this role as "the only really wonderful part I had in films."[5]

So while the movie does celebrate the qualities of stoic endurance, improvisation and collective endeavor, these are no longer *British* qualities. National differences become irrelevant when survival is at stake. As a contemporary reviewer put it, the film "shows, loud, clear and intelligently, that however much people will fight when they're told to, if you just leave them alone together they simply cannot help saving each other's lives."[6] It is this very human element, this de-emphasis on "us" and "them," that is so jarring. For while German characters had been portrayed sympathetically in some earlier films, they were very much secondary to the British officers. It would have been inconceivable to turn an enemy spy into a hero.

The Dunkirk evacuation (Operation Dynamo) in 1940 has been remembered as both a national humiliation and a miracle. Today it is fondly remembered for the small armada of boats that sailed across the Channel and for the much lauded "Dunkirk spirit" that galvanized the nation. It is equally remembered for the ignominious retreat from France that symbolized Britain's colossal military failure. Both these strands find their way into Ealing's *Dunkirk* (1958). In retrospect it seems surprising that such an iconic event in British history was not depicted earlier in the decade, but the tone of the film, at times bitterly cynical, perfectly captures the mood of the times.

The picture examines Operation Dynamo from both a military and civilian perspective. One part of the film centers on Corporal Tubby Binns (John Mills), an officer who reluctantly takes responsibility for getting a group of men to Dunkirk. Another examines the role of two civilians, one a journalist, Charles Foreman (Bernard Lee), who witnesses complacency in British circles, and another a businessman, John Holden (Richard Attenborough), who cares more about his family than the war. Both men become part of the civilian flotilla that sails to Dunkirk.

In *Dunkirk*, there is an unmistakable cynicism about Whitehall and "high politics," which Foreman quickly latches onto. He believes that the MOI expounds "the usual claptrap," and lambasts politicians who lie to the country and try to lull people into a false sense of security. The cynicism comes across even further when a British soldier Private Barlow (Ray Jackson) is discussing France's prospects with the French ambassador. The Frenchman questions what Britain has done so far with their men and then points to some raw recruits who are in the process of being trained for battle. He asks perhaps whether Britain will win the war with these new soldiers. Barlow replies that sometimes much can be said "for not being a realist."

While German troops march forward through France and Belgium, we are treated to a taste of just how comic British official propaganda really is. Inside a music hall, two singers offer a rendition of "Siegfried Line" and remind their audience that the washing will indeed be hung out, but only if the "line is still there." As the song continues, we see the French line of defense being pushed gradually further back by the German advance until the Allied troops are right on the coastline. This clever juxtaposition is designed to mock the government's jingoistic entreaties.

There is a specific anti-appeasement message in the film. At one point, Binns demands to know what caused this fiasco. He is told: "Stupidity.... The army could hardly be blamed, for they had what we gave them." The politicians were responsible for "shoving our heads in the sand." The idea that the army have been effectively abandoned by the reckless actions and decisions of British officials comes across forcefully towards the end.

With German attacks increasing steadily, one soldier asks almost comically, "Don't the Gerry ever let up?" Another replies, "What's to stop them?" In one extraordinary scene the soldiers kneel in prayer on the beach while, overhead, German planes lurk menacingly. Shortly after, the familiar merciless destruction rains down from the sky and scatters the religious huddle. The image of prostrate soldiers being left at the mercy of the enemy symbolizes in one sense the apotheosis of abandonment. Even the God they prey to for deliverance is unable to silence the fury of the enemy. It is as if they are part of a religious sacrifice, a grand ceremony of death that is necessary before the greater good is achieved. Despite the persecution, the men do not break ranks or lose morale, even if there are occasional murmurs of disapproval.

But the RAF is not the real enemy here, and the abandonment is seen as the result of political folly. This is clearly a post–Suez film, with its cynical and hostile attitude towards politicians, and its lack of deference to men in "high circles."

But the other side to the Dunkirk myth, the hope for national renewal, is equally present. The film invokes the defining myth of the "little ships" by presenting them as a mini armada, accompanied by stirring patriotic music and the great British national monuments in the background. Holden is transformed by the experience of 1940. Initially he is dismissive of the phoney war, caring only about the booming profits in his boat business and his private family concerns. Later he admits to his wife that he is not doing enough and decides to sail his boat to the beaches of France. This shows that the divide between the civilian and military is artificial, and whereas before there were fighting men and civilians, now there are only "people." *Dunkirk* can therefore be seen as a testament to the folly of war leaders and an inspiring reminder of British greatness in adversity.

Orders to Kill (1958) is a powerful psychological drama that explores the moral dilemmas of killing in wartime. The film focuses on an American soldier, Captain Summers, who is sent into France to kill a Parisian lawyer, Monsieur Lafitte. Lafitte is suspected of being a German collaborator who has betrayed members of the French Resistance. Summers, played by Paul Massie in an impressive debut performance, is selected for the task, but major doubts about his suitability are aired. An army psychologist describes Summers as a "nice, normal guy" who lacks "level-headed shrewdness," "maturity" and "tough, unimaginative nerve."

But what he really lacks is the ability to follow orders without exercising his own judgment. For when he meets Lafitte, he finds him to be a mild-mannered, henpecked husband with a curious affection for his cat. When he passes on his doubts about Lafitte's guilt to a member of the Resistance, Leonie (Irene Worth), he encounters a hostile response.

She takes him to task for his procrastination, demanding to know whether he was ordered to find out Lafitte's guilt or innocence. "It is not your business to sit in judgment on Lafitte, it is your business to kill him." She reminds him that as an air force pilot he would have carried out raids that killed innocent non-combatants.

Eventually he does execute Lafitte in the latter's office, but not before the Frenchman looks into his face and asks, "Why?" The experience of killing a man face to face is more than he can handle, and he descends into a spiral of alcoholism and despair, eventually winding up in a Parisian hospital. But it is there that he is finally told that Lafitte was indeed innocent, confirming his earlier suspicions. Far from suffering any further mental deterioration, he re-evaluates his previous role as an air force pilot, reflecting on the innocent people he would have killed in necessary military actions.

Orders to Kill may not be a strictly anti-war film, though it raises some highly disturbing issues. A decent soldier is compelled to kill an innocent man against his own better judgment. While we may put this down to the "fog of war," which often takes the lives of non-combatants, the film goes much further. Summers is reminded that when he was a pilot he dropped bombs that killed hundreds of innocent people, and without demur. When asked to explain the difference, Summers explains that as a pilot he "wasn't there at the other end to hear someone say 'Why?'"

War summons powerful moral dilemmas, which this film explores in a thoroughly convincing manner. Paul Gibbs was right to say that director Anthony Asquith "was trying to say something timely and unexceptionable about the sanctity of human life."[7]

Hammer's *Yesterday's Enemy* (1959), directed by Val Guest, examined the grittier and more disturbing aspects of jungle war. Though set in Burma, it was filmed entirely in the Shepperton and Bray studios, a factor that, for some, rendered the film unduly theatrical. In actual fact, the studio sets help create a powerful sense of oppressive claustrophobia throughout the production.

Stanley Baker gives a highly impressive performance as Captain Langford, a tough, no-nonsense leader of a stranded British brigade fighting its way through swampland in Japanese-occupied Burma. The men arrive in a Burmese village under enemy control and, after coming under fire from Japanese soldiers, overcome their adversaries. Langford discovers that among the dead is a Japanese commander who was in possession of a top secret map. The map appears to reveal plans for an impending enemy assault.

In an effort to extract a confession from a suspected Burmese collaborator, Langford orders two Burmese civilians to be executed, much to the horror of his unit. When some of the British soldiers then attempt to deliver vital information to headquarters, they find themselves under attack from the Japanese, who later capture the village. Langford is interrogated by Yamazuki (Phillip Ahn), a Japanese intelligence officer who wants to know how much the British captain knows about their military plans. In an ironic twist, Yamazuki places Langford in the same position as the Burmese collaborator, with Langford refusing to divulge information to protect his men.

Langford's utilitarian decision to kill innocent villagers pits him against war correspondent Max Anderson (Leo McKern) and a padre (Guy Rolfe), both of whom believe that his order is a "war crime." Anderson is especially cynical, believing that those who are sacrificed in "ugly" warfare are merely "dead and forgotten." But Langford is unrepentant, admitting that he cares only about his own men, and that in the midst of a retreat there is no place for a "cosy discussion on the ethics of war." In his view, the only way to fight a deadly enemy is "with the gloves off."

In an echo of the scene where Lieutenant Summers is reprimanded by the Frenchwoman Irene, Langford tears into their perceived moral obtuseness: "You don't mind when a bomber pilot presses a button and kills a few hundred civilians, you don't mind murder from a distance so long as you personally are not involved." This brings us to the film's central question: in total war, do the ends ever justify the means?

When we encounter the Japanese, we are made to look in a mirror and remember the barbarity of our own side. Both the British and the Japanese are willing to use lethal force against the innocent in order to outwit the enemy. As the Japanese officer, Yamazuki, points out to the protesting Langford: "This is total war. No quarter is asked. None is given." Yet the Japanese officer can salute the Englishman's bravery in refusing to divulge information, just as Saito recognizes in Nicholson his own code of honor. He is a man that Yamazuki would "prefer to fight with, not against."

The film is worth watching if only for Baker's performance. With his smoldering looks and brooding intensity, he plays the role of Langford to perfection. He was certainly suited to the part, having established a screen persona as a fiery, villainous character in films like *Richard III*, *Knights of the Round Table* and *Helen of Troy*. In this movie he is as far removed from the stiff upper-lipped hero as you can get.

In the film's campaign booklet, the producer acknowledged that the production "knocked the heroics out of war," while for Peter Newman, who wrote the play on which the film was based, it demonstrated "the utter futility of war for victor, vanquished and victim alike."[8]

Yet for all its cynicism there is enough in this film to suggest a modicum of honor. Langford, despite his earlier behavior, refuses to help the enemy and stubbornly withholds vital information. But when he continues to be intransigent, despite knowing that his men will die, we sympathize with his sense of self-sacrificial obligation. Despite the individualist sentiments expressed earlier in the film, it is duty which wins out. Unlike the true anti-war films of the following decade, this one finishes with a memorial to the fallen, even if their sacrifice had been questioned by the men themselves.

Chapter 12

How We Lost the War: Anti-Heroism and the New Wave

The 1960s is best remembered as a period of transformative social and cultural change which swept away the conventions of the past. It was the decade of pop music, free sex, drugs and experimentation—an unending assault on traditional society, culture and values. It witnessed a popular revolt against deference, duty, and patriotism—manifested in rocketing crime, the questioning of authority and a seemingly endless protest movement. Yet its roots lie very much in the upheavals of the previous decade.

In the late 1950s, a spirit of anarchic opposition to Establishment values had been gathering pace. John Osborne set the pattern with his *Look Back in Anger*, a play that raged against the pomp and pretensions of the upper classes. As one of the "angry young men," he helped establish the "kitchen sink" style of realist drama which explored gritty issues of social alienation, often from a left wing perspective.

At the same time, television produced its own anti-establishment satire with *That Was the Week That Was*. Every week a prime-time audience of some 12,000,000 would see political figures lampooned, with particular coverage given to the Profumo scandal in 1963. *Private Eye*, which first appeared in 1961, offered a similar brand of biting wit in an attempt to debunk the Establishment's leading figures.

This challenge to traditional values was given rocket fuel by the youth-centered revolution of the 1960s. The rising affluence and mass consumerism of that decade, combined with the post-war baby boom and the ending of national service, meant that a new young generation found itself in a position to influence social and cultural trends. As one contemporary put it, "Youth captured this ancient island and took command in a country where youth had always been kept properly in its place."[1]

What erupted was nothing short of a counter-cultural transformation in which the old values of paternalism, duty and hierarchy came under relentless assault. The global bloodshed of the Second World War had led many to question the willingness of people to subscribe to dictatorial power. Now the 1960s saw a generalized attack on authority in all its forms, with individualism the guiding moral principle.

The family, the bedrock of traditional British society, was undermined by the sexual revolution of the '60s. The widespread availability of the contraceptive pill gave women greater freedom over their sexual lives and began a process of normalizing "extra marital" sex. The divorce laws were also liberalized so that marriages could be dissolved more easily if one partner withdrew their consent.

Parliament legalized homosexuality between consenting adults in 1967, much to the horror of social conservatives, while the new experimental culture of "free love" was seen as a liberating alternative to the suburban family. Books, plays and films broke taboos by discussing sexuality in explicit terms, a process that started with the publication of *Lady Chatterley's Lover* in 1960. For many, it felt like a torrent of liberation from the stuffy conventions of an earlier era.

Popular music would be transformed by the advent of the Beatles, a rock band whose innovative rhythms made them an instantly recognizable cultural icon. Their hairstyles, clothing and progressive ideals were to influence a generation of youth across the globe. Recreational drugs, such as LSD, were increasingly prevalent and provided further evidence that the new generation was becoming narcissistic and rebellious. The term "generation gap" was a product of this period.

At the same time, youth protest became a defining feature of the decade. In America this manifested first in the civil rights movement and then in opposition to the Vietnam War. In Britain, the anti-war movement had spawned CND, an organization dedicated to the abolition of nuclear weapons. But in the 1960s the peace movement would also focus on Vietnam, with marches and demonstrations against American militarism.

All these forces were bound to affect popular notions of national character and identity. Instead of the traditional emphasis on duty and the stiff upper lip, the generational change of the 1960s produced a morality that was focused on individual pleasure, material comforts, libertarianism and freedom in sexual morality. Self-restraint (and emotional restraint) was replaced by a cult of hedonism and instant gratification. The idea of duty to the nation state was increasingly viewed as a dangerous anachronism, while the figure of the English gentleman, with all its associated traits, was now a moribund throwback to a discredited class system. Such old-fashioned values were seen as the cause of national decline.

Indeed, the whole notion of a group identity was increasingly disavowed by intellectuals working in the social sciences. They preferred to emphasize the individual personality and began to discredit the notion of a unitary personality type among the English.[2] This trend continued into the 1970s, summed up by the author A. S. Byatt, who wrote of the nation that it resembled "a bright mosaic of little, unrelated patches." As society became more atomized under the collective weight of media-driven materialism, the whole notion of national identity was increasingly seen as retrograde. Thus the influential historian, Asa Briggs, would later write that talk of national identity was "code for a reactionary nostalgia for past imperial glories."[3]

These analyzes were marked by a climate of "declinism" in which Britain, having lost its Empire and "failed to find a role," no longer enjoyed a preeminent position in the world economy. The war, and the common national project that led to victory, was but a distant memory. The lack of great national achievements in the 1960s (a World Cup and the occasional scientific triumph aside), and the erosion of trust in core institutions (the army, Parliament, monarchy), made it easier to deride patriotic sentiment than to celebrate it. In short, national identity was undergoing a radical, and perhaps irreversible, transformation.

Michael Balcon's 1961 *The Long and the Short and the Tall* (U.S.: *Jungle Fighters*) reflects the new rebellious phase in British film in which the old assumptions of deference and social solidarity were being eroded. This movie is very much a child of the angry new wave, an intriguing mixture of anti-militarism and kitchen sink. The end result is an uncomfortable anti-war production offering a most unflattering portrait of the British army. As with *Yesterday's Enemy*, the virtues that had epitomized army life—heroism, self-sacrifice and duty—come under biting scrutiny. Indeed, this film goes much further and questions the very purpose of war itself, together with the behavior of its central protagonists.

Set in the Burmese jungle in 1942, a seven-strong patrol who are specialists in sonic warfare arrive at a remote hut. The unit consists of squabbling, foul-mouthed recruits, the worst of whom is the rebellious Private Bamforth (Laurence Harvey). Bamforth's vulgarity and insubordination know no bounds, and he admits without embarrassment that he doesn't "go a bundle on all this death or glory stuff." His disdain for war is shared, in part, by Corporal Johnstone (Richard Harris). Johnstone questions why the unit has been sent into battle so under-resourced and describes their terrain as "rotten stinking jungle." It is far from the glorious heroism of an earlier age.

Tensions within the unit are heightened following the decision to kill their Japanese captive, Tojo, who has accidentally come across their hut. Johnstone believes in the motto "Never love your enemy, hate them" and wants the

The rebellious and loud-mouthed Private Bamforth (Laurence Harvey) holding a Japanese prisoner (Kenji Takaki) in the Burmese jungle, with Ronald Fraser on the left. *The Long and the Short and the Tall* (1961) offers a most unflattering portrait of the British army (Continental Distributing, Photofest).

captive killed immediately. Although initially scornful of the prisoner, Bamforth views Johnstone's ruthless approach as dangerous, old-fashioned bigotry. He defends Tojo against a charge of looting, pointing out that one of his fellow soldiers, Private Whitaker (David McAllum), is just as guilty of looting Japanese items. The British have no right to turn on their captive on a charge for which they themselves are guilty.

At the same time, Bamforth helps to humanize Tojo by showing others the photograph of his wife and children. These scenes help blur the moral distinction between the two sides. But more importantly, the use of the recalcitrant Bamforth to question the morality of more senior figures is a shocking reversal of the status quo.

Whereas some '50s films grapple with the dilemmas of conflict, none provide such a sustained critique of man's inhumanity in war or so vigorously question the purpose of fighting. So by the end, we are scarcely surprised when

Whitaker demands to "pack it in" and promptly surrenders to Japanese soldiers who have surrounded his unit. When his Japanese captors jeer at Whitaker and use their own threatening gestures, one can only feel that he is getting his comeuppance.

Sidney Lumet's *The Hill* offers an equally cynical perspective on the British army. The film is set in a military detention camp in the Libyan desert where a group of British soldiers, who have been found guilty of various disciplinary offences, are subjected to inhumane treatment. These include being forced to climb up and down a man-made hill while carrying a pack on their backs. In overall control is Regimental Sergeant Major Wilson (Harry Andrews) and, below him, the brutal Staff Sergeant Williams (Ian Hendry). They clash with a new group of 5 soldiers, particularly the recalcitrant Roberts (Sean Connery), as well as more humane figures, such as a medical officer played by Michael Redgrave. When one of the prisoners dies and another is beaten up by Williams, a fiery clash of wills becomes inevitable.

In some respects, this is a typical anti-war production capturing the essence of the anti–Vietnam zeitgeist. The recruits are the victims of the army's senseless and sadistic cruelty. They are subjected to a variety of horrendous abuses, including the repetitive climbing, long marches in the desert heat and periods of sleep deprivation. Yet in the face of such cynical treatment, the prisoners resort to fits of laughter, particularly at one moment when they have sand thrown at them on the hill by the defiant Connery. The hill itself becomes a comic-absurdist symbol of the futility of war, a modern-day Sisyphean punishment. As with many a Shakespearean tragedy, a soldier who holds up a candle to the monstrous treatment is derided as a madman.

But there is a more serious purpose to all this. We see the worst side of the British officer class here, its harsh and unforgiving punishments, its crude racism, its bullying officers who show a fondness for drunkenness, violence and prostitution. Attempts to make the men fitter merely expose the officers' inhumanity. The regime involves no deeper purpose than to satisfy the sadistic tendencies of those in charge. Redgrave's character serves as the conscience of the production, demanding to take Roberts to a hospital after he has been injured by Williams. He fits the character of the man of integrity standing up to injustice, a theme in many a Lumet film.

Sergeant Major Wilson himself displays some of the self-deceiving tendencies of Colonel Nicolson, with his sense of duty skewed by his amoral behavior. The punishments he dishes out are designed to reform the men and turn them into proper soldiers, a form of redemption through cruelty, even though he knows he will not be thanked for his work. As he points out at the start, "Nobody's going to pin a medal on us. But get this straight, one job is as important as the next."

Yet he is a far worse creature. He displays an utterly callous attitude when one of the prisoners (Stevens) dies because of exhaustion, denying all responsibility for his actions. When the prisoners riot in response, he orders one prisoner to be taken to the "mortuary" via the Hill. Such disregard for the men under his control would have been beyond the worst depredations of Nicolson or Captain Anson. But like Anson, Wilson's drunken revelries suggest that he too would rather avoid thinking about his brutal behavior. As Roberts tells Monty Bartlett (Roy Kinnear), "We are all doing time, even the screws."

The black and white cinematography and the clever camera angles are used to emphasize the darker, grittier and seedier side of war. Under Sidney Lumet's assured direction, this is one of the most thought-provoking war films of the decade.

A totally different, though no less scathing, treatment of the military comes across in Richard Lester's black comedy *How I Won the War* (1967). Based on the novel by Patrick Ryan, it offers an absurdist/comic treatment of the Second World War through satirizing the conventions of the older war movies.

The film stars Michael Crawford as Lieutenant Earnest Goodbody, a hopelessly incompetent and naïve officer who becomes a liability to the men serving under him. His task is to take raw recruits behind enemy lines in North Africa in order to set up a cricket pitch to impress advancing officers. Goodbody's ineptitude ensures that most of his men die, though in surreal fashion they reappear as monochromatic ghosts with netting over their faces. Most of the film is told in flashback after Goodbody has been captured by a German officer in 1945.

Everything about this film is subversive of the 1950s war genre. A soldier has his legs mangled and is told to "run them under a cold tap." Staff officers find amusement in exchanging bubble gum cards of the war. The British soldiers shoot down their own planes, with Crawford declaring it as "our first great victory." Col. Grapple (Michael Hordern) tells Gripweed, played by John Lennon, that being a fascist is nothing to worry about: "Fascism is something you grow out of." Gripweed later complains to the audience when his stomach is blown open, "I knew this would happen—*you* knew this would happen."

The familiar caricatures—Blimpish upper-class officers, stiff upper lips, unthinking patriotism—are pilloried mercilessly throughout the film. As Nina Hibbin put it, "This is not only an attack on the image of war, but an attack on the specific class image of war."[4] Throughout, the zany comedy and hilarious farce serve an unmistakably serious purpose.

Just as Hordern and Crawford extol the virtues of heroism, understatement and stoic fortitude, the film offers harrowing footage to show an inhuman side to conflict. These incongruities reflect an aversion to the drum-

These men are being readied for their next battle, building a cricket pitch behind enemy lines. A scene from Richard Lester's biting anti-war satire *How I Won the War* (1967). Front row, from left: Roy Kinnear, Ronald Lacey, John Lennon (United Artists, Photofest).

banging conventions of earlier war films and what Philip French described as "the nostalgia industry" in general.[5] How much is escapist comedy and how much trenchant satire is never entirely clear. Lester's previous films, particularly *A Hard Day's Night* (featuring the Beatles), perfectly captured the anti-establishment zeitgeist of the '60s and expressed the tension between the radical possibilities of youthfulness and the habits of an older generation. *How I Won the War* has a similar subversive quality.

Some may prefer to see the film as a vehicle for a purely comedic view of the war. From the late 1950s to the 1970s there were certainly a number of movies that treated the war in a more light-hearted vein. Among them were a Norman Wisdom outfit, *The Square Peg* (1958); *Operation Bullshine* (1959); *On the Fiddle* (1961); *Joey Boy* (1965), where a group of black marketers are offered the choice of army life or prison; *Dad's Army* (1971), based on the hugely popular TV series; and the Norman Cohen–directed *Adolf Hitler— My Part in His Downfall* (1973). But *How I Won the War* is more than pure comedy. Here the joke is on those who revere the war's traditional iconography, and the film's anti-war statements are too obvious to miss.

The Long Day's Dying (1968) is a somber and unsettling production from British director Peter Collinson. Like *The Long and the Short and the Tall*, this film focuses on a group of foul-mouthed, squabbling soldiers who face the dilemma of how to treat a prisoner of war. When we encounter them first, they are holed up in an isolated country house somewhere in battle-scarred Europe. They kill some Germans and capture one, Helmut (Alan Dobie), who pleads with them to save his life on condition that he takes them to his own men.

After discovering that the Germans in question are dead, the Englishmen try to escape across their own lines, only to die horribly in the process. The film is distinguished by the use of stream of consciousness on the soundtrack, a device which is rarely effective and often pretentious. Death is deliberately overdone, almost theatrical in its gore, as if to emphasize that war is the epitome of inhuman behavior.

John (David Hemmings) displays pacifist tendencies which capture the period's anti-war mood perfectly. At the end of the film he is gunned down by his own side after renouncing humanity: "I have nothing but contempt for the human animal, triumph of the animal, which is war." Stoicism, duty, self-sacrifice and courageous heroism have no place in this grim tale of death and destruction. These manly virtues are a gigantic hoax which traps men into destroying their humanity. The film's anti-war message is stark and uncompromising, spelt out by director Collinson with "all the vigour and passion of a street corner orator."[6]

Went the Day Well? imagined a typical English village living under Nazi occupation, albeit for a few days until liberation. *It Happened Here* (1964) takes this much further and provides a portrait of what England might have been like after four years of Nazi occupation. But unlike the wartime Ealing efforts, this movie offers little in the way of heroic redemption for its characters.

Nazis (actors unidentified) parade through the heart of London in *It Happened Here* (1964). The film offers a chilling reminder that not all British people would have resisted a fascist invasion (Lopert Pictures Corporation, Photofest).

The picture was shot in black and white on 16mm film, which gives it an earthy and authentic character. With no budget, the directors were reliant on unknown actors and borrowed equipment, including film stock donated by Stanley Kubrick. The resulting production, characterized by "jumpy, under-lit pictures, the muttering spontaneous dialogue," and a "nervy hand held camera," is triumphantly credible.[7]

Set in 1944, the film follows events in the life of a district nurse (Pauline Murray) who is sent to London to join a fascist organization. Her attitude toward the occupation is summed up realistically: "The only way to get back to normal is to support the forces of law and order." She later joins a hospital where she discovers, to her horror, that nurses administer euthanasia to sick European laborers. After she objects to this murderous brutality, she is arrested by the Nazis but, prior to her probable execution, is rescued by an American-backed partisan group.

The film's chilling evocation of life under the jackboot makes fascinating viewing today. A city center is left in ruins for harboring partisans; a British police squad enforces a brutal crackdown on subversives; a propaganda newsreel pays tribute to national socialist methods; and men freely exchange poisonous anti–Semitic views. The film is full of collaborators, fascists and fraternizers who demand the uprooting of international Bolshevism. The core message is that England would not have been immune to fascist collaboration had the Nazis launched a successful invasion.

However, the behavior of the "resistance" is equally brutal, giving the audience no sense of catharsis by the end. The movie instead is imbued with a "melancholy scepticism about the values of liberty."[8] The film garnered a negative critical reception from some quarters, including Jewish groups who objected to the fact that leading British Nazis were allowed to play themselves in the picture. As a result, certain scenes described by the *Jewish Chronicle* as a "foul outpouring"[9] were cut when the film was released.

Play Dirty (1969), a British version of *The Dirty Dozen* directed by Hungarian André de Toth, is one of the few British war films after 1960 to be set in the North African desert. But whereas in earlier films the desert was used to emphasize the heroism and Dunkirk spirit of army life, this movie's vision of war is unremittingly bleak from start to finish.

Colonel Masters (Nigel Green) is ordered by his senior officer, Brigadier Blore (Harry Andrews), to destroy a German fuel depot deep behind enemy lines. The man tasked with carrying out this operation is a BP employee, Captain Douglas (Michael Caine); but unknown to both men, Blore has planned to use Douglas' unit as a decoy so that his own force can take the glory by carrying out the operation. Tensions are raised within the unit by the arrival of the murderous and highly insubordinate Captain Leech (Nigel Davenport).

Leech openly defies Douglas but later reveals that he is to be paid £2,000 if he brings Douglas back home alive. Against the odds, the unit succeeds in transporting its equipment across the desert and reaches the fuel depot, only to find itself double-crossed in the end.

This profoundly cynical tale of amoral commanders and officers undoubtedly parallels public disillusionment over the Vietnam War. The film's gung-ho figures are indelibly associated with the perceived barbarity of the American military. They break all the accepted rules of waging war—they don enemy uniform, slaughter the innocent, revel in insubordination and accept bribes to bring back officers alive. The memorable ending, in which Douglas and Leech (disguised in German uniform), having decided to surrender to the British army, are gunned down by a trigger-happy British soldier, is quite fitting.

Brutal as it is, *Play Dirty* pales in comparison to Sam Peckinpah's Anglo-German production *Cross of Iron* (1977), perhaps the most brutal anti-war film ever made. It is typical Peckinpah, a rapidly edited *Wild Bunch*–style horror show replete with some of the most violent images committed to celluloid. The audience is treated to a dazzling display of destructiveness, with bodies hurled through the air in slow motion and blood spurting from the wounds of soldiers who writhe in agony on the ground. As with his Westerns, death is Grand Guignol.

The film is set on the Eastern Front and follows a German platoon in 1943. The platoon is joined by Captain Stransky (Maximilian Schell), a proud Prussian aristocrat who admits that he has joined up in order to win an Iron Cross. He clashes with the richly decorated but rather world-weary Captain Steiner, played masterfully by James Coburn. Steiner is the lone outsider railing against the system, an important trademark of the classic Peckinpah films. He declares quite freely that he hates "all officers, the iron Cross scavengers, the whole German army," and his uniform and "what it stands for." His only interest is personal survival, though he does not rate his own chances that highly. At the end Steiner ridicules the Prussian class system and military hierarchy by ordering Stransky (at gunpoint) to join him in the battle. Stransky accepts the challenge but only proves his incompetence by putting on his helmet back to front and unloading his weapon unnecessarily.

Though the film is visually impressive, its script is often weak and predictable. In one exchange, Colonel Brandt (James Mason) asks an adjutant, "What will we do after we lose the war," only to hear the reply, "Prepare for the next one." This has been the standard critique of most wars in the modern age, and Peckinpah is hardly telling us anything new with this unnecessary sermonizing. For some critics, the violence was excessive and self-indulgent, but in its brutal cynicism, one critic was right to say that it shows "palpable disgust for the events it is portraying."[10]

Overlord (1975) was made on a shoestring budget with a cast of virtual unknowns and failed to secure a release in America. Its lack of commercial success party explains why it remains so obscure today, which is all the more unfortunate when you consider that this is one of the most original and thought-provoking war films of the period.

Blending a wealth of archive footage with the fictional narrative, *Overlord* tells the story of the D-Day landings from the perspective of a twenty-one-year-old soldier, Thomas Beddows (Brian Stirner). Beddows is an innocent, middle-class everyman who is resigned to undergoing the harsh rigors of military training. Along the way he befriends a fellow soldier who complains about being turned into "cannon fodder" by the army. Beddows has a tentative love affair with a girl (Julie Neesam) before he departs for France, where he is killed as soon as he lands on the Normandy beaches.

This comes as no surprise to the audience, for throughout the film he has an eerie premonition of his death on D-Day. In an evocative sequence, Beddows dreams that he has been reunited with the girl after his death. She gently de-robes him in preparation for burial while giving him tender kisses. It is a hauntingly elegiac moment.

John Alcott's impressionistic cinematography, with its stunning sequences of falling bombs, charred bodies and burning buildings, gives this film a raw, disarming quality. Shorn of context or moral purpose, the war becomes a pointless, harrowing spectacle in which innocent men lose their lives.

None of the soldiers understand the direction of the war, a sentiment best summed up by one of the men when he describes their movements as a "game of musical bloody chairs." Another sums up the boredom of their routine by describing it as "nothing but film shows, housey-housey and lemonade in the naffy when the beer runs out."

It is the ordinary, boring side of war that is frequently absent from the unbridled heroics of the 1950s. Yet it is this very ordinariness that gives the film its sense of poignancy. A young innocent lad knows he will die yet never loses that sense of unfailing duty. This remarkable film is a subdued hymn to the fallen, which provides a timely reflection on "the bleakness of sacrifice."[11] It can also fit into the canon of anti-war cinema.

The Mackenzie Break (1970) was the last major POW film of the period and is worth mentioning at this point. This production subverts the convention because here the Germans are the prisoners trying to escape from British captivity. It is the British who seek to use force, albeit frequently unsuccessfully, to rein in German insubordination, and the Germans who display determination to outwit their captors. On the surface, it might appear as if there has been a complete role reversal. In actual fact, the British are one step ahead of their German counterparts because Captain Jack Connor (Brian Keith), assigned to the camp to investigate the prisoners' unruly behavior, has already learned of the escape plans. And while Will Schluter (Helmut Griem) leads a successful escape and heads to the coast for a waiting U-boat, Connor orders a motor torpedo boat to engage the vessel and leave Schluter stranded. There is the obvious danger that films such as this persuade an audience to empathize with the enemy and to hope that their ingenious schemes come to fruition, a criticism also levelled at *The Eagle Has Landed* some years later. Nonetheless, any sympathy for the German POWs is tempered by the fact that Schluter is a fanatical homophobe who is prepared to murder fellow prisoners.

Anglo-American productions were perfectly capable of offering up flawed anti-heroes. Philip Leacock gained attention in the 1950s with a series of thought-provoking films that tackled social and moral issues. *Appointment in London* (1953) featured Dirk Bogarde as a war-weary Wing Commander who struggles to maintain morale among his crew. Nonetheless, in its treatment of duty and heroic self-sacrifice, it largely fitted the conventions of the 1950s.

By contrast, Leacock's *The War Lover* (1962) offered a dramatic break with these conventions. Steve McQueen stars as Group Captain Buzz Rickson, an arrogant and egotistical womanizer whose defiance of authority is a danger to others and to himself. He freely admits a love of war and revels in his bombing missions.

But his brilliance as a pilot shields him from any sense of responsibility. On one bombing raid he finds that his target is obscured by cloud cover. Defying the instruction to return, he refuses to abort the mission and successfully hits the target, albeit at the cost of one bomber. On another occasion Rickson objects to dropping propaganda leaflets by flying dangerously low over the airfield. He allows personal differences with his men to put them at risk, as when he demands that Second Lieutenant Marty Lynch (Gary Cockrell) be transferred to another aircraft after he questioned Rickson's behavior. Lynch is later killed in an operation.

In the film's romantic subplot, Rickson and his co-pilot, Lieutenant Ed Bolland (Robert Wagner), vie for the attentions of the beautiful Daphne Caldwell (Shirley Anne Field). Sensing Rickson's boastful character, Daphne falls for Bolland, and they spend a great deal of time with each other. But later Rickson makes a move on Daphne, which she fiercely resists. Perhaps it is this rejection that causes Rickson to lose his confidence, and, at the end, he crashes his bomber into the Cliffs of Dover when he has an easy escape route. Describing Rickson, the army psychologist says there is a "fine line that separates a hero and a psychopath." Whether the film successfully explores that issue is open to debate.

Another air force film which questions the earlier conventions of heroic masculinity is *633 Squadron* (1964). Made by Mirisch films, *633 Squadron* is a modernized version of the classic *The Dam Busters* though it lacks that film's unquestioning paean to duty and self-sacrifice. Its central character, Wing Commander Roy Grant (Cliff Robertson), is a touch war weary and cynical, and lacks the intense dedication of Barnes Wallis.

Grant is asked to lead a dangerous bombing mission in Norway that involves targeting a mountain cliff which overhangs an important Nazi fuel factory. The factory itself is bomb proof and guarded by anti-aircraft defenses, making the mission even more perilous. There is a hint of daredevilry here, but Grant typically describes it as a "job, not the Holy Grail." Though the operation is successful, almost all of the planes involved are shot out of the sky, decimating nearly the entire squadron. But unlike *The Dam Busters*, no character is on hand to justify the high loss of life, and by the end, Grant is a bewildered wreck. Indeed, the film is most famous today for its spectacular aerial sequences and Ron Goodwin's justly famous score. A similar movie, *Mosquito Squadron*, was made in 1969 and starred David McCallum.

Revival of the War Epic in the 1960s and 1970s

Genuine war epics were a scarcity in British cinema until the late 1950s. At that point a spate of ambitious, high-drama productions were made, most notably *The Bridge on the River Kwai* and *Dunkirk*. The trend continued in the next two decades, with reconstructions of wartime events like *Sink the Bismarck!*, *The Heroes of Telemark*, *Operation Crossbow*, *The Battle of Britain* and *A Bridge Too Far*, as well as fictional adventure stories such as *The Guns of Navarone* and *Where Eagles Dare*. More unusual films included Michael Winner's *Hannibal Brooks* (1969), where a POW escapes from Germany to Switzerland with an elephant, and Sidney Lumet's exposé of British army cruelty, *The Hill* (1965). In some, such as *Sink the Bismarck!*, *Operation Crossbow* and *The Heroes of Telemark*, there are glimpses of old-fashioned heroism and a revival of the underdog, stoical mentality; in others, such as *The Guns of Navarone* and *The Hill*, the protagonists are more cynical and morally compromised.

Sink the Bismarck! (1960), directed by Lewis Gilbert, deals with the true story of how the Royal Navy relentlessly pursued and then sank Germany's largest battleship. In May 1941, at the height of the Battle of the Atlantic, the *Bismarck* and the cruiser *Prince Eugen* attempted to break into the Atlantic in order to sink British convoys. However, they were spotted by the Royal Navy and intercepted in the Denmark Strait. *Bismarck* then opened fire on one of Britain's major battleships, HMS *Hood*, and sank it, with huge loss of life. This led to Churchill's demand to "Sink the *Bismarck*," an operation successfully completed when the German ship was pummeled by a number of British battleships and cruisers. This is a *fin de siècle* celebration of a major British wartime triumph, something in keeping with the ethos of '50s war films.

This movie has a feel of semi-documentary realism, something partially owed to the use of several warships and cruisers loaned by the Admiralty. It helped that the producer, John Brabourne, was Lord Mountbatten's son-in-law.[12] The film also unusually features a number of broadcasts by the veteran pro–British journalist Edward R. Murrow.

The central character is undoubtedly the Admiralty's new Director of Operations, Captain Jonathan Sheppard, played by Kenneth More. He is a cold disciplinarian, not given to displays of warmth or sentiment. As he explains to his assistant Anne Davis (Dana Wynter), "Getting emotional about things is a luxury of peacetime. In wartime it is much too painful." He scarcely raises a murmur when he learns of the loss of *Hood* and maintains his cool composure under the most trying circumstances. But his English *sangfroid* is broken when he learns that his son, who was reported missing from a ship in the vicinity of the fighting, has been found alive.

The film contrasts the triumphalism of German Admiral Günther Lütjens (Karel Stepanek) with the more matter-of-fact professionalism of the English commanders. Whereas Lütjens celebrates the sinking of a British ship, there is an absence of rejoicing when the *Bismarck* is sunk, with Admiral Tovey (Michael Hordern) merely left to remark, "Gentleman, let's go home."

The Anglo-American production *The Guns of Navarone* (1961) was based on the 1957 novel by Alistair MacLean and featured a star-studded cast that included Gregory Peck, David Niven, Anthony Quinn and Anthony Quayle. In the story, an Allied commando team attempts to destroy two powerful German guns on the Greek island of Navarone which are threatening British ships in the Aegean Sea. Some of the men have specific skills that are necessary for the task: Captain Mallory (Peck) is a world expert in mountain climbing, Corporal Miller (Niven) is trained in explosives, and Private Brown (Stanley Baker) is lethal with knives. They are led by Major Roy Franklin (Anthony Quayle), with Colonel Andrea Stavrou (Anthony Quinn), a Greek soldier and a local native, and Spyros Pappadimos (James Darren) making up the six.

Together they engage on their daredevil "backs against the wall" mission which involves defying the Wehrmacht, a local saboteur and the hazardous Aegean terrain. They succeed in silencing the guns of Navarone, despite the deaths of some of the men. The plot is full of dramatic twists, with J. Lee Thompson's direction providing suspense throughout.

But this is not just a straightforward adventure yarn, and some of the film's characters display rather disturbing tendencies. Mallory is typical in that, far from being a conventional hero, he shows an alienating streak of ruthlessness. As he puts it, "The only way to win a war is to be as nasty as the enemy." In one scene he abandons the injured Franklin, knowing that when he is captured by the Germans, he will reveal to them a false account of the Allied plans under the influence of a truth drug.

During the film Mallory reveals that Stavrou has promised to kill him after the war following an incident in which he was inadvertently responsible for the deaths of Stavrou's wife and children. Miller, too, is given to frequent bouts of cynicism, while Brown appears unable to kill men face to face, traumatized by some deaths he has caused. The dramatic conflict between the characters gives the film added depth and complexity, though how much this is an anti-war film remains a matter of opinion. Certainly these mercenaries have a dark side that is distinctly anti-heroic and cynical. The 1978 film *Force 10 from Navarone* was an American-made sequel.

Two pictures from 1965 deal with attempts to destroy or retard parts of the German war machine. In 1944 and 1945 the people of London, and nearby counties, witnessed the terrifying destructiveness of Hitler's V1 and V2 rockets. Many thousands of these short-range ballistic missiles were fired at civilian areas, killing over 3,000 British civilians.

The only major film to explore this threat was *Operation Crossbow* (1965), directed by Michael Anderson, a fictionalized account of the countermeasures taken to deal with the rocket threat. As with his earlier classic, *The Dam Busters*, Anderson examines a technical operation carried out against fearsome odds, and that theme animates this production too.

Operation Crossbow is an engrossing account of how a small team of commandos managed to infiltrate the underground factory in Peenemunde that was producing the deadlier V2s. Using various cover identities, three specially selected commandos enter Holland en route for the factory, but almost immediately complications set in. It transpires that the identity of Robert Henshaw (Tom Courtenay) is that of a wanted murderer, and he is duly arrested by the Dutch police. He is released on condition he works for the Germans, only to then find himself interrogated by Bamford (Anthony Quayle). Bamford had earlier volunteered unsuccessfully for the project, but he turns out to be a German double agent. Henshaw is eventually tortured and shot for refusing to divulge his real identity. Then Nora (Sophia Loren), the wife of the man that U.S. Lieutenant John Curtis (George Peppard) is impersonating, arrives at his hotel just as the police are searching papers. She is eventually shot by the hotel owner, as she could have potentially compromised the mission. Eventually, Curtis and Phil Bradley (Jeremy Kemp) infiltrate the project and help British bombers destroy the factory, though at the cost of their own lives.

As in *The Dam Busters*, this film is sensitive to the tragic losses these operations entailed but never questions their necessity. We understand why Nora is shot, even if she is wholly innocent in the operation. The film is also noticeable for its scenes of high political intrigue, with sequences featuring Churchill (Patrick Wymark), his government minister Duncan Sandys, and his cantankerous advisor Frederick Lindemann (Trevor Howard).

Anthony Mann's *The Heroes of Telemark* (1965) is based on the true-life attempts by the Norwegian resistance to sabotage the German nuclear bomb program. A Norwegian resistance fighter, Knut Straud (Richard Harris), recruits a Norwegian nuclear expert, Professor Rolf Pedersen (Kirk Douglas), to destroy a heavy water factory. Heavy water is a vital component in the creation of an atomic bomb.

After carrying out a daring and successful raid, outwitting tight German security, they discover that the Germans have quickly rebuilt the factory and are planning to ship the heavy water back to Germany. Pedersen is caught but escapes his captors, eventually teaming up again with Straud, where they both plot to sink the ferry carrying the water back to Germany.

This is a thrilling drama with intense performances from Douglas and Harris. A number of sequences are visually impressive—the intrepid saboteurs skiing across the Norwegian snowscape, the clever use of shadows during the factory break in, and the finale with the blazing ferry. Throughout, the Norwegian resistance are cast as heroic underdogs who outwit the brutal Nazi occupiers. They too must "muddle through" with ingenious forms of subversion. That said, this adventure story lacks any "national" context. Unlike the resistance films of the '40s and '50s, we scarcely understand the culture or lifestyle that might induce a group of ordinary men to risk their lives to confront tyranny.

Whereas *The Heroes of Telemark* was based on real-life resistance, the Anglo-American *Where Eagles Dare* (1968) is entirely fictional. Based on the celebrated adventure novel by Alistair McLean, the story revolves around the daring rescue of a top-ranking American general from a German fortress in Bavaria. Major Smith (Richard Burton) and Schaffer (Clint Eastwood) lead the seven-man party, but their mission becomes ever more dangerous with the exposure of treachery in the highest places, and Smith's clever games of deceit and double bluff. In fact, the real mission is revealed to be the uncovering of German spies in Britain. The film is suspenseful throughout, enlivened by twists and turns, thrilling action sequences and a memorable score by Ron Goodwin. The production has all the hallmarks of a modern classic, though it does not pretend to make any serious comment on the war itself.

Battle of Britain (1969) is one of a number of war epics that tries to reconstruct a major event of the war, in this case the iconic battle between the RAF and the Luftwaffe in the summer of 1940. Harry Saltzman, producer of the Bond films, assembled a stellar British cast that included Michael Redgrave, Trevor Howard and Kenneth More, though Laurence Olivier stole the show as Air Chief Hugh Dowding. Despite its cast, this film never becomes a character study and centers instead on the air battles themselves. The close-up aerial sequences are visually impressive, though as the film is overly reliant on them, they become rather repetitive. Romantic subplots are few and far between in an attempt at pure filmic history.

On a superficial reading, the film might be seen to borrow from the mythology of 1940 in being a tribute to the "few," despite the multicultural slant that sees Polish and other nationalities represented among the pilots. Certainly this appears to have been the intention of director Guy Hamilton. Nonetheless, in an attempt at realism, the film moves away from the traditional narrative of earlier productions. Even though Dowding himself, played with consummate ease by Laurence Olivier, is a model of stoic restraint and maintains his composure even when the battle is going against Britain, the same is not always true of the pilots. In an attempt at realism, we see them display a broad range of quite realistic emotions, including fear, panic and anger, while the film highlights the squabbling over tactics from those on the ground. This gives the production greater credibility, but it also undermines the myth that was steadily built up around the few. Furthermore, by incorporating a German perspective, the film arguably lacks the emotional resonance of earlier tributes to the RAF.

The Eagle Has Landed (1977) was based on the Jack Higgins adventure novel and featured an all-star cast that included Michael Caine, Robert Duvall, Donald Sutherland and Donald Pleasence. It was the final film of Hollywood director John Sturges, whose memorable productions included *The Great Escape* and *The Magnificent Seven*. In some respects it mirrors *Went the Day Well?*, the wartime film about an imagined German takeover of an English village.

Here *Oberst* Kurt Steiner (Caine) leads a group of German commandoes, disguised as Polish parachutists, to infiltrate an English village in order to capture Winston Churchill and bring him to Germany. The plan is audacious and appears to be succeeding until one of the German commandos, after suffering a fatal accident, is revealed to be wearing a German uniform underneath his Polish clothes. Despite suffering this setback, Steiner escapes the village and manages to track down the wartime prime minister, only to find that when he shoots his target, it is an actor who has been hired to impersonate Churchill.

The film is tense and exciting, if over elaborate at times. It unfortunately suffers from poor casting, particularly Donald Sutherland as an unpredictable IRA loyalist, though Donald Pleasence stands out as Himmler. Sutherland would later feature in *The Eye of the Needle*, performing a chilling role as a Nazi agent desperate to send secrets about D-Day back to Germany.

The film is troubling because it forces the audience to empathize with the German unit to the point where, as *The Sun* put it, "you finish up wishing the Germans had won."[13] They become, like Van Der Poel in *Ice Cold in Alex*, "the moral and dramatic heroes of the piece."[14] This is achieved in two ways. First, the film sets them against an incompetent American colonel, played by Larry Hagman, who is eager for glory. His reckless tactics lead to his unit being decimated, demonstrating the superiority and discipline of the German paratroopers. Secondly, the film questions the evil of the German soldiers. Early in the movie, Steiner witnesses Jews being herded onto cattle trucks and rebukes an SS officer for this "senseless slaughter." One sympathizes at once with him, particularly when he is punished by being sent to the Channel Islands. Even the roguish IRA loyalist Devlin (Sutherland) has his more likeable side, and his anti–British rants echo the anti-imperialism of the day.

Towards the end of the 1970s there were a number of bigger budget wartime films, many Anglo-American, including *Escape to Athena*, *Hanover Street* and *Yanks*. Some have an explicit focus on wartime romances, in particular John Schlesinger's *Yanks* (1979), which features a trio of American servicemen enjoying romantic and sexual liaisons with English women in a northern town. *Hanover Street* (1979) too features a romantic entanglement between an American pilot, played by Harrison Ford, and a British nurse who happens to be married to a secret agent. The period was rounded off by *The Sea Wolves* (1980), featuring a group of ageing men from the Calcutta Light Horse, led by SOE officers, who are asked to destroy a German merchant ship in neutral Portuguese territory. It featured a stellar cast of British performers, including Trevor Howard, David Niven and Roger Moore.

However, the film which arguably stole the show was *A Bridge Too Far* (1977), perhaps the most ambitious British attempt at reconstructing wartime events on celluloid. Richard Attenborough assembled a glittering international cast in this epic recreation of Operation Market Garden, an audacious Allied attempt to end the war quickly by capturing the Arnhem bridge in Holland. An earlier treatment of this famous battle had been provided by Brian Desmond Hurst in *Theirs Is the Glory* (1946). But that post war production was far from being a spectacular, big-budget epic. It eschewed studio sets and professional actors, interspersing documentary footage with reconstructions of key battle scenes.

In some ways *A Bridge Too Far* shares a thematic affinity with war movies of the 1950s: a group of brave and stoic men rallying together against the odds in an attempt to secure wartime objectives. But unlike those films, and most of the war epics, this one has an unhappy conclusion. For Market Garden was a doomed affair almost from the start. The Allies had not reckoned on the strength of the Wehrmacht, particularly the Panzer SS divisions stationed at Arnhem, while communication problems and poor weather further hampered the operation.

As a result, the British 1st Airborne Division suffers terrible losses throughout the film, and its soldiers are a battered remnant by the end. The picture is a testament to their courage, albeit in an operation that was ultimately futile. The film received a hostile response in the U.S., hardly surprising in that it attempted to display the inadequacies of an Allied operation, and one set within the context of a British-American race to reach Berlin.

Despite occasional attempts to recapture the heroic conventions of earlier movies, particularly in *A Bridge Too Far* and *Operation Crossbow*, the films of the 1960s and 1970s are largely marked by an aversion to conflict and a deep-rooted skepticism towards rank and authority. Their lead characters are often highly flawed, dangerous individualists who exude a total indifference towards patriotic objectives. But the films of this period were a subtle reflection of a changing zeitgeist and altered perspectives on the war.

Chapter 13

The Dominance of Narcissism: British War Films from the 1980s and Beyond

A Bridge Too Far was the last major British war epic and perhaps the last attempt at a genuinely traditional war film. From the 1980s onwards, the war would continue to be addressed by filmmakers in Britain, but the narrative emphasis was subtly shifting. Instead of focusing on military or naval battles, reconstructions of major events or hagiographical profiles of military figures, the war would now become a backdrop to wider stories of human relationships and sexual intrigue.

Literary adaptations, for so long a staple of the British film industry, would become an ubiquitous feature of the modern war genre. These included such classics as Michael Ondaatje's *The English Patient*, Angela Huth's *The Land Girls* and Ian McEwan's *Atonement*, as well as two films based on the plays of David Hare (*Licking Hitler* and *Plenty*). Some of these films, in particular the Hare productions, are shaped by a strong anti–Establishment political ideology that is very much in keeping with the left-wing zeitgeist of the 1980s. But in many of these productions one can also discern very modern conceptions of national identity.

Ideas about nationhood, national character and national identity are thought to have taken a radical shift with the advent of Thatcherism in the 1980s. In some ways, Thatcher had sought to tap into the mythology of 1940 with its familiar traditional stereotypes of Englishness. Her attempt to restore patriotic pride in the nation was symbolized, above all, by Britain's surging victory in the 1982 Falklands War. The Prime Minister made several attempts to invoke national character, as in one postwar speech where she declared, with a Churchillian flourish: "We also fought alone—for we fought for our own people and for our own sovereign territory…. This generation can match their fathers and grandfathers in ability, in courage, and in resolution."[1] In a speech in 1992, she specifically evoked the image of a British underdog taking on Argentina against "impossible odds" and "the unbroken spirit" of the British "which lives on."[2]

Yet today the Thatcher experiment is associated above all with economic individualism and capitalism, the celebration of individual aspiration freed from the fetters of the state. Her policies of de-industrialization, privatization and deregulation were designed to empower communities and release them from the perceived harmful effects of state dependency. Self-reliance, that most important of Victorian values, became the new buzzword in her administration. In a now infamous interview from 1987, she decried the notion that government could ever solve society's problems. Talking of society, she declared, "There is no such thing! There are individual men and women and there are families, and no government can do anything except through people and people look to themselves first."[3]

Yet to blame Thatcher for the decline in national identity is to miss the point. In many ways her government's stress on individualism simply exacerbated trends that had been put in place in the 1960s. As cultural historian Richard Weight observed, "The cultural revolution of the 1960s had also been a celebration of individualism, entrepreneurial zeal and hedonism, though its movers and shakers dressed up their aspirations in prettier clothes and nicer politics."[4]

Despite her attempts to stir memories of 1940 and the national character that won the war, she could not shift three decades of economic and social changes that had fundamentally altered how the British perceived themselves. Society was becoming more atomized, more attuned to notions of individual rights and unfettered aspiration than perhaps ever before. This was an age of increasing narcissism.

From the 1990s onwards, this narcissistic ideology was influenced by a radical culture of human rights which elevated the needs of individuals to supreme importance. This was given rocket fuel by the Human Rights Act (2000), as well as various forms of equalities legislation that sought to entrench through law the fundamental entitlements of all individuals. Once such rights would have been balanced by responsibilities and duties, as well as the sacred promises and covenants made to others. Now such constraints (whether from the nation state, the church or the traditional family) were viewed as coercive and illiberal precisely because they stood in the way of individual freedom and lifestyle choice.

Militant advocates of human rights decried any notion that one culture deserved promotion, or that any individual was expected to have such "stifling" ties of obligation. Entrenched national narratives with their associated patriotism were the polar opposite of universal values, which promised a kind of utopian redemption to those who embraced them. Citizens had to embrace global values in the new age of ethical individualism.[5] Any institution promoting one lifestyle choice above another (i.e., the church promoting heterosexuality over gay marriage) was seen as fundamentally oppressive to the individual. Instead, non-judgmentalism and individualism became the order of the day.

The icons of popular culture too were changing. Whereas once the heroes of a younger generation were great soldiers, explorers and thinkers defined by a code of chivalry, they were now more likely to be the products of a shallow celebrity culture[6] whose lives were so often blighted by crime, drug abuse and sex scandals. Such individuals eschewed responsible lifestyle choices; indeed, their defiance of authority was often the hallmark of their popularity. This was the polar opposite of sexual and emotional restraint.

The cult of narcissism necessarily implied a weakening of those structures and institutions that once acted as a break on reckless impulses and anti-social behavior. The erosion of the traditional family, in part a consequence of welfare policy and changes in divorce law, was undermining the structures of moral authority that once regulated the behavior of the young. The result of such family breakdown was spiraling crime, educational failure, drug abuse and alienation among the young.

Indeed, authority in all its forms was coming under attack. Various scandals in recent decades had undermined the judiciary, the police and our political class, while the church, once a bastion of the moral order, had all but retreated from public life. The notion of "child centered" learning had progressively weakened the status of teachers and encouraged more liberal methods of discipline. Allied to this was an emerging cult of victimhood, according to which individuals were no longer primarily responsible for their misdemeanors. Instead, they were the victims of wider ills within society, whether exclusion, poverty or injustice. Within such a cult of victimhood, personal responsibility to others was shunned. Individual identity and fulfillment were all that mattered and all that the state and society had a duty to protect. It is an idea that the Victorian moralizers would have found most alienating.

But if any one modern event came to symbolize a departure from older, more traditional values, it was the national reaction to the death of Princess Diana in 1997. In life, Diana had been somewhat of a romantic rebel, a woman who decried and defied the Establishment. Now in death she was transformed into the "People's Princess," a woman whose common touch, emotional instincts and modern outlook offered an alternative to the Royal Family's formality and stuffiness.

In the week leading up to the funeral, tabloid emotion reached heights of hysteria almost unparalleled in modern Britain. There were somewhat totalitarian demands for the Queen to "show us she cared" and for the Royal Family to "bow to public pressure to show its grief." The *Sunday Mirror* spoke of a nation "suffering grievously," demanding by implication that Diana's relatives do the same in public. When the Royal Family did visit London, *The Sunday Times* declared, "The Palace bows to the People's Will."[7] Touchy-feely "Dianamania" was suddenly in the ascendant.

Not surprisingly, this outpouring of public emotion was viewed by some as a rebirth of national identity. Journalists talked of "the new British spirit," of Britain "reshaping itself" and how we were no longer "a nation known for its stiff upper lip."[8] All this was gratefully seized upon by a Labor administration which was desperately trying to rebrand Britain as a "young country." What the reaction to her death told us was that the old values of dutiful service, stoicism and emotional restraint were increasingly seen by a modern generation as a curious relic of a bygone age. In its place was a new ethic of hedonism, public emoting, and individualism.

Of course, there was still a powerful generational divide when it came to perceptions of national character. For many, Britain was still the land of composure, chivalry, emotional repression, inhibition and good humor. Some of the earlier values that had come to define Britishness, most especially understated humor and the love of the underdog, had survived the cultural revolution of the 1960s, and Britons remained as obsessed as ever by class and social positioning. Not everything had so obviously changed. But the new wave of values reverberating from the 1960s would nonetheless come to be reflected in many of Britain's contemporary war films.

In the early 1980s, two films based on plays by David Hare, *Rainy Day Women* and *Plenty*, offered disturbing and fresh perspectives on wartime experience. Before that, it is worth mentioning Hare's *Licking Hitler* (1978) for its exposé of the purportedly darker side of the British wartime experience. In that production, Anna (Kate Nelligan), a slightly naïve young woman from an upper class background, is recruited to work for a black propaganda unit that spreads malicious rumors across Germany. One rumor put forth is that blood transfusions are unsafe because the blood is non–Aryan and likely to carry syphilis. When she objects to these propaganda techniques, she is told by Archie (who leads this unit) that the British are only copying the tactics of that "great genius" Joseph Goebbels. Britain must serve its soldiers in the way that Goebbels served Germany, and if that means "covering the whole continent in obloquy and filth, then that is what we shall do."

David Hare had developed a reputation for being a scourge of the Establishment. In a recent interview he described how, in the sixties and seventies, he "had an apocalyptic feeling" about "the contradictions between what this country was pretending to be, the fantasy of influence and power ... [and] the reality of how things were around them."[9] *Licking Hitler* was designed to be an apt metaphor for the descent into corruption that Hare believes characterized Britain in the postwar years.

These themes also characterize *The Imitation Game* (1980), where a lower-middle-class 19-year-old Cathy Raine (Harriet Walter) decides to join the ATS in order to help the war effort. But she becomes disillusioned with the work and seeks respite in a pub with another girl. After an altercation with the barman, who objects to women being present in his pub, she is dispatched to Bletchley Park in order to carry out menial activities. She meets a mathematical don, Turner (Nicholas Le Provost), whom she eventually sleeps with. But Turner, presumably a repressed homosexual, accuses her of humiliating him, and when he finds her perusing military documents, her fate is sealed. She is incarcerated in a military prison for the rest of the war, exacerbating her sense of isolation.

Rainy Day Women (1984), another of the "Plays for Today," charts the way in which war hysteria allows people to descend into outright cruelty against the innocent. A Dunkirk veteran, John Truman, is sent by the MOI to the sleepy village of Darton to investigate rumors of possible spies. But the women who come under suspicion are innocent land girls, their alleged radio transmitter being nothing more than an electrolysis machine for removing hair. They are tortured and killed by members of the Home Guard, who are pictured as paranoid and depraved, leading the villagers to hush up the affair. Like *Licking Hitler*, this is a blatant attempt to highlight the darker and more cynical side of war. Yet in its scarcely subtle critique of war as a collective betrayal of decent values, it becomes too simplistic and black and white to be taken seriously. What makes this, and the other two productions, so disturbing is the sense that evil has triumphed and wrongdoing has been covered up. There is no satisfying closure here, and one is left to think that moral degradation overwhelmingly characterized wartime Britain.

One theme of the postwar interlude was the danger of ex-servicemen falling into a life of crime and destitution. The notion that war provided a sense of meaning now lacking in peacetime is taken up in *Plenty* (1985), based on another Hare play. Meryl Streep gives an unforgettable performance as an ex–French Resistance fighter struggling to come to terms with the realities of the postwar world. After the war she finds work in the worlds of business and diplomacy, and later marries an upper class diplomat. But gradually she goes into emotional decline, both from her inability to have children and her generally loveless marriage. Her sexual frustration is compounded by the fact that during the war she experienced an intense one-night stand with a young soldier (Sam Neill) which remains etched in her memory. Nothing can quite fill the void left by the excitement and purpose that the French Resistance provided, and the sexual satisfaction she once enjoyed.

Illicit, doomed love affairs feature in two films of the period, *Another Time, Another Place* (1983) and *The Eye of the Needle* (1981). Whereas the conflict is central to the latter, in that a German spy, played quite chillingly by Donald Sutherland, tries to warn the Germans that the Allies intend to land in Normandy for the 1944 Allied invasion, it plays an almost peripheral role in the former. *Another Time, Another Place* explores the relationship between a married Scotswoman, Janie (Phyllis Logan), and a womanizing Italian prisoner of war, Luigi (Giovanni Mauriello), one of a group of POWs that she has befriended. She is initially repelled by the Italian's amorous advances, and it seems obvious that she is more likely to fall for either of his co-patriots, Umberto or Paolo.

But slowly their relationship deepens when she sympathizes with his growing isolation and loneliness in the cold Scottish wasteland. Suddenly pity gives way to desire, and a sexual encounter results. The lovemaking is explosive, standing in contrast to the dull, mechanical sex that Janie has with her husband. Luigi allows Janie to feel an exhilarating sense of sexual satisfaction and to escape from the restraints of her tightknit, claustrophobic community. At the end, Luigi is falsely accused of rape, and Janie tries desperately to clear his name, sacrificing her marriage and reputation in the process. There is an unmistakable absence of the stiff upper lip here, and the restraint of desire that goes with it. What matters is her quest for liberating emotional fulfillment, even if this means illicit liaisons with the enemy. The distinction between nationalities has become a blur in her quest to break free from stifling relationships.

Perhaps the most original war film of the 1980s is John Boorman's *Hope and Glory* (1987). The film offers a semi-autobiographical account of war as seen through the eyes of a young child living in suburban London, and its strength lies in how well it captures a sense of youthful innocence. When Clive (David Hayman) is posted to Cumberland for wartime duties, his wife Grace (Sarah Miles) is left to look after 8-year-old Bill Rowan (Sebastian Rice Edwards) and his teenage sister. Bill's daily routine largely revolves around school, but in his spare time he engages in pranks with friends and scours through bomb wreckage in his neighborhood. He revels in the nightly air raids because they leave much-prized pieces of shrapnel in the garden. He witnesses his sister kissing a Canadian soldier but fails to fully comprehend its significance. He is joyful when his school is bombed because it will enable him to have more fun by the river.

Hope and Glory quite consciously distances itself from the traditional narratives of the past. Indeed, at one point it conflates Britain's war effort with

Sue and Bill Rowan (Geraldine Muir and Sebastian Rice-Edwards, in foreground) experience the thrills and fascination of the Blitz in *Hope and Glory* (1987). This is war from a child's perspective (Columbia Pictures, Photofest).

her imperial ambitions, as when Bill's schoolteacher tells his class, "What fraction of the earth's surface is British? Two-fifths. And that's what the war is all about. Men are fighting and dying to save all the pink bits for you ungrateful twerps."

There is no sentimental treatment of the family's endurance under fire, no celebration of English pluckiness and stoicism. This is all about youthful exuberance and what war might plausibly look like from a child's perspective. It is about Bill Rowan's freedom to roam around his bombed neighborhood without social constraint or disapproval. It is about the Blitz as a welcome distraction from the tedium of school life. It is about war as a youthful adventure in which death and destruction are never imminent. The perspective is refreshingly original and "unabashedly subjective,"[10] but it may be disconcerting for an earlier generation reared on the iconic memories of 1940.

Over the next two decades the British film industry produced a small number of carefully crafted literary adaptations where the war served as a backdrop to stories of human interest and romance. *The English Patient* (1996) is a hauntingly beautiful version of the award-winning novel by Michael Ondaatje. Towards the end of the Second World War, a young nurse in a Tuscan villa looks after a horribly burned and anonymous man who sustained severe injuries in a plane crash. At the start we know little about this enigmatic figure, beyond his love of Herodotus, whose *Histories* he has lovingly annotated. Gradually the pieces of his enthralling life are pieced together. Prompted by other visitors to the villa (Kip, an Indian Sikh in the British army, and Caravaggio, a Canadian spy), the "English" patient reveals that he is actually a Hungarian desert explorer called László Almásy.

During the 1930s he was accompanied on his missions by an English gentleman, Geoffrey Clinton, and his wife Katherine, with their plane aiding the Hungarian on his cartographical expeditions. Almásy falls in love with Katherine, and they begin an intense affair which she later breaks off. When war breaks out, they must move camp, and Geoffrey offers to fly Almásy out. But the betrayed husband has discovered the illicit affair and, in a fit of rage, tries to kill all three of them by crashing his plane. He dies in the ensuing crash and leaves his wife and the Hungarian severely injured. Almásy leaves Katherine in a cave and tries to get help, only to be caught by the British as a suspected spy. After escaping and then agreeing to help a German spy cross to Cairo, he flies over the cave to collect Katherine's body, only to be shot down again and suffer horrific injuries.

The English Patient is far more than an elegant tale of romance. It is about loyalty and betrayal, guilt and redemption, and the timeless and ultimately destructive power of love. Guided by Anthony Minghella's fluent direction, the film is complex and multi-layered, featuring a series of enigmatic characters who are masterfully portrayed onscreen. The cinematography too is breathtaking, with the audience left to admire the ravishing landscape of the North African desert.

But, as in *Hope and Glory*, the conflict itself forms the backdrop to a larger human story. Patriotism has no place here, for Almásy has erased his identity; he belongs to no nation. Perhaps that is why we are drawn to sympathize with him when he aids the Axis powers, for we know that this execrable action is the only way he can reach his beloved. In its handling of war, love and relationships, and particularly in the overriding triumph of romantic needs over selfless duty, *The English Patient* feels thoroughly conventional.

So too does *The End of the Affair* (1999), an impressive remake of the 1955 film based on the famous Graham Greene novel. (The original starred Deborah Kerr, Van Johnson and John Mills.) Ralph Fiennes stars as novelist Maurice Bendrix, who, during the Second World War, had a passionate affair with Sarah Miles (Julianne Moore), the wife of his best friend Henry (Stephen Rea). The affair is broken off in 1944, following a raid in which he nearly dies, but after the war he hires a private detective to follow Sarah in an attempt to rekindle their relationship. Later, she reveals to him why she broke off the affair. During the bombing raid, she assumed he had died, and in her despair

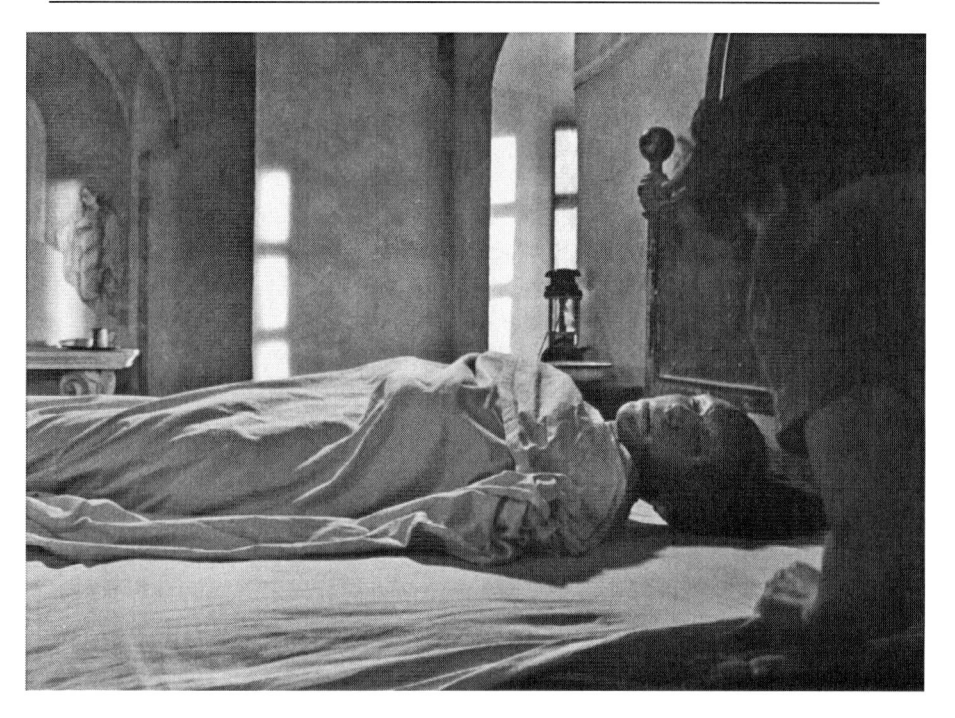

The haunting image of *The English Patient* (1996), László Almásy (Ralph Fiennes). He belongs to no nation, only to his beloved Katherine (Miramax Films, Photofest).

she made a promise to God that if he survived, she would never see him again. However, after the war, when he tracks her down, she tells him that she can no longer keep her promise to God.

It is a compelling and tragic story of love and obsession, with a religious dimension not found in other war dramas. The film is cleverly edited, with flashbacks of the affair set against the present day concerns of Maurice and Henry. Fiennes has a charm and intensity to suit the role, while Moore has never been more voluptuous; both are skillfully directed by Neil Jordan. As in *The English Patient*, Fiennes plays a tortured soul who has destroyed the sacred covenant of marriage for illicit personal lust.

David Leland's *The Land Girls* (1998) is a paean to the work of the Woman's Land Army, a name given to the many female volunteers who worked on farms to replace men who had gone to war. A trio of such volunteers descend on a farm belonging to the overworked Mr. Lawrence (Tom Georgeson). Stella (Catherine McCormack), Ag (Rachel Weisz) and Prue (Anna Friel) hail from different class backgrounds yet manage to form a lasting camaraderie under the strains of war. They all fall for the handsome Joe, played by Steven Mackintosh, a farm laborer who sleeps with all three but falls in love with Stella.

One of the film's themes is that of unrequited ambition. Joe is frustrated because his dreams of becoming an air force pilot are dashed by his heart problems. Stella turns down Joe for her fiancée, whom she later marries and then divorces, while Mr. Lawrence is heartbroken when his beloved farmland is ploughed under for the war effort. There is a conflict between love and duty, romantic attachment and the overriding needs of the war. It is a beautifully filmed and visually appealing production, with some enchanting performances by the three women.

The Brylcreem Boys (1998), directed by Terence Ryan, is a light-hearted account of life in an Irish prisoner of war camp. Two pilots, Miles Keogh (Billy Campbell) and Rudolph von Stegenbek (Angus MacFadyen), bail out of their stricken planes over Ireland, only to find themselves arrested and interned under Ireland's strict neutrality laws. Both men discover to their horror that the camp houses Allied and German servicemen, with both existing in a state of mutual animosity. Miles meets and falls in love with Mattie, played by Jean Butler, before discovering, to his chagrin, that she is the object of Rudolph's attentions. Eventually both men escape the clutches of their Irish captors after an audacious breakout.

But this has little in common with earlier POW productions and their celebration of the underdog spirit. There are occasional scraps between the Allied and German prisoners of war, their mindless brawling providing some compensation for their being detached from the war. But the prime battle between Miles and Rudolph is over the affections of the beautiful Mattie. Such is the bond that develops between them that Miles saves Rudolph's life when he is about to be killed by his co-patriots, and he helps him escape. When the two do eventually escape, Irish Commandant O'Brien (Gabriel Bryne) smiles, as he knows that the escapees will be recaptured the following day. This is not the "backs against the wall" stuff of *The Colditz Story*, and the film refuses to take itself that seriously.

The movie is marred by ineffectual characterizations, with the Germans portrayed as unthinking, robotic and humorless. Yet it is also enlivened by flashes of humor, such as a scene where British prisoners engage in a send-up of the Germans on parade. That and the appealing cinematography make this a fairly engaging production which sheds light on one of the less familiar aspects of the wartime experience.

In the early 2000s there was British involvement in a number of productions focusing on various aspects of the Second World War. *The Gathering Storm*, a made-for-TV production, offers a rounded and sometimes amusing portrait of Winston Churchill in his "Wilderness years" as a Conservative backbench MP. Albert Finney and Vanessa Redgrave are peerless as Mr. and Mrs. Churchill, with performances worthy of mention from Jim Broadbent

(Desmond Morton), Derek Jacobi (Stanley Baldwin) and Ronnie Barker (Churchill's butler, Inches). A sequel, *Into the Storm*, was made in 2009.

Some films dealt with the harrowing reality of the Holocaust, most notably *The Diary of Anne Frank*, *The Boy in the Striped Pyjamas* and *Charlotte Grey*. The largely British *The Boy in the Striped Pyjamas* (2008) breaks new ground by presenting the Holocaust from a child's perspective. In the film, Bruno (Asa Butterfield), the son of an SS officer who has been newly appointed to be a commandant of an extermination camp, strikes up a friendship with Shmuel, a young Jewish child in a nearby extermination camp. Bruno is a curious and disobedient child, and seeks the companionship of a fellow child. He forges a friendship with Shmuel, bringing him food and playing games with him on a regular basis.

When Shmuel reveals disturbing details about the camp, in particular that he has been imprisoned because he is Jewish, Bruno decides to enter it secretly and dress up in camp uniform. By having Bruno disregard his father's anti–Semitic propaganda, the film provides an effective contrast between his own youthful innocence and the growing fanaticism of his father and sister. The picture has a harrowing ending, as both Shmuel and Bruno (now mistaken for a Jewish child) are herded into a gas chamber for extermination, while Bruno's mother, suspecting that her son has entered the camp, wails in agony outside. While this film sheds no light on Britishness per se, it is invaluable for highlighting this most tragic part of the war.

Enigma (2001) offers a much deserved tribute to the code-breakers of Bletchley Park, a group whose story could not be told for decades due to the secrecy surrounding the project. It focuses on attempts by cryptanalysts in 1943 to crack a new German code prior to a huge U-boat attack on an Allied convoy. But the task is complicated by the sudden disappearance of a worker, Claire Romilly (Saffron Burrows). Claire is suspected of being a German mole passing vital secrets to the enemy, and a hunt for her ensues, both from her jilted lover and an MI5 agent, played by Jeremy Northam.

It later transpires that Claire discovered evidence of the Kaytn massacre of 1943, when thousands of Polish officers were murdered by the Soviets, as well as a subsequent cover-up by British intelligence. After a series of twists and turns, we discover that the real traitor was a Polish analyst (and Claire's lover) who, incensed by the massacre, was preparing to offer the Germans vital intelligence in revenge for the atrocity. *Enigma* is a fascinating film, bristling with multiple stories of deception and betrayal. Its exposé of British perfidy in covering up the Katyn massacre is somewhat reminiscent of Hare's anti-establishment plays of the 1980s. For all its heroic accolades to the code-breakers, the film's most compelling image is of Polish bodies lying in mass graves.

Charlotte Grey (2001), based on the Sebastian Faulks novel, traces the wartime career of a female SOE agent, played by Cate Blanchett, who served with the French resistance during World War II. The character has been taken to represent any number of actual agents, the most famous of whom were portrayed in films such as *Odette* and *Carve Her Name with Pride*. But this is not a straightforward case of fighting for the sake of patriotism. She enlists to help the French resistance at least in part because the man she has fallen in love with, Peter Gregory (Rupert Penry-Jones), has been captured there. When she is told by another member of the resistance that "Nobody fights for their country, they fight for their family, for someone they love," she scarcely demurs.

Once again, the pursuit of love and the triumph of affection are cloaked in duty and self-sacrifice. When she is told that he died in France, she is left heartbroken and distracted from her activities. But her alienation deepens further when she thinks that some members of the resistance may have been betrayed because they were communist, and also when she is unable to save two Jewish children that she was hiding from deportation. War, she later admits, "makes fools of us all." At the end she finds out that Gregory has survived the war, and they are later reunited. But when they meet again she is unable to resume their relationship and admits that he had been right to warn her against traveling to France earlier in the war. There is a strain of cynicism here that can be found in many an earlier production.

Two Men Went to War (2002) is a curious and somewhat whimsical film, based on a true story about two soldiers from the army dental corps who undertook a private and unauthorized mission to occupied France. They sail over the Channel on a stolen vessel, launching a series of raids against German targets, before returning home to face a court martial. The pair are loveable eccentrics in the best traditions of English comedy, and the movie has a light-hearted feel throughout.

This is a film enlivened by comic interludes in which bravery and pluck are not taken seriously. When they arrive, they are shown running along an unguarded section of the French coast to the sound of "Run, rabbit, run." At one moment Private Cuthbertson (Leo Bill) is held at gunpoint inside a French house, only to receive romantic attentions from his female captor, much to the chagrin of Sergeant King (Kenneth Cranham). At another, the two soldiers engage in a ferocious quarrel while, unbeknownst to them, German tanks roll through the fields close by. Instead of attacking a German operations room, they end up destroying the cook house, though it creates a diversion from an actual British operation in the area. They are continually stumbling upon enemy positions and seem to confuse the Germans as much as themselves.

This harks back to the comic-subversive style of the '70s, with elements of *Dad's Army* and *How I Won the War*. Enjoyable as it is, there is very little to turn this into a serious treatment of war.

One of the most significant films of the decade was *Atonement* (2007), based on the acclaimed novel by Ian McEwan. This is a beautifully filmed romantic drama about two tragic lovers whose lives are permanently altered after a mistaken accusation. The originality of its narrative devices, its artistic qualities and superb acting really give this film the feel of a modern classic.

The first part of *Atonement* focuses on life at a country estate in the 1930s. 13-year-old Briony Tallis (Saoirse Ronan), who harbors dreams of becoming a novelist, witnesses an erotic encounter between her older sister Cecilia (Keira Knightley) and a servant's son, Robbie Turner (James McAvoy), a man on whom Briony has a crush. Partly through misunderstanding and partly through jealousy, she begins to harbor suspicions about Robbie, believing that he had raped Cecilia. Later that evening she discovers that her cousin Lola has been raped and claims to have seen Robbie running away from the scene. The police believe her accusation, and Robbie is sent to prison, with Cecilia now estranged from her family.

In the next part of the film, Robbie is released from prison on condition that he serves in France. He has a fleeting meeting with Cecilia in London before he joins up with the 1st Battalion of the Royal Sussex regiment. He later arrives at Dunkirk, gravely ill and awaiting evacuation. Meanwhile, Briony, now fully understanding the gravity of her false accusations, has given up on the chance to go to Cambridge and opted instead to look after wounded French soldiers. Later, Briony decides to visit her sister, seeking forgiveness, and with a revelation about who really carried out the rape. But neither Cecilia nor Robbie, now reunited, will forgive her for what she did as a child.

In the third part of the film, the dying Briony, played masterfully by Vanessa Redgrave, gives an interview in which she reveals that she has completed her final novel, *Atonement*. She reveals that the encounter with Cecilia and Robbie in London never took place. This is because months earlier Robbie had died at Dunkirk from his illness, while in London her sister was one of the victims of the Balham tube disaster. Thus, in reuniting them in fiction, she is giving them the life they never had and attempting to atone for her past misdeeds. Like *The English Patient*, this film contains grandiose, haunting imagery, including a lengthy, continuous shot of the beach at Dunkirk.

In *Atonement* there is an implicit critique of the class system in the 1930s. Cecilia is forced to keep her romance with a servant's son hidden from her family, and that same family abandons Robbie to his fate. But there is also an implied critique of war too. When we see the dying Frenchman tended by Briony, or Robbie succumbing to disease at Dunkirk, there is little suggestion of heroic sacrifice. The war has deprived these men of their opportunity for romantic fulfillment and thus appears to be a futile enterprise which can never redeem its victims. One of Robbie's companions even jokes about giving Germany Europe because "Britain's got Africa," a subtle poke at imperialism that seems to fit well with an anti-colonialist zeitgeist.

While a few of the more modern war films, such as *Enigma*, suggest a return to more traditional formulas, there is a more subversive element in many others. The trio of Hare films question the role of authority in national life. A more fundamental theme in many others (*The English Patient, Another Time, Another Place, The End of the Affair, Atonement, Charlotte Gray*) is that it is right to question the older values of duty to the nation, self-sacrifice and stoicism. Romantic needs supersede national differences, and there is an emphasis on the power of individual expression and fulfillment. There is an unmistakable critique of the stiff upper lip and personal restraint here, and it is by no means confined to the modern war genre. It can also be found in a number of contemporary British heritage films, most particularly *Remains of the Day, Howard's End* and *Room with a View*.

In perhaps the greatest of these films, *Remains of the Day*, Anthony Hopkins plays Mr. Stevens, the highly efficient but emotionally repressed butler of Darlington Hall. Equal to him in the household hierarchy is Miss Kenton, played by Emma Thompson, who gradually develops feelings for the butler. But Stevens fails to respond to her warmth and concern, preferring to concentrate on professional matters of the household. He shows unquestioning loyalty to his master, Lord Darlington (James Fox), despite the fact that the latter is pursuing a controversial appeasement policy towards the Nazis. After the war, when Stevens is reunited with Miss Kenton, he begins to regret his earlier mistakes, though he is still unable to offer her any form of emotional attachment. Here, the stiff upper lip and a sense of duty are barriers to personal happiness and fulfillment.

The war films, like the heritage dramas just mentioned, reflect very modern notions of English (and British) national identity. They are subversive to the point of questioning duty, restraint and the stiff upper lip, and ultimately reflect the anti-establishment ethos of the '60s revolution. The war films, like those of other genres, have played some part in reflecting all the trends, values and ideas that have come to define modern Britain. But by the same token, they have surely helped to shape and legitimize them too.

Conclusion

The great new wave director Lindsay Anderson once described British cinema of the 1950s as "snobbish, emotionally inhibited, wilfully blind to the conditions of the present, dedicated to an out-of-date, exhausted national idea."[1] For many, Anderson's is an apt description of British war cinema as a whole, a genre whose output is often derided as a staid, unimaginative and absurdly patriotic tribute to the conflict. In caricature, British war films are dominated by a cavalcade of upper class officers who exude a stiff upper lip while dispensing reassuring *sang-froid* to the lower orders.

Yet it would be wrong to view all British war films this way. The British World War II war genre has evolved like every other, adapting to changes in historical circumstances and reflecting emerging social and cultural trends. It has strongly influenced, and been influenced by, prevailing notions of national identity and character since 1939, when the first war movies were being made. This is simply because, like almost all films, the war movies were designed for popular consumption, and, as Michael Paris says, "It is exactly this dependence upon a mass audience that makes films such a valuable reflection of popular opinion."[2]

Thus, throughout the 1940s and 1950s, war films were imbued with an ethos of social democracy, and emphasized emotional restraint, stoicism and duty. But the counter-cultural revolution of the 1960s, with its emphasis on immediate gratification and its corresponding attack on traditional values, put paid to the celebration of wartime glories. Old-fashioned "death and glory" heroics were held up to ridicule in *How I Won the War* and *Oh! What a Lovely War*.[3] Fundamentally, as perceptions of national identity shifted from one decade to the next, so too did the underlying ideology of war films. The most recent war movies, which offer tales of unrequited love and unfulfilled ambition, are an interesting reflection of our modern narcissistic culture.

How then can one understand the continuing fascination for the Second

World War, with its iconic ideology from 1940 (valiant underdogs, stoicism, restraint), and the fact that contemporary perceptions of national identity have altered so radically? The answer would appear to be that those iconic images, memories and myths matter to people of a certain generation who have reconstructed the war in precisely those terms.

While the war continues to be studied by young and old alike, it is less likely that the "myths" of the Blitz, Dunkirk or the few from 1940, with their invocation of English stoicism, duty and restraint, will be appreciated as much by a modern generation. Such behaviors are likely to be seen as outdated and outmoded, an anachronism in an age when emotional expression—indeed, expression of the most violent kind—has become the norm. It is not unfair to assume that a younger generation's fascination with World War II centers more on the military events themselves than the behavior of the national population under fire. For those of an older generation, by contrast, the heroic myths of 1940, and those additional events that signify the triumph of "muddling through," will continue to provide the definitive perspective on this conflict. And this is but one manifestation of the deep generational divide that exists in Britain today.

The radical shift in national identity does not necessarily mean that films about the war will dry up. Instead, they are likely to adapt to changing trends as well as the unique constraints that are imposed on British cinema. These constraints are evident the moment one takes a global perspective on the film industry. Hollywood continues to be the dominant force and, when it comes to the Second World War, has churned out big-budget blockbusters on an almost annual basis.

Saving Private Ryan (1998) dealt with the D-Day landings from a largely American perspective, with a stunningly filmed opening sequence showing young GIs being ripped apart by machine gun fire. *Stalingrad* (1993) and *Enemy at the Gates* (2001) both recreated the famous battle in 1942 in which hundreds of thousands of soldiers perished on both sides; while an equally epic blockbuster, *Pearl Harbor* (2001), examined the Japanese attack on the American fleet at Hawaii. Films such as the Oscar-winning *Schindler's List*, *Life Is Beautiful*, *Defiance* and *Jacob the Liar* dealt with the harrowing reality of the Holocaust. More recently, fresh perspectives on the war have been provided by *Australia* (which focuses on the bombing of Darwin in 1942), *Inglourious Basterds* (a Quentin Tarantino black comedy featuring a fictional plot to assassinate leading Nazis) and *Letters from Iwo Jima* (the battle told from a Japanese perspective). Many of these films are epic in scale, featuring dazzling technology and an impressive cast list.

During the same period, British cinema's contribution has been rather less noticeable. There have been no big-budget British combat movies to rival epics of the past like *Battle of Britain* or *A Bridge Too Far* (nevermind the all-star blockbusters made by Hollywood), and no large-scale recreations of the war's events told from a British perspective. But this is largely because the median budget for a British film stands at just £1.2 million (as of 2011). Despite the promised injection of £285,000,000 into the British film industry over the next five years,[4] it is clear that the British film industry simply lacks the resources to produce big-scale, spectacular war movies.[5] As a result, many recent movies have been collaborative efforts between a British and a foreign studio.

Thus British cinema has had to find its niche, and it appears to have done so by using the war as a backdrop to intriguing stories of relationships and romance, with military and political affairs usually in the background. Invariably these have been literary adaptations, in keeping with one of the great traditions of British cinema. This trend will surely continue for as long as the war remains an inspiration to writers, poets and playwrights.

One other thing is certain: for as long as films about the war reflect changing cultural trends in this country, they will continue to define what it means to be British for the wider world.

Chronological List of Films Covered

Documentaries

The First Days (1939)
London Can Take It (1940)
The Front Line (1940)
Island People (1940)
Christmas Under Fire (1941)
Spring Offensive (1940)
War and Order (1940)
Squadron 992 (1940)
From the Four Corners (1941)
Fires Were Started (1942)

Films

The Lion Has Wings (1939)
The Proud Valley (1940)
Convoy (1940)
Old Bill and Son (1940)
For Freedom (1940)
Pastor Hall (1940)
Sailors Three (1940)
Night Train to Munich (1940)
Contraband (1940)
Bulldog Sees It Through (1940)
Neutral Port (1940)
Ships with Wings (1941)
49th Parallel (1941)
Freedom Radio (1941)
Pimpernel Smith (1941)
The Prime Minister (1941)
This England (1941)
Lady Hamilton (1941)
Dangerous Moonlight (1941)
Crook's Tour (1941)
Secret Mission (1942)
Mrs. Miniver (1942)
The Foreman Went to France (1942)
Next of Kin (1942)
In Which We Serve (1942)
Unpublished Story (1942)
Salute John Citizen (1942)
Went the Day Well? (1942)
The First of the Few (1942)
The Big Blockade (1942)
One of Our Aircraft Is Missing (1942)
The Young Mr. Pitt (1942)
The Day Will Dawn (1942)
The Goose Steps Out (1942)
They Flew Alone (1942)
The Gentle Sex (1943)
The Silent Village (1943)
The Demi Paradise (1943)
They Met in the Dark (1943)

The Adventures of Tartu (1943)
The Bells Go Down (1943)
San Demetrio London (1943)
The Life and Death of Colonel Blimp (1943)
Nine Men (1943)
The Silver Fleet (1943)
Squadron Leader X (1943)
Yellow Canary (1943)
Millions Like Us (1943)
Warn That Man (1943)
Undercover (1943)
The Way Ahead (1944)
Henry V (1944)
A Canterbury Tale (1944)
Tawny Pipit (1944)
Two Thousand Women (1944)
For Those in Peril (1944)
This Happy Breed (1944)
The Way to the Stars (1945)
The Captive Heart (1946)
Night Boat to Dublin (1946)
Theirs Is the Glory (1946)
School for Secrets (1946)
Frieda (1947)
They Made Me a Fugitive (1947)
Night Beat (1948)
Portrait from Life (1948)
The Flamingo Affair (1948)
Against the Wind (1948)
But Not in Vain (1948)
Landfall (1949)
Silent Dust (1949)
Small Back Room (1949)
The Lost People (1949)
Landfall (1949)
Cage of Gold (1950)
Odette (1950)
They Were Not Divided (1950)
The Wooden Horse (1950)
Appointment with Venus (1951)
Angels One Five (1952)

Appointment in London (1952)
Malta Story (1953)
The Cruel Sea (1953)
Albert RN (1953)
The Intruder (1953)
The Sea Shall Not Have Them (1954)
The Purple Plain (1954)
They Who Dare (1954)
The Colditz Story (1955)
The Ship That Died of Shame (1955)
Cockleshell Heroes (1955)
The Dam Busters (1955)
Above Us the Waves (1955)
The Man Who Never Was (1956)
A Town Like Alice (1956)
Battle of the River Plate (1956)
Reach for the Sky (1956)
Ill Met by Moonlight (1957)
The Bridge on the River Kwai (1957)
I Was Monty's Double (1958)
Dunkirk (1958)
Carve Her Name with Pride (1958)
Ice Cold in Alex (1958)
Sea of Sand (1958)
The Camp on Blood Island (1958)
Orders to Kill (1958)
The Two Headed Spy (1958)
Operation Amsterdam (1959)
Yesterday's Enemy (1959)
Sink the Bismarck! (1960)
The Long and the Short and the Tall (1961)
The Guns of Navarone (1961)
The War Lover (1962)
633 Squadron (1964)
It Happened Here (1964)
The Hill (1965)
The Heroes of Telemark (1965)
Operation Crossbow (1965)
Joey Boy (1965)
How I Won the War (1967)
The Long's Day Dying (1968)

Chronological List of Films Covered

Where Eagles Dare (1968)
Battle of Britain (1969)
Play Dirty (1969)
Overlord (1975)
Cross of Iron (1977)
The Eagle Has Landed (1977)
A Bridge Too Far (1977)
Licking Hitler (1978)
Yanks (1979)
Hanover Street (1979)
The Sea Wolves (1980)
The Imitation Game (1980)
Another Time, Another Place (1983)
Rainy Day Women (1984)
Plenty (1985)
Hope and Glory (1987)
The English Patient (1996)
The Brylcreem Boys (1998)
The Land Girls (1998)
The End of the Affair (1999)
Enigma (2001)
Charlotte Grey (2001)
Two Men Went to War (2002)
Atonement (2007)
The Boy in the Striped Pyjamas (2008)

Chapter Notes

Introduction

1. John Whiteclay Chambers and David Holbrook Culbert, eds., *World War II, Film, and History* (New York: Oxford University Press, 1996), 4.
2. Philip M. Taylor, "Introduction: Film, the Historian and the Second World War," in *Britain and the Cinema in the Second World War*, ed. Philip M. Taylor (Basingstoke: Macmillan, 1998), 1.
3. Sarah Street, *British National Cinema* (London: Routledge, 1997), 119.
4. Grahame Allen and Joe Hicks, "A Century of Change: Trends in UK Statistics Since 1900," Research Paper 99/111, House of Commons Library, 21 December 1999, accessed 10 December, 2011, www.parliament.uk/commons/lib/research/rp99/rp99-111.pdf.
5. James Chapman, *British at War: Cinema, State and Propaganda, 1939–1945* (London: I. B. Tauris, 1998), 1.
6. Charles Drazin, *Korda: Britain's Movie Mogul* (New York: I.B. Tauris, 2011), 236.
7. Susan Hayward, *Cinema Studies: The Key Concepts* (London: Routledge, 2000), 192.
8. Raymond Durgnat, *A Mirror for England: British Movies from Austerity to Affluence* (London: BFI, 2011), 8.
9. Sir Ernest Barker, *National Character and the Factors in Its Formation* (London: Methuen, 1927), 8.
10. S. P. Mackenzie, *The Battle of Britain on Screen: "The Few" in British Film and Television Drama* (Edinburgh: Edinburgh University Press, 2007), 2.
11. Jeffrey Richards, "National Identity in British Wartime Films," in *Britain and the Cinema in the Second World War*, ed. Philip M. Taylor (Basingstoke: Macmillan, 1988), 43.

Chapter 1

1. *The Sun*, 30 June 2007.
2. Richard Weight, *Patriots: National Identity in Britain, 1940–2000* (London: Macmillan, 2002), 709.
3. *The Sun*, 25 June 2010.
4. Weight, *Patriots*, 710.
5. Henry Pelling, *Britain and the Second World War* (Glasgow: Collins, 1970), 122.
6. David Connelly, *We Can Take It! Britain and the Memory of the Second World War* (Harlow: Pearson Longman, 2004), 5.
7. Malcolm Smith, *Britain and 1940: History, Myth and Popular Memory* (London: Routledge, 2000), 7.
8. Connelly, *We Can Take It!*, 26.

9. Cato, *Guilty Men* (London: Gollancz, 1940), 11.
10. Connelly, *We Can Take It!*, 63.
11. Ibid., 65.
12. Jeremy Paxman, *The English: A Portrait of a People* (London: Penguin, 1998), 33.
13. Connelly, *We Can Take It!*, 130.
14. Ibid., 144.
15. Ibid., 132.

Chapter 2

1. Hamilton Fyfe, *The Illusion of National Character* (London: Watts & Co., 1946), 3, 23.
2. Ibid., 38.
3. Andrew Higson, *Waving the Flag: Constructing a National Cinema in Britain* (Oxford: Oxford University Press, 1997), 4.
4. George Orwell, *Collected Essays, Journalism and Letters* (Harmondsworth: Penguin, 1982), III, 21.
5. Kate Fox, *Watching the English: The Hidden Rules of English Behaviour* (London: Hodder & Stoughton, 2004), 14.
6. Anthony D. Smith, *National Identity* (Reno: University of Nevada Press, 1991), 9.
7. Maureen Duffy, *England: The Making of the Myth from Stonehenge to Albert Square* (London: 4th Estate, 2001), 38–9.
8. Francesca Wilson, *Strange Island: Britain Through Foreign Eyes 1395–1940.* (London: Longmans, Green, 1995), 12.
9. Ibid., 45.
10. Paxman, *The English*, 91.
11. Ibid., 87.
12. Paul Langford, *Englishness Identified* (Oxford: Oxford University Press, 2001), 75.
13. Ibid., 76
14. Roger Scruton, *England: An Elegy* (London: Chatto & Windus, 2000), 112–6.
15. Paxman, *The English*, 193.
16. Fox, *Watching the English*, 65.
17. J.B. Priestley, *The English* (London: Heinemann, 1973), 175.
18. Langford, *Englishness Identified*, 301.
19. Ibid., 250, 255.
20. Harold Perkin, *The Origins of Modern English Society 1780–1880* (London: Routledge & Kegan Paul, 1969), 280.
21. Jeffrey Richards, *Happiest Days: The Public Schools in English Fiction* (Manchester: Manchester University Press, 1988), 11.
22. Mark Girouard, *The Return to Camelot: Chivalry and the English Gentleman* (New Haven: Yale University Press, 1981), 7.
23. Mason, *The English Gentleman*, 12.
24. Girouard, *The Return to Camelot*, 233.
25. Ibid., 170, 235.
26. Michael Boyce, *The Lasting Influence of the War on Postwar British Film* (New York: Macmillan, 2012), 48.

Chapter 3

1. Robert Murphy, *British Cinema and the Second World War* (London: Continuum, 2000), 4.
2. Anthony Aldgate and Jeffrey Richards, *Britain Can Take It: The British Cinema in the Second World War* (Oxford: Basil Blackwell, 1986), 3.

3. James Chapman, *British at War: Cinema, State and Propaganda, 1939–1945* (London: I.B. Tauris, 1998), 42.
4. Nicholas Pronay and D. W. Spring, *Propaganda, Politics and Film, 1918–45* (London: Macmillan, 1982), 23.
5. Philip Taylor, *British Propaganda in the Twentieth Century: Selling Democracy* (Edinburgh: Edinburgh University Press), 1999, 67.
6. Pronay and Spring, *Propaganda, Politics and Film*, 24.
7. Ian McLaine, *Ministry of Morale* (London: George Allen & Unwin, 1979), 12.
8. Ibid., 13.
9. Anthony Aldgate, "Comedy, Class and Containment: The British Domestic Cinema of the 1930s," in *British Cinema History*, eds. James Curran and Vincent Porter (London: Weidenfeld and Nicolson, 1983), 245.
10. Stuart Hood, "John Grierson and the Documentary Film Movement," in *British Cinema History*, 99.
11. Anthony Aldgate, "Comedy, Class and Containment: The British Domestic Cinema of the 1930s," in *British Cinema History*, 256.
12. Murphy, *British Cinema and the Second World War*, 57.
13. Peter Stead, "The People as Stars: Feature Films as National Expression," *Britain and the Cinema in the Second World War*, 68.
14. Chapman, *The British at War*, 61–2.

CHAPTER 4

1. Michael Balcon, *Michael Balcon Presents ... A Lifetime of Films* (London: Hutchinson, 1969), 130.
2. James Chapman, "Cinema, Propaganda and National Identity: British Film and the Second World War," in *British Cinema, Past and Present*, Justine Ashby and Andrew Higson, eds., (London: Routledge, 2000), 194.
3. Balcon, *Michael Balcon Presents*, 126.
4. Ibid., 127.
5. Clive Coultass, "British Cinema and the Reality of War," *Britain and the Cinema in the Second World War*, 84.
6. For Lord Olivier's amusing account of how he learned to do a convincing Russian accent, see his *Confessions of an Actor*, 98.
7. Chapman, *The British at War*, 178.
8. "The Bells Go Down," *Sunday Times*, 18 April 1943.
9. Charles Barr, *Ealing Studios* (Moffat: Cameron & Hollis, 1998), 29.
10. Balcon, *Michael Balcon Presents*, 137.
11. Ibid., 135.
12. Barr, *Ealing Studios*, 27.
13. Aldgate and Richards, *Britain Can Take It*, 109.
14. Ibid., 110.
15. Taylor, "Introduction," 84.
16. "The Week's films," *Sunday Times*, 1 November 1942.
17. Geoffrey Macnab, "The Battle of Bramley End," *Time Out*, 25 August–1 September 1999, 167.
18. Frank Jackson, *Reynolds News*, 8 July 1956.
19. Murphy, *British Cinema and the Second World War*, 212.

CHAPTER 5

1. Balcon, *Michael Balcon Presents*, 129.
2. William Whitebait, "Convoy," *New Statesman*, 13 July 1940.

3. Pronay and Spring, *Propaganda, Politics and Film*, 242.
4. Balcon, *Michael Balcon Presents*, 148.
5. Ibid.
6. Barr, *Ealing Studios*, 37.
7. Balcon, *Michael Balcon Presents*, 148.
8. Caroline Lejeune, "The Films," *Observer*, 27 September 1942.
9. "Coward's War Service," *Daily Telegraph*, 12 December 1987.
10. Jeffrey Richards, "The Paradox of Colonel Blimp," *Daily Telegraph*, 10 July 1987.
11. Chapman, *The British at War*, 194.
12. Dilys Powell, "The Life and Death of Colonel Blimp," *Sunday Times*, 17 April 1943.
13. S. P. MacKenzie, *British War Films, 1939–1945: The Cinema and the Services* (London: Hambledon & London, 2001), 108.
14. *Manchester Guardian*, January 1943.
15. Durgnat, *A Mirror for England*, 244.
16. "The RAF on Screen," *The Times*, 31 October 1939.
17. S. P. Mackenzie, *The Battle of Britain on Screen*, 17.
18. *Kinematograph Weekly*, 27 March 1941.
19. Philip Warner, *World War II: The Untold Story* (Philadelphia: Coronet, 1990), 56.
20. Charles Drazin, *The Finest Years* (London: I.B. Tauris, 2007), 194.
21. Aldgate and Richards, *Britain Can Take It*, 283.
22. Michael Redgrave, *In My Mind's Eye: An Autobiography* (London: Weidenfeld & Nicolson, 1983), 171–2.

Chapter 6

1. Balcon, *Michael Balcon Presents*, 132.
2. Murphy, *British Cinema and the Second World War*, 46.
3. Aldgate and Richards, *Britain Can Take It*, 53.
4. Many have speculated that Howard's plane was shot down in 1943 on a direct order from Goebbels.
5. Aldgate and Richards, *Britain Can Take It*, 64.
6. Murphy, *British Cinema and the Second World War*, 102.

Chapter 7

1. John Keegan, ed., *The Oxford Companion to World War II* (Oxford: Oxford University Press, 2006), 796.
2. Robert Murphy, *Realism and Tinsel: Cinema and Society in Britain 1939–1949*, (London: Routledge, 1992), 9.
3. Louis MacNeice, "The Cinema," *Spectator*, 31 January 1941.
4. Drazin, *The Finest Years*, 192.
5. Murphy, *British Cinema and the Second World War*, 102.
6. Michael Powell, *A Life in Movies: An Autobiography* (London: Faber and Faber, 2000), 389.
7. Chapman, *The British at War*, 70.
8. *Documentary News Letter*, November 1941.
9. Balcon, *Michael Balcon Presents*, 140.

Chapter 8

1. Jeffrey Richards, *The Age of the Dream Palace: Cinema and Society in Britain 1930–1939* (London: Routledge & Kegan Paul, 1984), 265.
2. Pierre Sorlin, *The Film in History: Restaging the Past* (New York: Barnes and Noble, 1980), 19.

3. Durgnat, *Mirror for England*, 131.
4. William Whitebait, "The Prime Minister," *New Statesman*, March 1941.
5. *Picturegoer and Film Weekly*, 22 March 1941.
6. Caroline Lejeune, "The Films," *Observer*, 3 August 1941.
7. Chapman, *The British at War*, 246.
8. Caroline Lejeune, "The Films," *The Observer,* 26 November 1944.
9. Chapman, *The British at War*, 240.
10. *Picturegoer*, 19 August, 1944.
11. Murphy, *Realism and Tinsel*, 32.

CHAPTER 9

1. Christine Geraghty, *British Cinema in the Fifties: Gender, Genre and the "New Look"* (London: Routledge, 2000), 176.
2. Boyce, *The Lasting Influence of the War*, 54.
3. Balcon, *Michael Balcon Presents*, 171.
4. George Perry, *Forever Ealing* (London: Pavilion, 1985), 104.

CHAPTER 10

1. James Chapman, *Cinemas of the World: Film and Society from 1895 to the Present* (London: Reaktion, 2004), 273.
2. Peter Mandler, *The English National Character: The History of an Idea from Edmund Burke to Tony Blair* (New Haven: Yale University Press, 2006), 208.
3. T.S. Eliot, *Christianity and Culture* (New York: Harcourt, Brace, 1960), 124.
4. Phillip Taylor, "Film, the Historial and the Second War War," in *Britain and the Cinema in the Second World War*, 1.
5. William Whitebait, "Bombardment," *New Statesman*, 5 April 1958.
6. Neil Rattigan, "The Last Gasp of the Middle Class: British War Films of the 1950s," in W. W. Dixon, ed., *Re-viewing British Cinema, 1900-1992: Essays and Interviews*, (New York: State University of New York Press, 1994), 146.
7. S. P. Mackenzie, *The Battle of Britain on Screen* (Edinburgh: Edinburgh University Press), 53.
8. "New Films in London," *Manchester Guardian*, 22 March 1952.
9. *New Statesman*, 29 March 1952.
10. Reg Whitley, "The RAF Film We've Been Waiting For," *Daily Express*, 21 March 1952.
11. S. P. Mackenzie, *The Battle of Britain on Screen*, 66.
12. John Caughie and Kevin Rockett, *The Companion to British and Irish Cinema* (London: BFI, 1996), 114.
13. Kenneth More, *More or Less* (London: Book Club Associates, 1978), 167-8.
14. Lewis Gilbert, *All My Flashbacks* (Richmond: Reynolds and Hearn, 2010), 156-163.
15. John Ramsden, *The Dambusters* (London: I. B. Tauris, 2003), 108.
16. Durgnat, *Mirror for England*, 99.
17. Donald Sinden offers a fascinating account of how this scene was filmed, complete with stunt men, in his autobiography *A Touch of the Memoirs*, 158-160.
18. Caughie and Rockett, *The Companion to British and Irish Cinema*, 80.
19. Jack Hawkins, *Anything for a Quiet Life* (London: Elm Tree Books, 1973), 106.
20. Ibid., 94.
21. Derek Granger, "The Sea Shall Not Have Them," *Financial Times*, 6 December 1954.
22. V Graham, *Spectator*, 3 December 1954.
23. John Ezard, "Sexy Self-Image That Revved Up Dirk Bogarde," *The Guardian*, 2 October 2004.
24. Ian Mackillop and Neil Sinyard, "Celebrating British Cinema of the 1950s," in *British*

Cinema of the 1950s: A Celebration, Ian Mackillop and Neil Sinyard, eds. (Manchester: Manchester University Press, 2009), 2.
    25. Thomas Spencer, "Above Us the Waves," *Daily Worker*, 7 April 1955.
    26. Richard Attenborough and Diana Hawkins, *Entirely Up to You, Darling* (London: Hutchinson, 2008), 183.
    27. Derek Granger, "Heroism in the Jungle," *Financial Times*, 5 March 1956.
    28. *The Argus*, 18 July 1956.
    29. "Atrocities Recalled in Two British War Films," *The Times*, 21 April 1958.
    30. V Graham, "Colditz Story," *Spectator* 28 January 1955.
    31. Murphy, *British Cinema and the Second World War*, 214.
    32. Caroline Lejeune, "A Home Run," *Observer*, 30 January 1955.
    33. Michael Munn, *Trevor Howard: The Man and His Films* (London: Robson, 1989), 45-6.
    34. Virginia McKenna, *The Life in My Years* (London: Oberon, 2009), 131.
    35. Isabel Quigly, "Horrors Beyond Art," *Spectator*, 28 February 1958.
    36. Maurice Sellar, *Best of British: A Celebration of Rank Film Classics* (London: Sphere, 1987), 41.
    37. BFI Monthly Bulletin, Vol. 24, No. 278, March 1957, 28.
    38. Perry, *Forever Ealing*, 165.
    39. Rattigan, "The Last Gasp of the Middle Class," 146.
    40. Ibid., 149.

CHAPTER 11

    1. Durgnat, *Mirror for England*, 103.
    2. Ian Watt, "Bridges Over the Kwai," *The Listener*, 4 August 1959.
    3. Geoffrey Macnab, "Burning Bridges," *Time Out*, 23 August 1995.
    4. John Mills, *Up in the Clouds Gentlemen, Please* (London: George Weidenfield & Nicolson, 1980), 231.
    5. Anthony Quayle, *A Time to Speak* (London: Barrie & Jenkins, 1990), 340.
    6. Wayland Young, "A British Winner Takes the Alex Road," *Evening Standard*, 26 June 1958.
    7. Paul Gibbs, "Too Much Conscience?" *Daily Telegraph*, 29 March 1958.
    8. Andrew Spicer, *Typical Men: The Representation of Masculinity in Popular British Cinema* (New York: I. B. Tauris, 2003), 74.

CHAPTER 12

    1. Terence Conran and Juliet Gardiner, *From the Bomb to the Beatles* (London: Collins & Brown, 1999), 133.
    2. Mandler, *The English National Character*, 223.
    3. Ibid., 227.
    4. Nina Hibbin, "Comedy to Wipe the Smile Away," *Morning Star*, 18 October 1967.
    5. Philip French, "All Pacifists Now," *New Statesman*, 27 October 1967.
    6. Robert Ottaway, *Daily Sketch*, 19 September 1968.
    7. Robert Robinson, *Sunday Telegraph*, 15 May 1966.
    8. Harold Hobson, *Christian Science Monitor*, 31 October 1966.
    9. Sophie Walker, "'British Nazis' Film to Be Shown Uncut," *Independent*, 29 September 1996.
    10. Geoffrey Macnab, "War and Piss," *Time Out*, 13 August 1997.
    11. Stuart Cooper, "A Camera Instead of a Rifle," *Guardian*, 18 January 2008.
    12. Gilbert, *All My Flashbacks*, 199.

13. *The Sun*, 31 March 1977.
14. Colin McArthur, "Hitler's Soldiers as the Heroes," *Tribune*, 6 May 1977.

CHAPTER 13

1. Margaret Thatcher, "Speech to Conservative Rally at Cheltenham," 3 July 1982, http://www.margaretthatcher.org/document/104989, accessed 18 November 2012.
2. Weight, *Patriots*, 628–9.
3. Mandler, *The English National Character*, 232.
4. Weight, *Patriots*, 574.
5. See the lengthy discussion on nationalism in chapter 2.
6. Pop and rock stars, so feted by the Blair administration in the 1990s, were among the role models of this new generation.
7. Hal G.P. Colebatch, *Blair's Britain: Britain's Culture Wars and New Labour* (London: Claridge Press, 1999), 87–89.
8. Mandler, *The English National Character*, 236.
9. BBC Radio 3 interview with John Hare, http://www.bbc.co.uk/radio3/johntusainterview/hare_transcript.shtml, accessed 20 July 2012.
10. Murphy, *British Cinema and the Second World War*, 261.

CONCLUSION

1. Sarah Barrow and John White, eds., *Fifty Key British Films* (London: Routledge, 2008), 114.
2. Michael Paris, "Enduring Heroes: British Feature Films and the First World War," in *The First World War and Popular Cinema: 1914 to the Present*, Michael Paris, ed. (New Brunswick: Rutgers University Press, 2000), 53.
3. This film was actually about World War I, not World War II, but it captures the Zeitgeist of the time perfectly. It shows British soldiers as hapless victims of misguided and incompetent politicians and generals. It thus questions the idea of war as a noble enterprise.
4. This plan, dubbed "New Horizons," was announced by the British Film Institute in May 2012.
5. Mark Brown, "UK Film Production Hits the Doldrums," *Guardian*, 2 August 2011.

Bibliography

Ackroyd, Peter. *Albion: The Origins of the English Imagination*. London: Vintage, 2004.
Aldgate, Anthony. *Censorship and the Permissive Society: British Cinema and Theatre 1955–1965*. New York: Oxford University Press, 1995.
Aldgate, Anthony, and Jeffrey Richards. *Best of British: Cinema and Society from 1930 to the Present*. London: I. B. Tauris, 2002.
_____. *Britain Can Take It: The British Cinema in the Second World War*. Oxford: Basil Blackwell, 1986.
Anderson, Benedict. *Imagined Communities: Reflections on the Origin and Spread of Nationalism*. London: Verso, 1991.
Attenborough, Richard, and Diana Hawkins. *Entirely Up to You, Darling*. London: Hutchinson, 2008.
Balcon, Michael. *Michael Balcon Presents…A Lifetime of Films*. London: Hutchinson, 1969.
Barr, Charles. *Ealing Studios*. Moffat: Cameron & Hollis, 1998.
_____, ed. *All Our Yesterdays: 90 Years of British Cinema*. London: BFI, 1992.
Calder, Angus. *The Myth of the Blitz*. London: Pimlico, 1992.
Cato. *Guilty Men*. London: Gollancz, 1940.
Caughie, John, and Kevin Rockett. *The Companion to British and Irish Cinema*. London: Cassell, 1996.
Chambers, John Whiteclay, and David Holbrook Culbert, eds. *World War II, Film, and History*. New York: Oxford University Press, 1996.
Chapman, James. *British at War: Cinema, State and Propaganda, 1939–1945*. London: I.B. Tauris, 1998.
Colley, Linda. *Britons: Forging the Nation 1707–1837*. New Haven: Yale University Press, 1992.
Collis, Robert. *Identity of England*. Oxford: Oxford University Press, 2002.
Connelly, David. *We Can Take It! Britain and the Memory of the Second World War*. Harlow: Pearson Longman, 2004.
Conran, Terence, and Juliet Gardiner. *From the Bomb to the Beatles*. London: Collins & Brown, 1999.
Corrigan, Timothy. *A Short Guide to Writing About Film*. New York: Addison Wesley Longman, 2001.
Coultass, Clive. *Images for Battle: British Film and the Second World War, 1939–1945*. Cranbury: Associated University Presses, 1989.
Culver, Ronald. *Not Quite a Gentleman*. London: William Kimber, 1979.
Drazin, Charles. *Korda: Britain's Movie Mogul*. New York: I. B. Tauris, 2011.
Duffy, Maureen. *England: The Making of the Myth from Stonehenge to Albert Square*. London: 4th Estate, 2001.
Durgnat, Raymond. *A Mirror for England: British Movies from Austerity to Affluence*, 2nd ed. London: Palgrave Macmillan, 2011.

Eliot, T.S. *Christianity and Culture*. New York: Harcourt, Brace, 1960.
Fox, Kate. *Watching the English: The Hidden Rules of English Behaviour*. London: Hodder & Stoughton, 2004.
Fyfe, Hamilton. *The Illusion of National Character*. London: Watts, 1946.
Garnett, Mark, and Richard Weight. *Modern British History: The Essential A–Z Guide*. London: Pimlico, 2004.
Gilbert, Lewis. *All My Flashbacks*. Richmond: Reynolds and Hearn, 2010.
Gilbert, Sir Martin. *Finest Hour: Winston S. Churchill 1939–1941*. London: Heinemann, 1983.
Girouard, Mark. *The Return to Camelot: Chivalry and the English Gentleman*. New Haven: Yale University Press, 1981.
Glancy, H. Mark. *When Hollywood Loved Britain: The Hollywood "British" Film, 1939–1945*. Manchester: Manchester University Press, 1999.
Hawkins, Jack. *Anything for a Quiet Life*. London: Elm Tree Books, 1973.
Hayes, Nick, and Jeff Hill. *Millions Like Us*. Liverpool: Liverpool University Press, 1999.
Hayward, Susan. *Cinema Studies: The Key Concepts*. London: Routledge, 2000.
Hill, John. *Sex, Class and Realism: British Cinema 1956–1963*. London: BFI, 1997.
Hobsbawn, Eric. *Nations and Nationalism Since 1780*. Cambridge: Cambridge University Press, 2002.
_____, and Terence Ranger, eds. *The Invention of Tradition*. Cambridge: Cambridge University Press, 2002.
Hosking, Geoffrey, and George Schopflin, eds. *Myths and Nationhood*. London: Hurst, 1997.
Jeffrys, Kevin. *Finest and Darkest Hours: The Decisive Events in British Politics from Churchill to Blair*. London: Atlantic Books, 2002.
Keegan, John. ed. *The Oxford Companion to World War II*. Oxford: Oxford University Press, 2006.
Kracauer, Siegfried. *Theory of Film*. Oxford: Oxford University Press, 1968.
Kumar, Krishan. *The Making of English National Identity*. Cambridge: Cambridge University Press, 2003.
Langford, Paul. *Englishness Identified*. Oxford: Oxford University Press, 2001
Loyn, H. R. *The Making of the English Nation*. London: Thames and Hudson, 1991.
Mackenzie, John. *Propaganda and Empire: The Manipulation of British Public Opinion, 1880–1960*. Manchester: Manchester University Press, 2003. (New ed.)
MacKenzie, S. P. *British War Films, 1939–1945: The Cinema and the Services*. London: Hambledon & London, 2001.
Mandler, Peter. *The English National Character: The History of an Idea from Edmund Burke to Tony Blair*. New Haven: Yale University Press, 2006.
Mason, Phillip. *The English Gentleman: The Rise and Fall of an Ideal*. London: Pimlico, 1993.
McKenna, Virginia. *The Life in My Years*. London: Oberon, 2009.
McLaine, Ian. *Ministry of Morale*. London: George Allen & Unwin, 1979.
Miller, John. *Ralph Richardson: The Authorized Biography*. London: Sidgwick & Jackson, 1995
Mills, John. *Up in the Clouds Gentlemen, Please*. London: George Weidenfield & Nicolson, 1980.
More, Kenneth. *More or Less*. London: Book Club Associates, 1978.
Munn, Michael. *Trevor Howard: The Man and His Films*. London: Robson, 1989.
Murphy, Robert. *British Cinema and the Second World War*. London: Continuum, 2000.
_____. *Sixties British Cinema*. London: BFI, 1997.
Olivier, Sir Laurence. *Confessions of an Actor*. London: Weidenfeld and Nicolson, 1982.
Paris, Michael, ed. *The First World War and Popular Cinema 1914 to the Present*. New Brunswick: Rutgers University Press, 2000.
Parrinder, Patrick. *Nation & Novel: The English Novel from Its Origins to the Present Day*. Oxford: Oxford University Press, 2006.
Paxman, Jeremy. *The English: A Portrait of a People*. London: Penguin, 1998.
Pelling, Henry. *Britain and the Second World War*. Glasgow: Collins, 1970.
Perkin, Harold. *The Origins of Modern English Society 1780–1880*. London: Routledge & Kegan Paul, 1969.
Perkins, V. F. *Film as Film*. Harmondsworth: Penguin, 1986.

Perry, George. *Forever Ealing.* London: Pavilion, 1985.
_____. *The Great British Picture Show.* London: Pavilion, 1985.
Porter, Roy, ed. *Myths of the English.* Cambridge: Polity Press, 1994.
Powell, Michael. *A Life in Movies: An Autobiography.* London: Faber and Faber, 2000.
Priestley, J.B. *The English.* London: Heinemann, 1973.
_____. *English Humour.* London: Heinemann, 1976.
Pronay, Nicholas, and D. W. Spring. *Propaganda, Politics and Film, 1918–45.* London: Macmillan, 1982.
Quayle, Anthony. *A Time to Speak.* London: Barrie & Jenkins, 1990.
Ramsden, John. *Don't Mention the War: The British and the Germans Since 1890.* London: Little, Brown, 2006.
Ramsden, John. *The Dambusters.* London: I. B. Tauris, 2003.
Rattigan, Neil. *This Is England: British Film and the People's War, 1939–1945.* Madison: Fairleigh Dickinson University Press, 2001.
Redgrave, Michael. *In My Mind's Eye: An Autobiography.* London: Weidenfeld & Nicolson, 1983.
Reeves, Nicholas. *The Power of Film Propaganda: Myth or Reality?* London: Cassell, 1999.
Richards, Jeffrey. *The Age of the Dream Palace: Cinema and Society in Britain 1930–1939.* London: Routledge & Kegan Paul, 1984.
_____. *Films and British National Identity: From Dickens to Dad's Army.* Manchester: Manchester University Press, 1997.
_____. *Happiest Days: The Public Schools in English Fiction.* Manchester: Manchester University Press, 1988.
_____. *Visions of Yesterday.* London: Routledge & Kegan Paul, 1973.
Rose, Sonya O. *Which People's War? National Identity and Citizenship in Wartime Britain 1939–1945.* Oxford: Oxford University Press, 2003.
Scruton, Roger. *England: An Elegy.* London: Chatto & Windus, 2000.
Sellar, Maurice. *Best of British. A Celebration of Rank Film Classics.* London: Sphere, 1987.
Sinden, Donald. *A Touch of the Memoirs.* London: Hodder & Stoughton, 1982.
Smith, Anthony. *Nations and Nationalism in a Global Era.* Cambridge: Polity Press, 2002.
Smith, Malcolm. *Britain and 1940: History, Myth and Popular Memory.* London: Routledge, 2000.
Spicer, Andrew. *Typical Men: The Representation of Masculinity in Popular British Cinema.* New York: I. B. Tauris, 2003.
Street, Sarah. *British National Cinema.* London: Routledge, 1997.
Taylor, Phillip. *British Propaganda in the Twentieth Century: Selling Democracy.* Edinburgh: Edinburgh University Press, 1999.
_____, ed. *Britain and the Cinema in the Second World War.* London: MacMillan, 1988.
Tidrick, Kathryn. *Empire & the English Character.* London: I.B. Tauris, 1992.
Wakelin, Michael. *J Arthur Rank: The Man Behind the Gong.* Oxford: Lion, 1996.
Warner, Philip. *World War II: The Untold Story.* Philadelphia: Coronet Books, 1990.
Weight, Richard. *Patriots: National Identity in Britain, 1940–2000.* London: Macmillan, 2002.
Welch, David. *Propaganda and the German Cinema 1933–1945.* London: I. B. Tauris, 2001
Wilson, Francesca. *Strange Island: Britain Through Foreign Eyes 1395–1940.* London: Longmans, Green, 1995.

Index

Numbers in ***bold italics*** indicate pages with photographs.

Above Us the Waves 128, 131, 140, 143
Adolf Hitler—My Part in His Downfall 174
The Adventures of Tartu 91, 96
Against the Wind 126
Albert RN 128, 145–146
Alfred, King 27–28
Anderson, Lindsay 201
Anderson, Michael 182
Andrews, Harry 161, 171, 176
Angels One Five 131–132, 138, 143
Another Time, Another Place 193, 200
Appointment in London 133, 179
Appointment with Venus 134, 148
area bombing 12, 13, 85
Arne, Peter 147
Arnold, Thomas 37
Asherson, Renée 87
Asquith, Anthony 40, 53
Atonement 187, **199**–200
Attenborough, (Lord) Richard 4, 143, 156, 185

Back Room Boy 90
Bader, Douglas 4, 12, 132–134
Baker, Stanley 158, 165, 181
Balcon, Michael 42–43, 49–50, 58–59, 69, 74, 107, 126; *see also* Ealing studios
Banks, Leslie 61, 70, 84
Barrie, Wendy 108
Battle of Agincourt 29, 114
Battle of Britain (1940) 14–15, 19–20, 82–83, 131–133, 203
Battle of Britain (film) 183–184

Battle of the Atlantic (1939–1945) 16–17, 71
The Battle of the River Plate 131, 141
Baxter, Jane 70
BBFC (British Board of Film Classification) 41
Beaverbrook, Lord 41, 51
The Bells Go Down 55, 78
Bentham, Jeremy 32
The Big Blockade 84–86
Blanchett, Cate 198
Blitz (1940–1941) 15–17, 20–21, 45–47, 52, 55–56, 60–61, 120, 132, 192–193
Bogarde, Dirk 4, 132, 139, 153–154
Boorman, John 192
Boulting Brothers 40, 99
The Boy in the Striped Pyjamas 197, 202
Bracken, Brendan 76
The Bridge on the River Kwai 4, 128, 143, 145, 158–159, ***160***, 180
A Bridge Too Far 180, 185–186
British Council, 42
British national identity 31–39
Brook, Clive 69, 100
The Brylcreem Boys 196
Bryne, Gabriel 196
Buchan, John 89
Bulldog Sees It Through 91
Burrows, Saffron 197
Burton, Richard 183
But Not in Vain 124

Cage of Gold 122
Caine, Michael 4, 176, 184

Index

Calvert, Phyllis 6
The Camp on Blood Island 128, 143, 145, 157
Campbell, Billy 196
A Canterbury Tale 109, 116–117, **118**–119
The Captive Heart 125
Carve Her Name with Pride 7, 128, 146, 151, **152**–153, 198
Cavalcanti, Alberto 40, 49, 122
Chamberlain, Neville 18,
Charlotte Grey 198, 200
Christmas Under Fire 46
Churchill, Sir Winston 12, 13, 15, 18–19, 43, 58–59, 71, 76, 98, 107, 110, 143, 196–197
Clark, Sir Kenneth 44, 105; see also Ministry of Information
Clements, John 69, 78, 101, 107
Coburn, James 177
The Cockleshell Heroes 128, 131, 139–140
Cold War 129
Colditz Castle 12
The Colditz Story 7, 117, 128, 145, **146**–147, 196
Columbus, Christopher 27
common law, characteristics of 33
Connery, Sean 171
Contraband 91–92
Convoy 49, 57, 69, 84
Coulouris, George 148
Coward, Noël 74, 75
Craig, Michael 143
Cranham, Kenneth 198
Crawford, Anne 66
Crawford, Michael 172
The Crook's Tour 92
Cross of Iron 177
The Cruel Sea 1, 7, 128, 131, 136, **137**–138, 156, 157
Culver, Ronald 52, 101
Cummings, Constance 115

Dad's Army 174
Daily Express 19, 133
Daily Mail 77
Dalton, Hugh 84
The Dam Busters 4, 7, 11, 125, 128, **135**, 155, 157, 180, 182–183
Danger Within 147
Dangerous Moonlight 86
Davenport, Nigel 176
The Day Will Dawn 103–104, 154
declinism 169; see also sixties revolution
The Demi Paradise 53, 86, 119
Denham, Maurice 144

Denson, Michael 121
De Toth, André 176
Dickens, Charles 31
Dickinson, Thorold 50, 60, 111
Diffring, Anton 146
Disraeli, Benjamin 111
Dobie, Alan 174
Donald, James 160
Donat, Robert 96, 108, 111
Douglas, Kirk 183
Drake, Sir Francis 18
Dunkirk (film) 131, 156, 158, 162–163, 180
Dunkirk evacuation (1940) 12, 14–19, 60, 98, 162–163
Durgnat, Raymond 5, 79, 111, 138, 160
Duvall, Robert 184

The Eagle Has Landed 96, 179, 184–185
Ealing comedies 121
Ealing studios 43, 49
Eastwood, Clint 183
Eden, Sir Anthony 41
Elliot, Denholm 155
The End of the Affair 194–195, 200
The English Patient 187, 193, **195**, 199, 200
Enigma 197, 200
Evans, Clifford 57
Der Ewige Jude 4
Eye of the Needle 185, 192

Farrar, David 76, 122, 123, 124
Fawlty Towers 13
Ferrer, Jose 140
Fiennes, Ralph 195
Fifth Column, threat of 58, 61; see also *Next of Kin*
Finch, Peter 144
Fire Over England 82, 108–109
Fires Were Started 55
The First Days 44
The First of the Few 4, 47, 82
Flaherty, Robert 49
The Flamingo Affair 122
Flynn, Errol 112
For Freedom 68
For Those in Peril 75
Force Ten From Navarone 182
The Foreman Went to France 55–58, 74–75
Forty Ninth Parallel 102, 105–106, 117
Freedom Radio 100
Frend, Charles 84
Frieda 123
Friel, Anna 195
Frobisher, Martin 18

From the Four Corners 47
The Front Line 45
Fyffe, Will 68

Genn, Leo 145
The Gentle Sex 65
Gentleman, cult of 36–37; *see also* national identity
George VI, King 19
Georgeson, Tom 195
The Gift Horse 141
Gilbert, Lewis 146
Gilliat, Sidney 64–66, 91
Gladstone, Herbert 31
Goebbels, Joseph 5, 41; *see also* propaganda
The Goose Steps Out 90
Gordon, General Charles 31
Goring, Marius 99
Gough, Michael 123
Graf Spee 68–69, 141
Graham, Morland 51
The Great Escape 17
Green, Nigel 176
Greene, Graham 61, 194
Greene, Richard 60–61, 97
Gregson, John 131–132
Grierson, John 42
Guest, Val 164
Guillermin, John 149
Guinness, Sir Alec 155–156, 158–159
The Guns of Navarone 180–182

Hagman, Larry 185
Hamer, Robert 50
Hanley, Jimmy 52, 80
Hannibal Brooks 180
Hanover Street 185
Hare, David 187, 190–191
Harker, Gordon 97
Harris, Arthur (Bomber) 85
Harris, Richard 169, 183
Harrison, Rex 91, 96
Hartnell, William 80
Harvey, Laurence 169
Hawkins, Jack 3, 4, 64, 122, 130–132, 137–139, 151, 155–156
Hayakawa, Sessue 159
Hendry, Ian 171
Henreid, Paul 91
Henry V (film) 109, 114
Henry V (play) 29
Herbert, Percy 143
heritage films 115–119
The Heroes of Telemark 180, 183

Heydrich, Reinhard 51, 96
The Hill 171–172, 180
history as propaganda 108–115
Hitchcock, Alfred 89, 91
Hitler, Adolf 13, 41
Hoare, Samuel 41
Hobbes, Thomas 32
Hobson, Valerie 96
Holden, William 160
Holloway, Stanley 80
Home Guard 15, 77, 191
Hope and Glory 192, **193**
Hordern, Michael 172, 181
How I Won the War 172, **173**–174, 199, 201
Howard, Joyce 93
Howard, Leslie 47, 65, 83, 93–94, 106
Howard, Trevor 122, 131, 140–141, 152, 183, 184, 185
Hue and Cry 121
Huntley, Raymond 80, 126
Hurst, Brian Desmond 86, 185
Hyman, David 192

I Was Monty's Double 149–151
Ice Cold in Alex 1, 131, 142, 158, 161, 185
ideology in film 5
If War Should Come 44
Ill Met with Moonlight 128, 151, 153–154
The Imitation Game 190–191
In Which We Serve 3, 4, 74, **75**, 78, 86, 131, 139
Indian Mutiny 30
Inspector Hornleigh Goes to It 91
internment in WWII 13
The Intruder 122
Island People 46
It Happened Here 174, **175**–176

Jackson, Gordon 57, 66
Jennings, Humphrey 45–46, 51
Jew Suss 5
Joey Boy 174
John, Rosamund 87
Johns, Glynis 148
Johns, Mervyn 55, 59, 73
Johnson, Celia 53, 74
Jordan, Neil 195

Katyn massacre 197; *see also Enigma*
Kerr, Deborah 4, 77, 104, 194
The Key 141
Knightley, Keira 199
Korda, Alexander 5, 42–43, 81, 108
Kubrick, Stanley 176

Lady Chatterley's Lover 169
Lady Hamilton 8, 109, 112–114
Lambert, Jack 78
Lanchester, Elsa 108
The Land Girls 187, 195–196
Landfall 121
Laughton, Charles 108, 159
Launder, Frank 64–66, 91
Laurie, John 126
Lawson, Wilfrid 99–100
Lean, Sir David 40, 53, 74, 161
Lee, Bernard 162
Leigh, Vivien 113
Leland, David 195
Lennon, John 172
Lester, Richard 172
Let George Do It 90
Licking Hitler 187, 190–191
Lidice, destruction of 51; *see also The Silent Village*
The Life and Death of Colonel Blimp 76, 141
The Lion Has Wings 81, 115
Livesey, Roger 77
Locke, John 32
Lockwood, Margaret 91
Logan, Phyllis 192
London Can Take It 45
The Long and the Short and the Tall 169, **170**, 174
The Long Day's Dying 174
Loren, Sophia 141, 182
The Lost People 124
Lovell, Raymond 124
Low, David 19, 76
Lumet, Sidney 171

The MacKenzie Break 178–179
Malta Story 7, 131, 155–156
The Man Who Never Was 149, **150**
Manchester Guardian 79, 133
Mason, James 93, 101
Massie, Paul 164
McAllum, David 170
McAvoy, James 199
McCormack. Catherine 195
McKenna, Virginia 4, 138, 144, 153
McKern, Leo 165
McQueen, Steve 179
Mers-el-Kebir 13
Michael, Ralph 75
Miles, Bernard 74, 99, 117
Miles, Sarah 192
Mill, John Stuart 32, 36
Millions Like Us 65

Mills, John 3, 4, 51, 64, 74, 86, 131, 140, 158, 161–162, 194
Minghella, Anthony 194
Ministry of Information, 42–44
Mitchell, R.J. 82, 135
Montgomery, General Bernard 150
Moore, Julianne 194
Moore, Roger 185
More, Kenneth 3, 4, 64, 133–134, 148, 181
Morley, Robert 111
Mowbray, Alan 113
Mrs. Miniver 2, 8, 55
Murray, Pauline 176
Murray, Stephen 107, 122

Napoleonic wars 109–110, 113, 115; *see also The Young Mr. Pitt*
national identity 5, 6, 23–27
nationalism 26–27
Naumann, Michael 12, 13
Neagle, Anna 97, 115, 152
Neill, Sam 192
Nelson, Lord Horatio 30
Neutral Port 69
Newton, Robert 53, 126
Next of Kin 59
Niemoller, Pastor Martin 99
Night Beat 122
Night Boat to Dublin 125
Night Train to Munich 91
Nine Men 55, 78, **79**, 161
Niven, David 4, 80, 148, 181, 185
Northam, Jeremy 197
Northcliffe, Lord 41
nuclear age 129–130

Oberon, Merle 82, 108
Observer 75, 147
Odette 128, 131, 151–152, 198
Old Bill and Son, 51
Old Mother Riley Joins Up 90
Olivier, (Lord) Laurence 4, 53, 105, 113, 159, 184
Olympia 5
On the Fiddle 174
One of Our Aircraft Is Missing 102, 117
Operation Amsterdam 151, 154
Operation Bullshine 174
Operation Crossbow 180, 182–183, 186
Operation Frankton 140
Operation Market Garden 185–186
Operation Mincemeat 149
Orders to Kill 163–164
O'Rorke, Brefni 61

Orwell, George 24
Osborne, John 167
Overlord 178
Owen, Bill 156
Oxby, David 153

Passport to Pimlico 121
Pastor Hall 99
Pavlow, Muriel 155–156
Peck, Gregory 144, 181
Peckinpah, Sam 177
Penry-Jones, Rupert 198
Peppard, George 182
Phoney War 18
Pimpernel Smith 47, 84, 91, 94, **95**, 100
Play Dirty 176–177
Pleasence, Donald 184
Plenty 187, 190–192
Plunkett, Patricia 121
Portman, Eric 66, 105, 116–117, 147
Portrait from Life 124
POW films 125, 145–148, 178–179
Powell, Michael 43, 77, 82, 102, 105, 154
Pressburger, Emeric 43, 77, 82, 102, 105, 154
Price, Dennis 116
Priestley, J. B. 52, 56
The Prime Minister 109, 111
The Private Life of Henry VIII 108
propaganda 5, 41
The Proud Valley 50
public schools 38
The Purple Plain 128, 143

Quayle, Anthony 4, 161–162, 181–182
Quinn, Anthony 181

Radford, Basil 91–92, 125
Rainy Day Women 191
Rea, Stephen 194
Reach for the Sky 1, 4, 7, 128, 133–134, 146, 157
Redgrave, Michael 4, 86, 88, 125, 135, 171, 184
Redgrave, Vanessa 199
Reed, Carol 40, 91, 110
The Remains of the Day 200
Rennie, Michael 70
Reynolds, Quentin 45
Rice-Edwards, Sebastian 192
Richard II 29
Richardson, Sir Ralph 103, 126
Robertson, Cliff 180
Robeson, Paul 50
Robson, Flora 64, 108, 124

Roc, Patricia 64–65
Rolfe, Guy 165
Rorke's Drift 30
Ryan, Terence 196

Sailors Three 90
St. George 28
Salute John Citizen 52
San Demetrio, London 55, 72, **73**, 75, 79
Schell, Maximilian 177
School for Secrets 126
Scott, Sir Walter 37
Sea Hawk 112
Sea of Sand 128, 131, 142–143
The Sea Shall Not Have Them 125, 139, 146
Sea Wolves 185
Secret Mission 101–102
Seven Days to Noon 121
Shakespeare, William 29, 114
The Ship That Died of Shame 156
Ships with Wings 49, 57, 70, 84, 141, 146
Signoret, Simone 126
Silent Dust 122
The Silent Village 51
The Silver Fleet 103, 154
Sim, Sheila 116
Simmons, Jean 122
Sinden, Donald 137
Sink the Bismarck! 128, 180–181
Six Three Three Squadron 180
sixties revolution 167–169
Sixty Glorious Years 108–109
Small Back Room 122
Smiles, Samuel 36
social levelling 16, 21, 49, 52, 55, 69, 74; see also Blitz
Spanish Armada 30, 82, 108, 112, 115
Special Operations Executive 98–99, 126, 198
Spring Offensive 46
Squadron Leader X 106
Squadron Nine Nine Two 47
The Square Peg 174
Stalag Seventeen 125
Steel, Anthony 145
Stirner, Brian 178
The Story of an Air Communiqué 47
Streep, Meryl 191–192
Sturges, John 184
Suez Crisis 7, 158–159
Sullivan, Francis 94, 104
Sun 11, 185
Sunday Times 56, 60, 53, 78, 190
Sutherland, Donald 184

Sydney, Basil 62, 70
Szabo, Violette 153

Tallents, Stephen 42; *see also* Ministry of Information
Tawny Pipit 109, 117–119
Taylor, Valerie 62
Tennyson, Penrose 50, 69
Thatcher, Baroness Margaret 187–188
Theirs Is the Glory 185
They Flew Alone 115
They Made Me a Fugitive 122
They Met in the Dark 91, 93
They Were Not Divided 128
They Who Dare 154
This England 109, 115
This Happy Breed 131
The Titfield Thunderbolt 121
Tito, Josip 107
Todd, Richard 136
Tomlinson, David 88, 126
Tomorrow We Live 101
A Town Like Alice 128, 143–144
Trinder, Tommy 55–57, 90
Triumph of the Will 5
The Two Headed Spy 151
Two Men Went to War 198

UK Film Council 8
Undercover 106–107
Unpublished Story 60
Ustinov, Sir Peter 80

Valk, Frederick 147
Vansittart, Sir Robert 43

Veidt, Conrad 92–93
Victoria the Great 108

Wagner, Robert 179
Walbrook, Anton 77, 86
War and Order 47
War Lover 179
Warn That Man 96
Watt, Harry 45, 50, 78
The Way Ahead 79, 86, 131
The Way to the Stars 86, **87**–88, 131
Wayne, Naunton 91–92
Webb, Clifton 149
Weisz, Rachel 195
Went the Day Well? 61–63, **64**, 174, 184
Where Eagles Dare 183
Whisky Galore 121
Wilcox, Herbert 108
Wilding, Michael 70
Williams, Hugh 71, 101, 103
The Wind Cannot Read 143
The Wooden Horse 125, 128, 145, 147
Worth, Irene 164
Wyler, William 55
Wymark, Patrick 183
Wynter, Dana 181

Yanks 185
Yesterday's Enemy 145, 158, 164
The Young Mr. Pitt 109

Zetterling, Mai 124
Zulu Wars 30